THE GHOSTS OF EUROPE

ANNA PORTER

THE
GHOSTS
OF
EUROPE

*Central Europe's Past
and Uncertain Future*

ANNA PORTER

THOMAS DUNNE BOOKS
ST. MARTIN'S PRESS
New York

FOR MARIA,
the keeper of memories

THOMAS DUNNE BOOKS.
An imprint of St. Martin's Press.

Editing by Barbara Berson and Stephanie Fysh
Jacket and text design by Jessica Sullivan
Jacket photograph by Robert Capa ©2001/Magnum Photos

www.thomasdunnebooks.com
www.stmartins.com

Library of Congress Cataloging-in-Publication Data

Porter, Anna.
    The ghosts of Europe : Central Europe's past and uncertain future / Anna Porter.—1st U.S. ed.
        p. cm.
    "First published in Canada by Douglas & McIntyre"—T.p. verso.
    Includes bibliographical references and index.
    ISBN 978-0-312-68122-7
    1. Europe, Central—Politics and government—1989- 2. Post-communism—Europe,
Central. 3. Democracy—Europe, Central. 4. Social change—Europe, Central—History.
5. Europe, Central—Social conditions—1989- 6. Europe, Central—Economic condtions—1989-
7. Europe, Central—Ethnic relations. 8. Porter, Anna—Travel—Europe, Central.
9. Interviews—Europe, Central. I. Title.
    DAW1051.P67 2011
    943.0009'049—dc22

                                                                                    2010037316

First published in Canada by Douglas & McIntyre, an imprint of D&M Publishers Inc.

First U.S. Edition: January 2011

10 9 8 7 6 5 4 3 2 1

CONTENTS

PREFACE

THE OTHER EUROPE

IN 1989, the Soviet Empire began to crumble and Central Europe, as local pundits and Western journalists were fond of saying, returned to history. Between 1946 and 1989, historians, journalists and politicians tended to dismiss these lands from discussion of Europe, as if they had somehow absented themselves from their own geography. Now the great cities of Warsaw and Budapest, Kraków and Prague, Bratislava and Vilnius would no longer be viewed as sitting stolidly on the far side of the Iron Curtain's unfathomable chasm, a divide between "us" and "them."[1]

Poland was the first Soviet satellite to rebel against the hegemony of the Soviet Union, whose red czars, from Stalin to Chernenko, had provided their acolytes with the means to suppress opposition. In February 1989, the leaders of the formerly banned Solidarity trade union and the Communist Party leaders of Poland settled around a table to discuss how the country would recover from the human and economic disasters that the Party's rule had wrought. On June 4, 1989, Poland held the first semi-free elections in a Soviet satellite country.

On June 16, 1989, Hungary's former prime minister Imre Nagy, executed for his role during the ill-fated 1956 revolution, was reburied with the pomp and circumstance due a national leader. On July 6, he was formally rehabilitated by the Supreme Court. Thirteen days later, the last Communist prime minister of Hungary allowed several hundred East Germans free passage to the West. It was the first time since 1946 that East Europeans had been able to freely cross the Iron Curtain. When a reporter asked Soviet president Mikhail Gorbachev whether he would like the Berlin Wall to be taken down, Gorbachev replied, "Why not?" Tadeusz Mazowiecki, Poland's first non-Communist prime minister since 1947, took his seat in the Sejm (parliament) on August 24.

On October 18, Erich Honecker, the strongman of the East German Communist Party, stepped down.

On October 25, President Gorbachev's foreign ministry spokesman, Gennadi Gerasimov, voiced the end of Soviet hegemony over its satellites. When asked whether the Soviet Union would still follow the Brezhnev Doctrine of military intervention if needed, Gerasimov replied, in the spirit of the Frank Sinatra song "My Way," "So every country will decide in its own way which road to take."[2] The implication was obvious: the Soviet Union would not come to the rescue of other Communist leaders. They were, as of now, on their own.

On November 9, the Berlin Wall was breached, peacefully. Amid breathless, televised jubilation, East and West Germans met and embraced over the divide that had, for twenty-eight years, seemed impenetrable. East German guards who only weeks before would have shot their fellow East Germans for attempting to escape to the other side were now dancing with West German girls and giggling with delight.

On December 10, when the new national unity government was announced, the Czechoslovak Communist Party—one of the most repressive regimes of the Soviet Bloc—gave up power.

During a mass meeting in Bucharest on December 21, 1989, the usually submissive Romanian crowd booed the Communist dictator Nicolae Ceauşescu and no one was arrested. When Ceauşescu's shocked face appeared on national television, everyone knew that his reign was over. A few days later, he and his wife were arrested, tried by a military court and, on December 25, executed.

On New Year's Day 1990, Václav Havel, the new president of Czechoslovakia, stepped out on a balcony in Wenceslas Square and promised a government based on fairness and morality. He ended his speech with a quote from Tomáš Masaryk, the Czech politician and national hero who had successfully carved a country out of the Austro-Hungarian Empire in 1918: "People, your government has returned to you."

In a move that would have been unthinkable a few months earlier, Havel welcomed world leaders to Prague. The list of dignitaries included President George H.W. Bush, Chancellor Helmut Kohl, Prime Minister Margaret Thatcher and President Gorbachev, who said he grasped the opportunity for his own country to "open up" to democracy and for the world to escape from the threat of nuclear war.[3] But, as Gorbachev saw it, the USA was not ready to deal with Russia as a partner, only as a defeated enemy.

At the end of 1989, there were 300,000 nuclear weapons-equipped Soviet troops in Poland, Czechoslovakia and Hungary. Four years later, they had all gone home.

When it was all over, and credit was claimed or assigned, there were many contenders: Ronald Reagan, who had challenged Mikhail Gorbachev to take down the Wall; Solidarity, the Polish trade union that refused to be intimidated; Pope John Paul II, the Polish pope, who defied the system and told people who opposed it not to be afraid; Germany's successful *Ostpolitik*, the effort to open the door between East and West; and Gorbachev's perestroika, or "restructuring" of the Soviet economy, and glasnost, or openness. Whether Gorbachev had a premonition about the future of his country and the rest of Europe or he was trying to reform Communism (as the general secretary of the Czechoslovak Communist Party, Alexander Dubček, had done some twenty years previously) is still uncertain. Looking back, what is sure is that few in 1989 foresaw the events that ended the Communist era in Europe.

One might form the mistaken impression that the West was unified in its delight at the sight of all the walls collapsing. It was not.

British prime minister Margaret Thatcher, for one, aggressively opposed the unification of Germany. French president François Mitterrand worried about integrating the rebellious East into the orderly West. Americans, however, forgetting that some democratic elections have contributed to the world's insecurity, imagined that the West's export of democracy to the newly opened East would give them more security. The notion that democracy, like a commodity, is exportable is still prevalent among many Western politicians and continues to provide them with ample opportunities for disappointment. Unlike exotic fruit or fancy cars, democracy is best if it is grown locally. It may take root in the common desire of the people who choose to adopt it, but it cannot be imposed from the outside. While it has found fertile ground in most of the former Iron Curtain countries, it has not taken root in Iraq, and its Russian version excludes criticism of the government, as has been proven by the bodies of dead journalists.

ADVENTURES IN DEMOCRACY

During the years that followed, the former satellites had a chance to ask themselves what sort of countries they wished to be. They experimented with governments of various stripes; with judiciaries both old and new; with "shock therapy," market-driven economics and the "third way"; with the reform of social programs and the end of large government subsidies to massive industrial complexes. They saw the beginnings of stock markets and the emergence of new wealth and of a widening gap between rich and poor.

As Western advisers moved in—to create new lines of communications between two different ways of thinking (Communist and capitalist), new strategies, a new vocabulary that favoured "restructuring," "open society,"[4] "civil society" and a "return to Europe"—Poles, Czechs, Slovaks and Hungarians determined that they were not, and never had been, part of the East. They were "Central Europeans." Money poured in from the West to assist with the transformation. Much of the aid turned out to be export credits and loans, and a large portion of the funds intended for quick starts in the new economy was siphoned off by overpaid foreign consultants and local bureaucrats.[5] Most Western consultants were paid six to seven times as much as the people they were advising, and the whole aid package turned into a financial bonanza for the well fed and expensively accommodated—the Poles called them the "Marriott brigade"—who had little knowledge of local issues and tended to move on after a few weeks to the next victims of their expertise.

Fast privatization plans created instant millionaires. Corrupt officials and immoral entrepreneurs were quick to take advantage of the new opportunities. The Czech writer Ivan Klíma, surveying some of the damage inflicted on his countrymen as a result of quick economic changes, remarked, "We asked for freedom and you gave us the market."

Yet, overall, Central Europe was successful in reforming its moribund economies and writing its own democratic constitutions while improving the lives of most of its citizens. It was a considerable achievement that came with a significant price tag. Much of the new economic elite emerged from the old *nomenklatura,* the pre-'89 elite and its children. Justice, again, seemed to have failed those who had been dispossessed for fifty years.

There was also the unpleasant fact that millions of citizens of all social strata had been willing and unwilling tools of the postwar Soviet-dominated state police. There were secrets that had been hidden or half-hidden from all, except from the perpetrators, many of whom are now dead, their acts preserved in state security archives. Each country tried to deal with the mountains of documents its secret services had compiled during forty-five years of Communist dictatorships that spied on individuals and bribed or threatened people to report on their friends. Some countries set up truth commissions; some allowed the documents to be destroyed or pilfered; some stuffed them into new archives. Some managed it better than others, but none resolved the issues nor succeeded in delivering tangible justice to those who had been imprisoned, exiled, broken by the system.

Nobel Prize–winning author Herta Müller said in a Frankfurt newspaper that over 40 per cent of those in power in her native Romania are veterans of the dreaded Securitate, Ceauşescu's most powerful weapon against his own people. "In Romania," she said, "they're pretending that the past disappeared into thin air."

Under the thick ice of Communism, those east of the Iron Curtain had not fully dealt with their role in the Shoah, the genocide of their Jewish populations. Except for the immediate postwar executions of well-known collaborators, a complicit silence shrouded the six million dead, despite the fact that most of the extermination centres were here, east of the Oder-Neisse line, in the full knowledge of the locals and, in some places, with their complicity. The people in the East did not have the handy excuse of the French or the Dutch that they did not know where their neighbours were taken in those murderous boxcars. Here, the stench of death was an everyday event, as was the robbing of the dead.

The Holocaust did not easily fit into the Communist mythology about World War II: the Red Army's "Great Patriotic War" and its final victory over Fascism. Even the Fascists had to be redefined to eliminate an association with the clean-living East Germans versus the capitalist-imperialist West Germans. In the workers' paradise, it was vital to specify one's enemies. Not even Auschwitz, where 1.5 million Jews were killed, escaped the cleansing of Communist ideals: the victims were identified only as Polish, Hungarian, German, French—not as Jews. After 1989, no one had an excuse for evading the brutality of history. Yet there continued to be a resentment for the Jews' place in the order of suffering—as if each horror had to be measured against other horrors and judged on some scale of the relativity of evil.

These are the lands where, under both Nazism and Communism, brutality had been an everyday event, where expulsions of whole populations were explained as inevitable, where disappearances had to be borne in silence, where whole villages were emptied to supply slave labour, where millions were murdered. Thirty-one million people were violently moved from their homes, according to historian Paul Robert Magocsi,[6] and the rape and murder of conquered peoples by the German and Soviet armies were neighbourhood events. Whole populations were charged, collectively, with war crimes. The accused included the German-speaking populations of Poland, Czechoslovakia, Hungary, Romania, Yugosalvia and the Soviet Union, and the Hungarians in Czechoslovakia, Romania, and Yugoslavia. They were expelled from their homes and countries and alternatively degraded, killed, beaten. In the East, the punishment for collaboration was swifter and less circumscribed by laws than in the West. The dismissal of whole classes of citizens as traitors gave the new postwar regimes a blank slate to remake society to suit their Marxist ideology. In Hungary, 300,000[7] people were hauled before the people's courts; in Austria, fewer than 150,000.

At Communism's end, the ghosts of history returned with a vengeance, a reminder of half-forgotten events, old ethnic rivalries, borders drawn and redrawn, ghosts that had lurked, unacknowledged, under Communism's force-fed stories of peaceful coexistence and a common front toward the Western enemy.

In 1989, Central Europe came "as a messenger not only of freedom and tolerance but also of hatred and intolerance. It is here, in Central Europe, that the last two wars began," said Adam Michnik, one of the architects of Poland's first democratic government. Michnik, the much-admired resistance hero, a man who would rather stay in prison than leave his country, is now the editor of Poland's largest, most profitable liberal daily newspaper, and a regular on the talk circuit.

Very soon, the powerful, inspired, charismatic groups that had in 1989 led their countries out of the thickets of totalitarian rule fractured into separate parties and fought one another at the polls over precisely these old schisms, differences, perceptions of history.

WHEN BERLIN set out to celebrate the twentieth anniversary of the fall of the Wall, it dressed itself in its post-Communist best. There were fireworks and light shows, U2 played a free concert, a two-kilometre domino chain was symbolically toppled and the East Side Gallery showcased the retouched murals on its two-kilometre-long stretch of the Wall along the river Spree. Angela Merkel, the first East German to be elected chancellor, welcomed world leaders to a long, self-congratulatory talkfest that included the requisite number of former dissidents.

Most of the stalwart members of the Soviets' Warsaw Pact are now members of the European Union and NATO, all facing West, with cautious backs to a glowering, nationalistic Russia that uses its gas and oil reserves, much as it had used its armies, to threaten and cajole. Russia's violent foray into Georgia, its former dominion, has served its cautionary purpose. Europe, eager to continue to purchase energy from Moscow, has made disapproving noises but has failed to pose a meaningful threat against Russian aggression.

NATO celebrated its sixtieth birthday in April 2009 amid questions about its role and effectiveness. Its original boast that an attack against one of its members is an attack on all has foundered on its roles in Iraq and Afghanistan and on its cautious response to Russia's invasion of Georgia. For longer than a decade now, Russian "diplomats" have been accredited to NATO, free to wander about the Brussels headquarters and spy on planned actions, if there are any. Despite the free access, Prime Minister Vladimir Putin has protested all attempts to enlarge NATO membership. He was particularly incensed at the invitation to Georgia and the Ukraine, both of which he considers Russia's "near abroad."

Most Russians have had enough humiliation at the hands of the United States and enough of their own attempts to emulate Western-style capitalism as espoused by the disastrous Yeltsin years. The results of those attempts were a small coterie of monumentally wealthy oligarchs, gangs of violent enforcers, general lawlessness and continued poverty for the masses. Now Russia is redefining its relationship to the West and reconsidering its own history. Even Stalin's crimes have found a gentle apologist in Putin: "We have never used nuclear weapons against civilians," he told a gathering of historians in 2007, "and we have never dumped chemical weapons on thousands of kilometres of land as was the case in Vietnam. We can't allow anyone to impose a sense of guilt on us."

Alarmingly, in a December 2008 Russian opinion survey to determine Russia's greatest historical figure, Stalin came in third, trailing turn-of-the-century prime minister Peter Stolypin and the medieval prince Alexander Nevsky. There were some suggestions that the results were cooked to avoid international embarrassment; otherwise, Stalin would have been voted first.

THE SEPTEMBER 11, 2001, Islamist terrorist attacks on the United States brought all the former Iron Curtain countries to America's side. The determination to spread democracy acquired new urgency, as if democracy would resolve differences between the fervent adherents of Islamic traditions and the open societies advocated by the United States. When President Bush announced that "the global expansion of democracy is the ultimate force" against tyranny, none of Central Europe's new member countries argued. They sent armies to Iraq, where, once more, democracy proved to be unenforceable.

By 2010, much of the goodwill born of America as victim has been eroded by America as aggressor in Iraq and by the trillion-dollar collapse of its financial sector. Europeans are no longer the enthusiastic endorsers of American policies. Western Europeans have shown consistent signs of suspicion and disdain for Americans, fuelled by America's role as the world's sole superpower. Central Europeans' hopes for a robust U.S. response to Russia have been dashed by President Obama's open-arms approach to Prime Minister Putin. Plans for U.S.-funded defensive missiles have been postponed, and, while Poles and Czechs are still supporters of the United States, their unalloyed keenness for sending troops to America's wars is a thing of the past.

Seven leaders in the former Soviet Bloc sent an open letter to President Barack Obama expressing their concerns about his friendly overtures to Russia. Their fear that the United States has lost interest in its former allies, that the bloom is off the new democracies' rose, is palpable even through the diplomatic prose, as is their insistence on their own strategic importance in the region. Presidential hopeful Barack Obama's heartfelt 2008 speech in Berlin, praising the East Germans for tearing down the wall that divided East and West and opening doors to democracy, seems long ago. The April 2010 Prague ceremonial dinner that President Obama hosted for leaders from all the Central European countries did little to assuage their fears that they are no longer in the United States' sightlines. Central Europe had hoped to play a vital role in U.S. foreign policy during the early years of the twenty-first century—its knowledge of Putin's politics and probable expansionist plans can be useful for Americans—but plaintive appeals for special status are unlikely to impress Washington.

The sense of unfairness and failed expectations has led to a toxic atmosphere in Central Europe at the end of the first decade of the new century. The 2009 Slovak presidential elections resounded with nationalist, anti-minority voices. In Hungary, anti-government, anti-minorities, anti-Semitic demonstrations grew in number and ferocity. Those who are disappointed with the results of cozying up to the West, of adopting its capitalist credo, are beginning to yearn for the security of the old order. As philosopher-politician Ralf Dahrendorf predicted, when economic conditions deteriorate, "the *ancien regime* begins to look to many like the good old days."[8]

In preparations for the April 2010 elections in Hungary, Viktor Orbán, leader of the FIDESZ party, spoke of "Greater Hungary," the pre–World War I version that included most of modern-day Slovakia and parts of Romania and Serbia. His populist platform guaranteed his sweeping victory. In Poland, the nationalist-clerical Euroskeptic Law and Justice Party continued its vehement criticism of the liberal government. Slovak prime minister Robert Fico's chauvinist platform, his poisonous attacks on international finance and his anti-EU demagoguery have kept him in power even as his government totters under accusations of corruption. Czech president Václav Klaus kept the European Union waiting for his approval of the Lisbon Treaty, which granted the Union greater powers. His ransom demand in the end boiled down to no more than a final whack at the old enemies: the Sudeten Germans expelled more than fifty years ago.

Czechoslovakia's interwar president, Tomáš Masaryk, famously remarked, "We now have democracy. All we need are some democrats." When asked how long he thought it would take for his country to become a democratic state, he answered, fifty years. That was in 1918. It is now just twenty years since the advent of democracy in Central Europe.

With the benefit of hindsight, looking at our crumbling economies in 2010, it is difficult to remain wholeheartedly wedded to the romantic notion that cozying up to the West could solve Central Europe's problems. Economic solutions are difficult to implement in catastrophically declining markets, as previously rich corporations reach for the most convenient ways to fix their own ships, and the dream of social justice is even more difficult to realize.

Democracy has not delivered on all its promises of stability and security, nor has majority rule guaranteed a willingness to listen to different points of view. In welcoming democracy, Central Europe became plagued by the bugbears of other democracies: public demonstrations of hatred and spite, the need to espouse freedom of expression while keeping the genies of racism and intolerance in the bottle. Democracy is messy, irreverent and, in its drive to be inclusive of everyone, often exclusionary of some. It lacks the thunderous attractions of other nineteenth- and twentieth-century ideas such as nationalism, liberalism, Fascism and Marxism. Marxism in particular drew such a broad coterie of intellectuals from all countries, such enthusiasm and devotion, that we face a great challenge to present democracy in an equally attractive light. This is particularly so in countries where democracy already exists, where freedom of expression and the vote for democratic governments are no longer in question.

IN 2006, I set out to discover whether democracy had taken root behind the Iron Curtain. I chose Central Europe because this part of the world had been the dividing space between East and West, or, as Stalin and Churchill deemed, between spheres of conflicting influence. My second reason is that I am a Central European.

I was born in Budapest at the end of World War II and the beginning of Communist Hungary. My grandfather and mother served time in Communist jails—my grandfather because he expressed his outrage at state controls on his freedom, my mother for having tried to emigrate. I was a child when the 1956 revolution reminded the world that all was not well in the "people's republics." I grew up in one democracy, New Zealand, and now live in another, Canada. When I undertook to find out how Central Europe is faring with its sparkling new democracies, I thought I knew what questions to ask and where the shadows lurked. But the reality surprised me. I have travelled in Poland, Slovakia, the Czech Republic and Hungary, listened to politicians, writers, Roma, shopkeepers, former prisoners, exiles, priests, students, musicians, millionaires, interpreters, entrepreneurs, the new elites and those on the outside looking in. I have tried to be fair in presenting them, their convictions, resentments, dreads and joys. My journey was one of discovery rather than of proving or disproving an existing theory. The one prejudice I carried with me was what I had learned while researching my last book, *Kasztner's Train*. That book took me into the heart of darkness, the horror of the Holocaust. Its ghosts continued to haunt me throughout the writing of this one.

The year 2009 was the twentieth anniversary of the miracle that ended Communist rule in Central Europe. It has been twenty years since the new beginnings, twenty years of experiments with freedom of choice. It was, I thought, a good time to reflect on how the transformation has affected the lives of people who live there. It seemed to me also a good time to ask a question: In the midst of a world more and more inclined to accept dictators (Zimbabwe, Venezuela, Nicaragua, Belarus, Russia, China, to name a few), can this chunk of Europe, with its own ghosts and its own dreads, resist the pull and cling to its hard-won freedoms? Will the power of ideals prevail over the fears, insecurities, resentments and the search for scapegoats?

When talking with young people in Bratislava, Budapest, Warsaw and Prague, it is clear that they are the least anxious about their place in the world and that they take for granted that their future is in their own hands rather than at the whim of politicians they neither know nor care to know. They are less inclined than their parents to linger over historical grievances, and even when they parrot time-worn phrases of racism and intolerance, they seem to do so out of a desire to shock rather than from conviction. Twenty-year-old football hooligans screaming for trains to cart their opponents to Auschwitz have only a faint notion of what that word means to those who know.

THE STATE OF THE UNION

In September 1946, on receiving an honorary degree from the University of Zürich, Sir Winston Churchill, Britain's wartime prime minister, mentioned for the first time his idea for a "United States of Europe." It was an outrageous notion such a short time after the fighting had stopped, but Churchill foresaw that the combatants could knit together a new kind of federation that would end war in Europe.

Sixty-four years later, the European Union has twenty-seven members, has the largest single market in the world and, despite the decline of the past two years, still exports more than it imports. The euro has replaced the national currencies of most of its members, with the venerable French franc and the equally venerable Deutschmark leading the way into history. Slovenia was the first of the former Soviet satellites to adopt the euro. Slovakia followed. The global economic crisis has jolted confidence in the euro, but the fiscal prudence the wealthier members are forcing on the more profligate will, I think, serve the Union well in years to come.

The Union has close to 500 million people, a constitution and a relatively new presidency with some defined powers. After years of haggling and debate, all members agreed to sign the Lisbon Treaty, transferring some national rights to the new president and foreign minister. While journalists criticized the choices of both Belgium's Herman Van Rompuy and Britain's Lady Catherine Ashton—neither has an international profile, and both are bland, relative unknowns—their election brought to a close the vicious bargaining for position within the Union. If the new president can lend a human face to what most Europeans imagine as a vast collection of fat, faceless gnomes in Brussels's glittery glass palaces, the European Union could still become the powerhouse the German-French postwar agreements promised. There is a real possibility now of a common EU foreign and security policy, something that would make it a real global "player," as so many of its member states have wished. Henry Kissinger may still get his wish for a single number to dial when the U.S. wants to contact Europe.

Unfortunately, 2009 did not end well. The demand for higher wages by the 45,000 EU officials was received with derision by the cash-strapped member states.[9] Unlike the EU's previous blunders—regulating the size of condoms and the contents of British bangers—this sign of its disengagement from reality failed to amuse.

It is too soon to know how generously the wealthier members of the European Union will help their new colleagues during the economic crisis that has borne down on the world at the beginning of the twenty-first century, how the new realities of the market and the catastrophic collapse of financial institutions will affect decisions in Europe. But as Polish prime minister Donald Tusk observed with growing alarm, "the European ship is rocking and they may start throwing the weaker passengers overboard." Some of the old member states have openly questioned the wisdom of allowing the newcomers to become full members. A few EU countries have demanded restrictions on foreign workers, and others are objecting to what they see as a free ride for reckless Southerners, such as Greece and Spain, and spendthrift Easterners, such as Hungary and Latvia, on the backs of more prudent economies. Policies proposed to counter this have undermined the Union's open-markets base and threaten to destroy the sense of safety and community that belonging to the EU has signalled to the new entrants. Being viewed as those "slightly disreputable, pesky relations" is no longer to be so easily tolerated.

Hungarian prime minister Ferenc Gyurcsány, a few short weeks before his forced resignation, noted that a new Iron Curtain was being lowered between the established and recent members of the EU. "In the beginning of the nineties," he told a group of leaders in Brussels, "we reunified Europe; now the challenge is whether we will be able to reunify Europe financially."

As the financial crisis deepened, the IMF, the leadership of the EU and its bankers had to show what true solidarity is. They examined ways to bail out older members, such as the desperately moribund Portugal, Italy, Ireland, Greece and Spain—the so-called PIIGS—who have lived beyond their means. Their eleventh-hour 750-billion-euro rescue and stabilization plan with back-breaking terms and nasty conditions guaranteed further protests in Athens. By contrast, the former satellites seemed to manage without broken windows and anti-Brussels slogans. In its March 20, 2010, issue, *The Economist* praised the "grim patience of ex-communist voters, whose living standards have plunged." Their forbearance and resilience in the face of declining fortunes compared favourably with the Greeks' protest riots.

There is little doubt that by 2010, the EU had lost its enthusiasm for enlargement. Even the drawn-out discussions about the admission of Turkey and the more progressive Balkan countries have stalled. The Orange Revolution failed to bring Ukraine near EU standards, and President Viktor Yanukovych is likely to steer the country closer to Russia.

The June 2009 elections to the European Parliament demonstrated the renewed strength of ultranationalist parties that have nothing in common except their fear and suspicion of those who do not fit their self-definition as the representatives of their country's *volk*. The British BNP advertised its in-your-face stance of "Putting British People First." A most uncharacteristic debate continued to rage in Holland about national identity and the Dutch desire to define a recognizable community at home, one with shared stories and shared morality. The debate has succeeded in punishing the governing parties and rewarding Geert Wilders's Euroskeptic, right-wing populist Party for Freedom.

French president Nicolas Sarkozy's yearning for a new definition of French identity has created a cultural storm in the European country with the largest Muslim minority. If he hoped to entice Muslims into some form of nationalist self-expression, he has failed. If the idea was to delineate the difference between the French and their new immigrants, he may have succeeded. The government has also succeeded in uniting various, usually rival, liberal groups in defending a symbol of women's subjugation: the niqab.

The right-wing populist Danish People's Party increased its proportion of the vote to 15 per cent; Italy's anti-immigrant Northern League is exerting its influence in that country's parliament. During the past five decades, the mostly Muslim non-white population of the continent has increased sevenfold, and it is expected to rise further even if no new immigrants are added. While the white population is becoming a vast old people's home, Muslims are having children. As Europe's population ages, it needs new immigrants to keep its workforce functioning and paying for the increased benefits its old people require. It remains to be seen whether Europeans' fears of being overrun by anti-democratic, religious fanatics with a penchant for suicide bombings (Spain), revenge murders (Holland), honour killings and chador-wearing will prevail over their economic needs and urge to believe that the silent majority of Muslims are law-abiding citizens.[10]

So far, there is little indication that Muslims are inclined to settle east of the Elbe River. Local economists predict that the influx will start when the financial markets recover and Central Europe improves its social benefits programs for immigrants.

For now, Central Europe's prevailing racial concerns are over homegrown linguistic minorities as well as the timeworn "others": gypsies and Jews. In 2009, the Greater Romania Party won 9 per cent of the national vote and two seats in the EU; in the April 2010 elections, Hungary's Jobbik party won almost 17 per cent of the vote, and it has three seats in the European parliament; Austrian and Polish extremist parties gained voter support, even as the more liberal, democratic parties declined. Despite Jörg Haider's death at the wheel of a car (he was drunk at the time), his populist, racist, anti-EU Alliance for the Future of Austria won with a new leader who campaigned with Haider's old placards. Now the Carinthian provincial Haider party is teaming up with the other extremists, the Freedom Party of Austria, to form a clear threat to the democratic parties that rule in Vienna.

These extremist parties rely mostly on support from the angry, resentful, envious underachievers in their countries. While it is unlikely that they will do much to influence EU policies, what remains to be seen is how they fare in local elections and whether their popularity tempts their governing parties to borrow, as they have in Slovakia, chunks of their ideological platforms.

Václav Havel, who has remained a stalwart supporter of the European Union, if only in contrast to his Euroskeptic Czech colleague President Václav Klaus, criticizes the EU's impenetrable bureaucracy and its technocratic, materialistic approaches to the key issues facing its members. "The European Union is letting itself be dragged, with no resistance, in the same general direction as the rest of global civilization: it's driven by the idea of growth, growth for the sake of growth, the creation of profit at any price," he says in *To the Castle and Back*. He sees Europe heading toward a soulless society where morality has no place and where there is no room for questioning the prevailing culture of economic success, a society devoid of a spiritual dimension, obsessed with trivialities, a society whose "best-known representative is the multi-national corporation."

Klaus, true to form, characterized the European Union as a cipher, an entity with no real meaning, a false construct "at variance with the original principle, the European idea of freedom . . . [I]t does not have a common idea and it won't ever have one." In the words of Mark Eyskens, Belgium's foreign minister in 1991, the European Union has chosen to be "an economic giant, a political dwarf, and a military worm."

ON DECEMBER 16, 2008, the European Parliament unanimously agreed to create a vast multi-million-dollar museum called the House of European History. The project was proposed by Hans-Gert Pöttering, then president-for-six-months of the European Parliament, who thought such a project would "promote an awareness of European identity." It was a lovely idea, following Central Europe's much-vaunted re-entry into European history. However, given the various contentious bits of history still hotly debated to the east of Brussels, the plans, as outlined in a twenty-eight-page document, ran onto the shoals of the myriad painful memories and political debates over World War II and its aftermath. Debates continued through 2009, with French attacks on the United States and its Middle Eastern policies, and Polish insistence on the recognition of its role during World War II and in the ending of Communist rule. Now the notion that an acceptable museum and common history could be created by 2014, as originally announced, seems rather remote.

NOSTALGIA

FOR THE

HABSBURGS

CENTRAL EUROPE, as Polish journalist Konstanty Gebert suggests, is a state of mind. According to Czech novelist Milan Kundera, it "is a culture or fate. Its borders are imaginary and must be drawn and redrawn with each new historical situation." It is made up of small nations that contend with their precarious lives between large nations that are uninterested in their existence. Hungarian playwright Ödön Horváth billed himself as the typical Central European: "I was born in Fiume, grew up in Belgrade, Budapest, Pressburg, Vienna, and Munich, and I have a Hungarian passport... I am a typical mix of old Austria-Hungary: at once Magyar, Croatian, German and Czech."[1] Horváth, incidentally, like Kafka, wrote in German.

Central Europe has several recognizably common architectural features that make some towns in Galicia look remarkably like towns in Transylvania and Slovakia; shared musicians—Liszt, Chopin, Mahler, Dvořák, Smetana, Bartók, Kodály; shared writers, such as Musil, Gombrowicz, Koestler, Brod, Mickiewicz, Kafka, Roth, Zweig, Faludy; and some peculiar shared traditions, such as the tiny coffee spoon and the oversweet desserts with whipping cream.

British author Jan Morris writes of trams as "emblematic mechanisms of Austro-Hungary which trundled down the imperial streets in Poland as in Transylvania" and, of course, in Budapest and Vienna. But Central Europe is certainly not a geographical designation in the way that Finland or Sweden is: it lacks permanent borders, and it has no single common denominator, except perhaps that much of it had once belonged to the Habsburgs.

Some four or five centuries ago, the Habsburgs proudly claimed to rule over an empire "on which the sun never set." From 1278 till 1918, the Habsburg dynasty dominated the largest chunk of Europe. They lorded it over the Czechs, having beaten them in Moravia and Bohemia during the Hussite wars of the fifteenth century. They were eager to grab the southern, or Galician, chunk of Poland in 1772. Empress Maria Theresa, outwardly sorrowful at taking part in the dismemberment of another Roman Catholic country, took her piece of Poland when the opportunity arose. She said that owning this piece of Europe would come back to haunt the Habsburgs, and it did.

They left behind grand baroque churches, convents, castles and gaudy palaces. When, under Maria Theresa, their attention shifted from Prague to Vienna, Prague lost its imperial lustre and became a provincial city—a fact the Czechs never forgave and awaited their opportunity to avenge.

The Habsburgs beat the Hungarians into submission during two wars of independence but, after Austria's disastrous war with Prussia, signed an agreement with them for a semblance of joint rule in 1867. They still shared the same supreme authority: Franz Joseph, emperor of Austria and king of Hungary. The emperor-king had to be crowned twice—once in each country—and swear allegiance to each, in glittering ceremonies that took days to complete. Each country had its own parliament and each was independent in some other ways, but for the joint administration of such dull business as postage, money, foreign affairs, defence.

Some historians still maintain that had the empire remained intact, had the victorious Allies not insisted on its dismemberment after the First World War, there would not have been a Second World War. The empire would have honoured its ancient role of preventing the Cold War's "clash of civilizations."[2]

The Austro-Hungarian Empire governed a variety of nationalities, languages, customs, extremes—the kind of diversity the twenty-first century holds dear and praises as a harbinger of equitable times. Its administrators and judges performed a mostly reasonable, if slow-moving, series of tasks; their rules helped to keep enemies apart, and their laws did provide some protection for minorities. A large bureaucratic system ruled by professional civil servants managed the empire's every jurisdiction. There was diversity of religion and there were myriad languages. The function of the central government was to ensure that the boring bits of life ticked along within the law. While philosopher-politician Ralf Dahrendorf allows in *After 1898* that the reality "was not quite as appealing as the warm glow of memory," he concluded in his September 1992 keynote address to German historians that the European Union could do far worse than to follow the Habsburg format. This model includes no push for federalism, but it respects civil and human rights and the rights of citizenship.

Could the empire have resisted the urge to go to war over a young Bosnian Serb's assassination of the Archduke Franz Ferdinand? It certainly could have, but the strain of holding all those divergent national interests at bay was beginning to fray its cloth. The senseless war led by the czar and emperor—cousins, really—ended with the partitioning of the Habsburg lands and the end of the dual monarchy.

There are historians who believe that the central catastrophe of the twentieth century was World War I,[3] because it gave rise to Nazism, Communism and all the other evils that bestrode what had once been European civilization.[4] Emperor-King Karl's 1917 attempts to sue for peace on behalf of his peoples fell on deaf ears. After the defeat of 1918, a variety of independent states emerged from the ruins of the empire, and after the next world war, all but one, Austria, found themselves ruled by the Soviet Union.

Now, a century after the empire's demise, there is a sense of nostalgia in some of these borderlands for the predictable bureaucracies and the multinational landscapes of the Habsburgs. "Galicia has retained its own, rather Habsburg character even after all these years," says Krzysztof Jasiewicz, professor of social theory at Washington and Lee University. "It is socially conservative, traditional,

Catholic, a stronghold of the Law and Justice party that yearns for the old, small-town ways. During the '80s, it was utterly committed to Solidarity. They are different from the rest of Poland where the Habsburgs had no base."

And the grand castle in what is now Bratislava (once Pozsony for the Hungarians and Pressburg for the Austrians) retains an air of empire. The elite here used to be Hungarian, Austrian or German. "Always on the periphery of someone else's centre," Fedor Gál, a Slovak intellectual, tells me. "When there was a census under the Habsburgs, only about 100,000 people admitted to being Slovaks—being Slovak meant you were a shepherd."

In 1918, the Habsburgs were banished from the spanking-new country of Czechoslovakia. They lost their palaces, citizenship and permission to visit their former homes. Prince Friedrich's magnificent palace is now the Slovak president's home in Bratislava, but in a friendly gesture toward the past, the palace displays a copy of an old baroque statue of Maria Theresa, the original having been beheaded and smashed in Nitra during the ebullient days of the new republic.

THE LAST almost emperor-king of the Habsburg dynasty lives in Pöcking, a distant suburb of Munich, the second to last station of the s6, on the way to Tutzing. It is a long way from the imperial glory of the five-hundred-year-old court in Vienna, or the royal castles in Buda, Bratislava and Prague. The station itself is a grey concrete bunker; an underpass directs you to either side of the road. One leads to Lake Starnberg, the other to a steep country road that winds between two rows of neat, small houses, modest gardens, a gas station, a motel, a bar.

The emperor-king's house is near the top of the hill, across the road from a motel. Its gate has no number. Considering his numerous inherited honours and titles, the long history of his name, these are surprisingly modest surroundings. I was there on a gloomy April afternoon in 2000, marching uphill and passing by the unmarked driveway, then returning to ask for directions at the motel. The proprietor was eating his dinner in back of the bar, his white napkin tucked into his collar. When I asked about the driveway across the street, he said he had no idea what number it was but he was certain they would not welcome visitors. When I enquired whether it was Otto von Habsburg's house, he shook his head and continued eating, warily.

The iron gate was open. A sign warned of vicious dogs, but all I saw were two ancient dachshunds, their tails raised half-heartedly as they lumbered toward me. The house sits at the end of the winding, narrow driveway. From a distance, it had seemed bigger and more imposing than it was up close. It rises like a poor man's Bavarian castle, all bevelled windows and towerettes, stairways, a long balcony, stone flowerpots.

The dogs accompanied me up the short staircase, under the brown awning to an even narrower door. When the door opened, they both dashed inside with a sudden agility that belied their advanced age. The old gentleman who stood in the doorway uttered some gentle warning at them, but he made no move to bar their way.

He then opened the door wider and stretched out his hand. His fingers were thin and long, his grasp surprisingly strong. "Otto Habsburg," he said. "Come in," in English. In German, he asked to take my coat and hung it in the dark hallway. He asked, in Hungarian, whether I preferred Hungarian. For him, all three languages were equal, interchangeable. He had learned German as a young child in Austria, Hungarian in preparation for ascending to the dual monarchy's throne, and finally English, Latin and Portuguese at school. His mother, the ironhanded Empress Zita, believed that Otto would need all this and more to discuss matters of state with his European counterparts, the kings and princes of royal Europe. But it was not to be.

In 1918, Otto's father was forced to abdicate his titles and his inheritance that included Austria, Hungary, Slovakia, the Czech Republic and large parts of Poland, Romania and the former Yugoslavia.

There was nothing to prevent the individual nationalities from grabbing for one another's throats. The treaties of Versailles (or, as it's known in some parts, Trianon) lit fires that became impossible to put out. It was on the coattails of that sense of aggrieved entitlement that Miklós Horthy, a former aide to Otto's grandfather Franz Joseph, maintained power in Hungary from 1920 till October 1944. Horthy, the self-styled "regent," had no intention of ever returning the crown to the Habsburgs. He prevented Otto's father's return to Hungary and pushed the country further and further into Germany's arms after Hitler came to power. He traded his support for the Nazis for pieces of the old Hungary, forcibly returned from its neighbours.

When I asked Otto about the "regent," he gave a wintry laugh, then said he refused to discuss "that man." It is interesting that while Otto avoided all contact with Hitler, Miklós Horthy was often his unwilling and unwelcome guest. Hitler disdained Horthy, and Horthy thought Hitler was mad—sometimes usefully mad, but nevertheless mad.

As for more recent racial tensions in what had once been his family's backyard, Otto does not like to comment; his interests now, as then, are the future of a united Europe. Central Europe may have absented itself after 1945, but it has always been part of Europe. It never fell off the map, and Otto sees himself as a vital link between Central Europe's past and its future.

A passionate opponent of the Yalta system to carve up Europe, Otto travelled throughout the world to persuade leaders of the need to combat Communist tyranny. He joined the pan-European movement while he was in his twenties and was elected to the European Parliament in 1979. From the beginning, he championed the cause of the larger Europe. He insisted that there should be an empty chair at all meetings, representing the missing countries of Europe.

In August 1989, he sponsored the Pan-European Picnic near Sopron, at the Austria-Hungary border. As if by happy coincidence, 661 visiting East Germans who had taken refuge at the West German embassy in Budapest were given maps to easily locate Sopron and the picnic. They were welcomed on behalf of the Pan-European Union by Otto's daughter Walburga, a lawyer and member of the Swedish Parliament, and sent on their way to Austria. It was the first time a satellite country refused to honour another satellite's laws of not allowing Easterners to go to the West. And it was one of the opening acts to the demolition of the Berlin Wall.

Once the barriers came down, Otto focussed his considerable energies on bringing Poland, Hungary and Czechoslovakia into the EU, and most recently, he was anxious to persuade the European Union to grant membership to Croatia. Hungary, he said, enjoyed several great advantages: the world's perception of the 1956 revolution was, clearly, one of them; the opening of the gates to the East Germans was another. Perhaps the fact that the Communist system had become sufficiently relaxed to allow foreign investment—that there was some private enterprise already—helped.

WHAT OTTO did not mention was how he had worked to promote Hungary's image. That information comes from his second son, George, who would have been an archduke and second in line to the throne had the monarchy survived. George is an exceptionally tall man with the slight stoop of the shoulders very tall men seem to develop in their forties. He has dark, curly hair and the somewhat jutting chin of his illustrious ancestors, a chin that became most pronounced on the Spanish side of the family. Poor Velásquez had a devil of a job trying to minimize the chins when he became the royal artist in Madrid during the 1600s.

We had lunch at Budapest's Gresham Palace Four Seasons Hotel, undoubtedly the city's most prestigious accommodation. It was a sunny day in September 2008. George had his own table, a round one against the wall, from where he could look out the high picture windows over the square where his great-grandfather Franz Joseph had sworn allegiance to the Hungarians on June 8, 1867. Dressed in the uniform of a Hungarian general, the newly minted emperor-king had ridden his white horse across the Chain Bridge and mounted what they called "Coronation Hill" because it was made of soil from every county in the realm. He then waved his ceremonial sword at the four corners of the kingdom, indicating that he would defend the land from all its enemies. I craned my neck a bit to look across the bridge at the Royal Castle on the Buda side of the Danube. It's where the Habsburgs stayed when they were in residence here, rather than at the larger, more opulent and more comfortable Hofburg Imperial Palace in Vienna or their summer residence, Schönbrunn Palace.

The June 1867 "Compromise" with the Habsburgs guaranteed peace after the bloody revolution of 1848. A short walk from the hotel, along the Danube Corso there is the bronze statue of Sándor Petőfi, poet and revolutionary, killed during that revolution. It was no accident that the 1956 revolution began to take shape at the foot of this statue. In 1848, as it happened, the Habsburgs called on the Russians to help them put down their unruly Hungarian subjects, and a little more than a hundred years later it was the Soviet army that put down the October 1956 revolution.

The Habsburg properties were confiscated by the state when the monarchy was dissolved in 1919. With a little smile, George tells me his father had not been allowed to take even his favourite toys with him. While numerous buildings here and in Vienna are still adorned with the Habsburgs' crowned, double-headed eagle, there is no statue to the last emperor-king of the Habsburg Empire. George, as head of the Hungarian Red Cross, takes no salary, as he accepted none when he was Hungary's ambassador to the EU.

He has learned to love Hungary since he moved here in 1992, but he stays out of public affairs. This allows him to represent the country irrespective of which party rules. In terms of politics, he says, "My only interest is that the Habsburg name should not disappear from history books"—a remarkably modest ambition for a name that dominated Europe for more than five centuries.

In 2010, Georgia chose as its new ambassador to Berlin Gabriela Maria Charlotte Felicitas Elisabeth Antonia von Habsburg-Lotheringer, Princess Imperial and Archduchess of Austria and Hungary, the fourth of Otto von Habsburg's seven children. Like all Otto's children, she is educated in several languages and has the refined manners, bearing and charm of an aristocrat—most of the prerequisites needed to persuade the Europeans that Georgia, despite its recent troubles, is one of them.

ONE

POLAND

THE RETURN OF MEMORY

The past is never dead, it is not even past.
HANNAH ARENDT, quoting William Faulkner

IN STAŚ Pruszyński's smoke-filled Radio Café, everyone wants to discuss history. Perhaps they are encouraged by the framed, faded photographs of former Radio Free Europe celebrities that decorate the walls; perhaps it's the Old World atmosphere of the restaurant-bar, the bare wooden tables. Or maybe it's Staś himself (who used to be "Stash" when he lived in Montreal), drawing them deep into his own tales of a childhood irreparably damaged by war. His father escaped from a German concentration camp and joined the Polish resistance army in Brittany. His mother was smuggled out of Belarus and, hiding with friends, barely survived the war in Kraków. Staś remained with a Belarusian peasant family until his mother came for him after the war. Communism was kind to Staś's father, naming him the People's Republic of Poland's ambassador to Holland. It was less kind to his mother, who never learned to keep her thoughts to herself.

As he talks, Staś leans across the polished mahogany table, his arms folded, his broad shoulders hunched, wishing to share confidences, but his voice carries over the others in the room. When he steps out into his kitchen, I listen to the group of students debating whether Communism and Nazism are comparably evil. Nazism is leading by a hair's breadth when Staś comes back, bearing a platter piled high with pork ribs, veal chops and chunks of beef. He says he returned to Poland in 1992 because there was hope in the air and, no matter how far he had gone, no matter how successful he had been in Canada and the United States, at heart he had remained a Pole.

He tells me that the Germans killed his grandfather in 1941. Did I know that the Germans were going to kill all the Poles who were not suited for manual labour? Did I know how the Allies traded the Poles to Stalin at Yalta? The price was counted in the millions of Soviet lives, the Red Army's cost in driving the Germans out of Eastern Europe, all the way to Berlin. Of course, the essential deal had been struck already in Moscow in October 1944 between Churchill and Stalin, Stalin using a blue pencil to tick his desired "spheres of influence."

Yalta, February 1945, merely sealed the agreement.

A resort town in the Crimea, on the Black Sea, designated vacation spot of favoured Soviet bureaucrats and select sanatorium of the proletariat for its warm climate and verdant mountains, Yalta is where the legendary leaders of the victorious powers met to decide the fate of Europe after the not yet predictable German and Japanese defeat, where, as legendary Polish philosopher Leszek Kołakowski put it, "the fate of millions was decided by three old men: a bloodthirsty tyrant, a terminally ill statesman who knew little about the issues, and a Realpolitker of a declining empire."[1] Yalta is where Winston Churchill and Franklin Roosevelt sealed the deal with Stalin. Everyone seemed to have forgotten that, in September 1939, Britain and France had declared war on Germany because of their treaty to defend Poland. It had made scant difference that Poland had fought the war on the side of the Allies. Stalin grabbed his reward.

Some historians have argued that Churchill had no choice in the matter: that Soviet troops were already in place and the

Moscow-trained Communist government was already in Warsaw. Poland lost about 20 per cent of its territory in the east. In compensation, the thoughtful Allies presented the Poles with a chunk of Germany mostly inhabited by Germans for the previous three hundred years. More than three million Germans and three and a half million Poles were moved to accommodate the border changes. Oh yes, the Poles remember Yalta.

Some sixty-five years later, they still talk about that meeting as if it happened a week ago. Poland was betrayed, its wartime service ignored, its people condemned to Russian slavery—"the Christ of Nations," the sacrificial lamb. In this rather confident, democratic part of Europe, it is still impossible to escape the Poles' sense of victimhood. Memories of past wrongs invade conversations; examining the past occupies writers. History is, according to a 2008 survey, one of the top two categories that readers choose regularly. Much of Polish history had remained blanketed by the heavy and impenetrable layers of denial that was Communism. Now, after the thaw, it is as if everyone has a stake in correcting misconceptions, getting the facts right.

"We learn history not to know how to behave or how to succeed, but to know who we are," according to Kołakowski. The author of thirty books, including a three-volume history of Marxism,[2] Leszek Kołakowski had a keen appreciation of the need to understand history.

THE POLITICS OF MEMORY

Poland's top-grossing film in 2007 was Andrzej Wajda's *Katyń*. Its subject: the 1940 massacre of Polish officers by Soviet troops. Germany and the Soviet Union signed a mutual non-aggression pact in August 1939[3]—a deal that allowed their armies to invade Poland from two directions, splitting the Polish defence. The film tells the story of the Polish officers who had surrendered to the Red Army, their murder at Stalin's orders and the cover-up that followed.

In 1943, two years after Hitler launched his attack on the Soviet Union, the Germans discovered the shallow mass graves of 4,500 Polish officers (of the over twenty thousand killed there) in the Katyń forest. Each man had been shot through the back of the head;

all were still wearing their army uniforms. Stalin, who was now Churchill's and Roosevelt's ally against Germany, denied responsibility. At the Nuremberg Military Tribunals, the Soviet prosecutor, General R.A. Rudenko, accused the Germans of the crime but failed to provide any credible evidence. As the tribunal had been set up specifically to investigate war crimes by Germany and its allies, there was to be no further investigation. Britain's prime minister, Winston Churchill, who certainly suspected the truth, decided that the "issue should be avoided." When the BBC aired a documentary about Katyń in 1971, the People's Republic of Poland's embassy in London protested, but by then no one, other than Poles, seemed interested in the massacre.

The Polish Communist Party not only lied about the perpetrators, but it also used questions about Katyń to test the loyalty of party members wishing to climb the bureaucratic ladder. Everyone knew the truth, but there was a common bond of silence.

Wajda's father was murdered at Katyń.

Stalin's reasons for this particular massacre were, in hindsight, obvious. Polish officers were the "cadre" of the old order. In civilian life they were teachers, lawyers, doctors, government officials—in short, the intelligentsia—whose ties to the past could have obstructed the way Moscow defined the future. Stalin had been concerned about the Poles' military skills since their victory over the Soviet army. He often made nasty comments about the Polish gentry—the *szlachta*, or hereditary ruling nobility—whose very existence was anathema to Communist ideology. Perhaps Stalin, who seemed fearless to his own people, was afraid of Poles. He even ordered the murder of his own loyal Polish Bolsheviks and their wives.

The various reasons for Stalin's hostility toward Poland have been discussed and debated by a number of historians and will, no doubt, continue to fascinate them and their successors if more of the Kremlin's archives are opened to the public.

In 1987, the USSR's last president, Mikhail Gorbachev, announced that the "blank pages" of Polish-Soviet history should now be filled to heal the wounds. On April 4, 1990, TASS, the Soviet news agency, finally admitted that the NKVD (the People's Commissariat for

Internal Affairs) had murdered the Polish officers at Katyń and others at several other locations in Belarus and the Ukraine. Prime Minister Putin has been somewhat less forthcoming on the subject.

Russia's current high school history curriculum must be applied
"in accordance with the objectives of protecting and strengthen-
ing our state sovereignty [and] rearing citizens who are patriots of
Russia." In Putin's patriotic views, the "Katyń assassinations" were
regrettable but may have been a justified response to the mistreat-
ment of Red Army soldiers in Polish prison camps after the war of
1920.[4] Perhaps the Russian archives are awaiting Putin's decision
about what Soviet history he wishes the world to know.

Naturally, Katyń was not a subject that Polish children were
taught after 1945. The 1962–70 thirteen-volume Polish encyclopedia
has no entry for Katyń. Nor is there a reference to the mass murders
in the second edition of the *Great Soviet Encyclopedia*. The Molotov-
Ribbentrop Pact is also excluded. Fascists were, by definition, and in
all textbooks, the sworn enemies of Communists, so it was impossible to deal with a time when they were allies.

When I asked Piotr Wróbel, a former history lecturer at Warsaw
University, what he had taught about the murders, he said, very little until the early '80s. Wróbel's own professor, Krzysztof Jasiewicz,
says that by the late '70s, when a student asked, you could say that
according to one theory, the soldiers had been executed by the Soviet
army. But only a fool or the very brave would talk about the massacres in the presence of a known Party official or his son or daughter.
The ruling regime was quick to punish those who broke the bond of
silence. The same official obfuscation surrounded the Warsaw Uprising, the Polish Underground army and the government-in-exile. The
books that were published had to be submitted to the censors. The
role of the Soviet army had to be pristine, though everybody knew at
least a part of the truth.

Today, there is an impressive monument in the centre of Warsaw
dedicated to "those who died or were murdered in the East, the victims of Soviet aggression of 17 September, 1939." The gigantic bronze
and concrete construction includes a long piece of railway track
and displays the names of the places where Polish prisoners died in

Soviet captivity. It culminates in a series of tall bronze crosses leaning over an open wagon sealed on one side with the Polish eagle in
bondage. The monument is presented by "The Nation." Even on a
cold winter day in late January 2009, there are bouquets of red and
white flowers laid over some of the markers with the names of faraway prison camps. One large wreath leans against the wheels of the
cart. On either side of the monument, cars speed toward a modern
traffic circle.

Shortly after its occupation of Kraków in 1939, the ss rounded
up most of the academics at Jagiellonian University and transported
them to Buchenwald for later disposal. I once took a bus tour that
ground to a halt in front of the university's neo-Gothic red brick
facade, allowing our soft-spoken young Polish guide an opportunity
to tell us that this is Europe's second-oldest university, founded in
1364 by Kasimir III the Great, and that its world-renowned professors were among the Nazis' first victims. She had the practised delivery of a seasoned tour guide, but when she reached the end of the
story, she wiped tears from her eyes.

The university was closed, looted, much of it destroyed. In the
German view of the world, Poles would have no need for education;
they were useful only for hard labour. In defiance of Nazi rules, the
few survivors continued to give courses in private homes throughout the city. About a thousand students were educated this way, most
of them receiving their degrees when the horror of German rule was
over.

Under German occupation, Poles developed an underground
society with schools, banks, newspapers, social security and, of
course, an army. This complex organization, which by 1943 involved
over a half-million people, was a mirror image of an ordinary state,
except that its entire existence was forbidden and its employees, if
caught, could be shot.

Poland never capitulated to the Germans. The Polish government-
in-exile, formed in Paris shortly after the German-Soviet occupation,
relocated to London after the French capitulated. It was recognized
by all Allied governments. Thousands of Polish soldiers and much
of the navy escaped and formed military units in Britain and France

under the command of the prime minister, General Władysław Sikorski. They fought in Norway, France, the Battle of the Atlantic, North Africa. The large, semi-circular military cemetery of the 2nd Polish Corps at Monte Cassino attests to their sacrifices in Italy.

In April 1943, Sikorski demanded a Red Cross investigation into the Katyń massacre. He died three months later in a mysterious plane crash. There is much speculation among historians that Stalin, worried that Sikorski might interfere with Churchill and Roosevelt against his plans for Poland, was responsible for his death.

On November 27, 2008, forensic scientists removed General Sikorski from his coffin among the country's royals and long-dead heroes in Kraków's Wawel Cathedral. His decayed body was still wrapped in the blanket that had been all the honours afforded this military hero when he was returned to Poland in 1993. The remains were tested to determine whether the general died when his plane crashed, as reported on July 4, 1943, or had been murdered, as so many have suspected. The results of this inquiry, as many others before now, were inconclusive.

THE MODERN, four-storey Warsaw Rising Museum celebrates the bravery of both civilians and soldiers who endured the sixty-three days of the German bombardments. Opened during the 2004 anniversary year, the museum's thirty-five-metre-high tower is cut to look like it has been hit by shrapnel; its peak displays the symbol of "Fighting Poland." Adjacent to the museum is a designated "place of memories," a 156-metre-long grey granite memorial wall displaying the names of those killed. The list is continually updated with new names as they become known.

Crowds of schoolchildren listen with rapt attention as guides, some of them survivors of the Uprising, narrate day-by-day accounts of what happened. The children can talk to other survivors on telephones installed at various windows. There are take-away sheets of paper explaining every stage in the critical decision to fight the Nazi occupation, and each heroic moment. There is a "little insurgents' room" designed for young children, where they can watch enactments of battles and the work of medical orderlies. I was amazed to see a couple of ten-year-olds begging their teacher to photograph them with wax figures of child heroes.

There are mock barricades and a twenty-five-metre-long sewer to show how the fighters moved under the city, and the sounds of explosions, nose-diving Stukas and streaking bullets reverberate. In its "Memory and History" segment, the museum talks of the Communists' attempts to erase the Uprising from "social memory."

Textbooks, at least until the early 1970s, claimed that the insurgents were in the pay of "the proprietary classes," enemies of the new proletariat. The Polish encyclopedia claimed that those who took part were young, irresponsible and misled, that their true motivation was provided by the bourgeoisie and the landowners.

During the afternoon of August 1, 1944, after consulting the government-in-exile, the Underground Home Army rose against German occupation. The uneven battle was encouraged but went unaided by Britain and the United States. Red Army forces waited on the east bank of the Vistula while the Germans killed almost 250,000 Poles, most of them civilians, and bombed Warsaw into rubble. Stalin was determined that this war was to have only one set of heroes, and they were to be Soviet.

Several units of the Polish Home Army fought alongside the Red Army against the Germans, but when the war ended, many Polish soldiers were rewarded with a passage to Soviet prison camps, where most of them perished.[5] Between the winter of 1939 and the end of the war, more than two million Poles—about one and a half million between the 1939 Soviet invasion and 1941[6]—were deported to the Soviet Union, most of them to Siberia. Thousands died on their way to their final destinations. Once there, two-thirds perished from the cold, the beatings, lack of adequate food and medication, overwork and sheer despair.

Wojciech Jaruzelski, Poland's last Communist Party boss, was one of the few who survived the Soviet-forced settlement. He joined the Red Army while he was in Siberia. The reason, he told me, was his unshakeable belief in the rightness of the Communist ideals and his "desire to see social justice in his own class-ridden society." He was the son of a landowner and, he said, had grown up embarrassed by his own privileges. In the interests of what he saw as the greater good, he was willing to overlook the fact that the Soviet machinery failed to provide the necessities of life to so many of his countrymen.

Under Communist rule, there were to be no memorials to the resistance. In the Soviet view, the liberation of Europe could not have begun "until the Soviet army crossed... the river Bug on July 1944."[7] As the Home Army could not be classified as Soviet-inspired, its sacrifices could not be recognized.

Many of the heroes of the Warsaw Uprising were imprisoned, its leaders discredited or sent to Siberian work camps. Anniversary commemorations, even church memorials, were forbidden. The mere fact of having taken part in the Uprising was sufficient reason for arrest. Wladyslaw Bartoszewski, a young stretcher bearer during the Uprising, an Auschwitz survivor, was sentenced to six and a half years in prison on trumped-up espionage charges in 1946.

Despite official threats, every year on August 1 people tried to pay homage to their dead at Warsaw's Powązki Cemetery. By the 1980s, the government had relented enough to allow relatives to clean the graves, light candles, sing a few old insurgent songs.

By contrast, the sixtieth anniversary of the Warsaw Uprising in 2004 was a grand affair, commemorated by government dignitaries and distinguished visitors, including Germany's Chancellor Gerhard Schröder and U.S. secretary of state Colin Powell. To mark the occasion, British professor Norman Davies's *Rising '44: The Battle for Warsaw* was published in all its 752-page glory, and the author himself led a tour through the capital, pointing out where the fighting had been and where the Soviets had waited. "If any Soviet soldier tried to cross the river to help the Poles, both sides fired at him," he said, taking a run at one of the local myths.[8] Not only were the Soviet soldiers forbidden to help the Poles by their own commanders, Polish high command would not have allowed the Soviets to take control of the Uprising once it had begun.

This news would have been something of a shock to General Zygmunt Berling, commander of the Polish army in the USSR, who issued his own orders to engage the Germans. In any event, Berling's intervention failed to make a difference in the outcome.

Of course, with the floodgates of history opened, there is inevitably debate and discussion. Now, historians and survivors openly debate whether the Uprising was folly, whether those who gave the orders were willing to sacrifice the capital and its people to their own glory in the mistaken belief that Poland's last resistance would change the British and American deal with the Soviets. A 2003 CNN documentary about the events of August 1944 immersed itself in the debate, much to the grief of emigrant Polish communities. Poland's futile battle with Nazi Germany, waged while the Soviets watched the Poles die, remains one of the sustaining stories and enduring tragedies in national memory, and the debate does nothing to change that.

The massive bronze Warsaw Rising monument—two groups of grim and weary figures—was erected near the Old Town, above the entrance to the city's sewers that the insurgents used to reach key destinations underground. Here, as in the museum, children roam and get their photos taken grinning up at the awesome figures; older people place flowers on the pedestal; a man climbs to stand with the statues, proudly proclaiming his kinship with the dead.

Close by is the brooding statue of astronomer Copernicus. Appropriated by the Germans during the occupation, defaced and finally moved outside the city, he is now restored to his massive base.

The Old Town is a UNESCO World Heritage Site. Though it looks as medieval as other European old towns, it is really a painstakingly detailed recreation of a past completely destroyed by German bombardments. The mullioned windows, the arched doors with their handmade iron handles, the heraldic ornaments, the Gothic spires and marble floors of the Royal Castle were lovingly recreated by craftsmen after the war.

In the Old Town's large squares, at cafés with outdoor tables and cheery umbrellas, nattily dressed waitresses offer service in three languages, not including Russian.

"WHAT POLES share in equal measure is the desire to be a normal, stable, prosperous, perhaps even a boring European country," Staś Pruszyński tells me when I return to his Radio Café. Staś says he loved Montreal but he never felt at home. There, too, he had opened a café—Stash Café-Bazaar—famous for its garish, everything-is-for-sale philosophy and the thick Polish soup cooked in massive pots. In Warsaw, he is at home.

TO COMMEMORATE the seventieth anniversary of the beginning of World War II, European leaders gathered at the Westerplatte monument, near Gdańsk, on September 1, 2009. The monument commemorates Germany's first attack on Poland in September 1939 and the endurance of the small Polish force of only two hundred soldiers that held out against the German army and air force for seven days.

It was a sombre occasion, with national flags, military honour guards and the unspoken memory of the Molotov-Ribbentrop Pact that tore Poland apart. In his now famous "Letter to the Poles," delivered prior to his arrival at Westerplatte, Putin spoke of "the most disastrous and slaughterous war in Europe" and went on to explain the Molotov-Ribbentrop Pact with the Munich compromise, "where France and England signed a well-known treaty with Hitler and thus destroyed all the hope for a united front to fight fascism." As a result, the Soviet Union faced the prospect of war on two fronts—with Germany and with Japan. It would, he said, have been "unwise to reject Germany's proposal to sign the Non-Aggression Pact when the USSR's potential allies in the West had already made similar agreements with the German Reich." He even mentioned Katyń: "The people of Russia, whose destiny was crippled by the totalitarian regime, fully understand the sensitivity of Poles about Katyń where thousands of Polish servicemen lie. Together we must keep alive the memory of the victims of this crime."

With Putin's decision that Russians could again celebrate Stalin as a war hero, this seemed like the perfect moment for the grand gesture that could produce a shared history of the two countries. And, indeed, prime ministers Tusk and Putin did agree on just such a project, but Putin was quick to point out to waiting reporters that "mistakes were made by both sides." Then he referred to Russians' deeply felt pride in their victory over Nazi Germany, making sure that everyone was still aware the war could not have been won without the Red Army.

At about the same time as the Westerplatte ceremonies, Russian state television showed a documentary special that managed to imply the Poles were responsible for their own invasion. Some Russian historians in the documentary went so far as to blame Poland for the outbreak of war. After those strange decisions, it came as something of a welcome surprise that Putin invited Tusk to a formal commemoration of the Katyń massacre in April 2010. But the long-awaited memorial ended in a horrific tragedy. On Saturday, April 10, just three days after the Putin-Tusk ceremonies, the plane bringing President Lech Kaczyński and ninety-six others from Poland, many of them military, government and business leaders, crashed near Smolensk, killing all aboard. They were on their way to the Polish ceremony at the site of the massacre.[9]

Thousands of mourners gathered in front of Warsaw's presidential palace, lighting candles and placing bouquets of flowers. It will take many years for Poles to absorb the full impact of the catastrophe. Former prime minister Aleksander Kwaśniewski, still in shock from the news, talked of Katyń proving, once more, to be "a cursed place, a terrifying symbol" in Polish memory.

In sympathy with the grieving Poles, Prime Minister Putin announced a day of mourning in Russia and ordered Andrzej Wajda's film *Katyń* to be shown on Russian television.

ONE OF MY Warsaw cab drivers said that watching Poles die had always been a favoured Russian pastime. The driver spoke remarkably good French, having spent several years in France after the declaration of martial law. He returned after the Communist regime drew its last breath. "We beat them once," he told me with a happy smirk. "Our armies invaded Russia. We took their capital. No one else has ever taken Moscow intact. We did it once, we can do it again, if we must. *Bien, on doit savoir ça.*"

This is the land of lost battles and persistent dreams. During the 123 years after the Russians and Austrians dismantled the country, all that kept Poland alive was its memories. My guide wants me to see Jan Matejko's 1870s paintings of Polish valour in the National Gallery. They were all painted while there was no Poland. Political scientist Jan Kubik[10] told me that I would not understand what this country is about till I saw Matejko's *Battle of Grunwald*. Flanked by smaller paintings by Matejko and his school, it covers an entire wall of the largest room in the building. It is a dark, foreboding painting teeming with bodies of fighting men and confused horses. Although it celebrates the 1410 victory of Polish and Lithuanian forces over the Teutonic knights, it is really symbolic of the Polish determination to exist as a nation.

Back in my stylish boutique hotel, I search the Internet for when the Poles took Moscow, and all I can find is Stanisław Żółkiewski marching into Muscovy in 1610. How did a cab driver dredge that up in rush-hour traffic in 2009?

THE INSTITUTE OF NATIONAL REMEMBRANCE

The grandly named Institute of National Remembrance (IPN in Polish) is a grey high-rise building with narrow windows divided by blue upright features that were probably meant to be decorative. The low, sheltered entrance is guarded by two uniformed security guards who ask for identification with the same impassive glares that used to greet tourists to Communist countries before the regimes collapsed under the weight of their citizens' fury and their own incompetence. I remember that look from the Czech border when I crossed no man's land by car from Austria, and I remember it on arrival at Budapest's Ferihegy airport—armed men with impassive faces, guns at the almost ready. I used to be afraid of them, and I was sure they knew it and enjoyed it. They could smell the fear on those who had been touched by their states' terror apparatus, the well-oiled machinery that controlled citizens.

In 2009 Warsaw, there is no reason to be afraid. My student IPN guide waves his identity pass at the guards and they let me walk through the metal detectors with only a cursory glance into my purse. We hurry past rooms with large grey metal cabinets and men working at grey metal desks with papers piled high.

The Institute of National Remembrance-Commission for the Prosecution of Crimes against the Polish Nation was established by the Polish parliament on December 18, 1998, and began to function in July 2000. Its "mission" as set out on its website is "primarily to preserve the memory of the losses which were suffered by the Polish Nation as a result of World War II and the post-war period" and to celebrate the patriotic traditions of fighting Nazi and Soviet occupations in the interests of an independent Polish state. Its duty is "to prosecute crimes against peace, humanity and war crimes" and to compensate those who had been harmed by the state: "no unlawful deeds of the state against its citizens can be protected by secrecy or forgotten." The IPN's public education department has the added responsibility of engaging the public in its discoveries through staged exhibitions, seminars and books.

But most of the IPN's time has been devoted to exposing Communist crimes from September 17, 1939, to December 31, 1989. Its investigations would include tasks performed by the old regime's satraps and enablers, the spies and their handlers, the day-to-day activities of officers within the secretive Ministry of Internal Security.

The IPN also stores the state security police files—mountains of secrets about everyone, including the agents themselves. The autocracy could trust no one.

Often it was the tiny, petty indiscretions, the infidelities of wives or husbands, the quiet meetings in coffee houses or bars, that turned victims into victimizers. How would you ever know that your wife or husband was spying on you? That your boss was noting your choices of lunch companions, that your new office boy was taking an unhealthy interest in your phone messages, that there were listening devices sunk into the light fixtures in your bedroom, in your toilet, in the faucets of your hand basin? That your lover was no longer just a lover, that your son was earning his Communist Youth badge by reporting on your reading habits?

The Ministry of Internal Security threatened, cajoled and beat a vast array of citizens into becoming tools of its mission to stamp out all independent thinking—thinking that could lead to resistance. By one estimate, during the 1970s more than a million people were spying on their fellow citizens, submitting regular reports and meeting with their state police handlers.

In his 1953 book *The Captive Mind*, Czesław Miłosz, one of Poland's great poets, winner of the 1980 Nobel Prize for Literature, described the process whereby an entire society became self-policing, a society in which "terror becomes socially useful and effective. The conviction grows that the whole world will be conquered by the dialecticians of Moscow." If a person could not be sure who the informers were, he kept his mouth shut and his thoughts to himself. At first, Miłosz, like so many other young intellectuals, had been attracted to the outwardly moral stance of Communist ideology. He served as cultural attaché for the People's Republic of Poland in Paris and Washington. He would write of the difficulty he had trying to separate himself from his religion, his civilization, his nation's history, in order to serve what he believed was a higher purpose. How easy it had been to ridicule the capitalism of the West, the "charlatans of the stock exchange, feudal barons, the self-deluding artists."

Eventually, he returned to what he had known before he had espoused Marx's ideas.

The moment of recognition came in early 1949, after "a reception where people in those highest circles drank and danced. We were on our way home at four in the morning; it was summer but the night was cold. And I saw jeeps carrying prisoners, people just arrested. The soldiers guarding them were wearing sheepskin coats, but the prisoners were in suit jackets with the collars turned up, shivering from the cold. It was then that I realized what I was part of."[11]

In 1950, still serving as the second secretary at the Washington embassy of the People's Republic of Poland, he had the daily urge while walking in the U.S. capital to "grab every passerby and beg his pardon for my appearing as someone I was not."

He defected in 1951, never an exile from the language of his country, only from its system. He returned after 1989.

The Institute of National Remembrance assumed the task of locating those who had committed crimes "against the dignity of others" by torture, beatings or murder between 1939 and 1989. My young guide tells me it was too late to find most of the perpetrators, let alone the government officials who had given the orders. Smart Party members had been quick to recycle themselves as aspiring capitalists, entrepreneurs, avid nationalists, populists, bodyguards, devoted public servants—whatever it took to blend in with the order. There were rumours about the suddenly rich, about brazen benefits amassed by the few who had the inside track—the former civil servants, members of the security police, those with good connections, the old *nomenklatura,* some of whom became the newly minted tycoons of the democratic era.

Was it too late now for justice, too late for retribution? I ask the guide as he leads me through the labyrinthine grey corridors of the Institute. He is a tall, friendly man in his early twenties. He has no memory of the events the Institute is charged with uncovering, yet he believes in the rightness of its cause. In his view, someone must be held responsible for the devils that beset his country. That so much time has passed is irrelevant. As a youthful graduate of Communist repression myself, I carried this view with me to the former satellites, along with the conviction that victims deserve justice, even if it is less than what they wished for in their darkest hours.

PROFESSOR ANTONI DUDEK'S office is on the twenty-second floor of the second building. A tall, broad-shouldered man in his early forties, with a high forehead and blond hair cut short, he favours me with a fierce handshake from behind his desk. He comes around to my side, reluctantly, after a long Polish explanation by the guide. He sits, cautiously, at the long table that provides a formal area for visitors.

Professor Dudek is suspicious of outsiders. The Institute has been accused of using its archives against opponents of the rather boastfully named nationalist Law and Justice party. Established in 2001 by Lech and Jarosław Kaczyński, twins and former child stars of the film *The Two Who Stole the Moon,* the party advocates a return to traditional ways, opposes most modern social reforms and is suspicious of libertine Western Europe. In 2006, Law and Justice sponsored the "lustration" or purification law to purge the country's professional classes of former collaborators. The word *lustration* has its roots in the Latin *lastrare,* "to purify through sacrifice," but meant, in Poland, the public unveiling of an individual's connections with the secret services, and it affected only those who held public office or candidates for public offices. Lustration did not exclude people from political life: its purpose was to provide citizens with the information to make informed decisions.[12] It required all those employed in private, public or government sectors, politicians, judges, lawyers, managers of public companies, journalists and school principals to admit, in writing, if they had worked for the state security apparatus. If they failed to disclose their past, they could be fired from their jobs and banned from practising their professions. Furthermore, the Institute could shame them by publishing its research into their lives.

When the lustration law was adopted by the Sejm, the Polish parliament, only the former Communist representatives voted against it. Afterward, as the new law applied to everyone who had ever worked for the Ministry of Internal Security, at least 700,000 individuals were required to file affidavits attesting to their guilt.

The Institute's fact-checking investigations, according to Professor Dudek, could take fifteen to twenty years. Two thousand people work here—so many that they have spilled over into another nearby tower with a large parking lot and more up-to-date facilities. There are also eleven branch offices throughout the country. In 2009 alone, IPN published over one hundred books, and since 2000 about eight hundred. Its publication list includes a series of over twenty books, one per region, on individual state security policemen. The books feature the men's (most of them are men) photographs, their personal data and "their crimes against the Polish nation." These now-diminished "vermin fed like lice on the Polish soul," Dr. Dudek told me. Now, at least, their neighbours will know who they are. It will be harder for them to pretend they were tiny cogs in the big wheels of a long-dead government.

Not unexpectedly, the judiciary, in the form of the Constitutional Tribunal, extracted many of the new law's teeth: elected officials and anyone employed by private enterprise would not, after all, be subject to lustration, and automatic penalties for lying or refusing to file were eliminated. Professor Dudek spreads his elegant hands over the table. "Nothing," he says, "has been done about the judges. They now preside over the trials of those they used to serve. These are the same judges who sentenced Solidarity members and their supporters to prison." It is a travesty, he says, that only about fifty people have been convicted of crimes, and that they are on the bottom of the pyramid of power—they are the order-takers, the torturers, not the men at the top who gave the orders.

When a certain judge died last year, his victims' families signed a petition demanding that he should not be allowed to rest in the same cemetery where his victims are buried.

In recent years, even the word *lustration*, Dudek says, has been sullied, ridiculed. When it was first coined, it was intended to embrace Poles' renewed understanding of who they were and how far they had come. Lustration punished neither membership in the Communist Party nor its *układ*,[13] only lying about it. While these modest measures could not right the wrongs, as Dr. Dudek saw it, they would at least provide some illusion of retribution.

Those against the process have questioned the validity of the documents in this building. How many of them have been doctored? How many of the state's spies have lied to protect themselves? "Our dilemma," he says, "is that if nothing is done about the past, there can be no sense of justice. If even South Africa could accept the need for a Truth and Reconciliation Commission, why not here? What are we afraid of?" The crimes of the past should not be overlooked in the interests of peaceful coexistence. Too many lives had been wasted.

"The students of '68 should know who was responsible," he adds.

March 1968 is one of several iconic dates in Poland that serve as communications shorthand, establishing connections, links, shared-memory signposts among people. I noticed that sometimes the mere mention of a date, such as 1920 (when the Poles defeated the Russian Bolsheviks) or 1772 (the date of the first partition of Poland), 1795 (when the independent nation of Poland ceased to exist) or August 1939 (the signing of the Molotov-Ribbentrop Pact), is enough to elicit a nodding of heads. No explanations are needed.

March 1968 was the first large-scale student protest in Poland. The trigger event was the government's closing down of a theatrical production of a nineteenth-century patriotic drama by revered

Polish poet Adam Mickiewicz. The play, intended by its long-dead author to be anti-czarist, was taken by the authorities to be anti-Soviet. References to repression and occupation fit the current realities of life in Poland, and the audience's wildly enthusiastic reception of this production seemed to reflect its views of the present regime's friends, the Soviet Union.

After the play was banned, the students published anti-repression articles, spoke passionately about freedom of expression, democracy and human rights. The regime responded by arresting the student leaders, among them a young man called Adam Michnik.

The protests persisted and grew.

On March 8, the Ministry of the Interior called upon Communist Party workers to deal with the rebellious young. Setting industrial workers against students could have been a stroke of genius, but it turned out to be a disaster. The leather-jacketed, truncheon-wielding men who descended from the buses were instantly recognized as state police stooges. The spontaneous confrontation between proletariat and spoiled students was revealed to be what it was: a brutal attack by the state on unarmed young people.

Demonstrators were beaten; hundreds were arrested; some were tortured; many, including a few sons and daughters of the Party elite, were jailed. Books were pulped, writers banned; suspect academics were fired; scientists had their research destroyed. A few professors held evening tutorials in their homes, reading from banned literature and telling students the truth about history. The government responded by sending ambitious Communist students to break down doors and beat both professors and fellow students with cudgels. Jacek Kuroń, a lecturer at Warsaw University, recognized one of his students in the group of stick-wielding thugs and tried to expel him from the university, only to be formally notified that he would be denied that privilege.

Dudek asks: Isn't it time for some measure of punishment for those who ordered these reprisals and those who executed them with unflinching obedience? The students who were beaten in 1968 are entitled to know who ordered the violence and the names of the men who beat them.

The Wujek and Silesia miners are also entitled to know who killed their fellow strikers when they protested the high price of food, and they are entitled to know who were the trained sharpshooters and who selected those to be murdered. It was not until June 2007 that fifteen members of the former Communist police finally went on trial for killing the striking miners. When twenty-two police officers who had acted under Jaruzelski's orders were acquitted in the 1981 killing of nine miners, Katarzyna Kopczak, the daughter of one of the miners, had this question, as reported by AP: If they were innocent, "Who killed my father?"

The Gdańsk shipyard workers who had erected the forty-two-metre monument to honour those killed by militia should know who had ordered those shootings. The "thick line" that Solidarity leaders wished to draw over the past failed to convince. Old wounds festered. Suspicions, accusations, mistrust of those in power persisted. The tortured found it difficult to live cheek by jowl with their former torturers.

I ASK Lena Kolarska-Bobińska, president of the Institute of Public Affairs, a Warsaw public opinion research firm, what Poles thought about lustration. We meet in her office, where all surfaces are stacked high with documents except for the space occupied by a photo of her daughter. The past is now a matter for historians, she says. An attractive blond with a PhD in economics, she moves fast and talks fast. She views herself as a pragmatist.

"I think we should know about those in power. And the criminals who killed or shot or beat others should be prosecuted. And leave it at that. But do I really need to know that my respected colleague, a man I have always liked, worked for the state security police?" She starts stacking some papers on her desk, her hands flying. Her smile fades. "Well, perhaps it would have been better..." She glances down the corridor where I imagine her colleague is still working but now has only one occupation, not two.

Ultimately, the sense of betrayal is personal. While historians usually reveal their biases, they rarely feel betrayed by those they write about.

ACCORDING TO the IPN, the present political elite is reluctant to judge even the most obviously guilty. General Wojciech Jaruzelski comes to mind. He is the man who ordered martial law in 1981, had thousands imprisoned and empowered the military police to fire on demonstrators.

The 1991 Sejm proceedings against Jaruzelski had been an embarrassment: the government could not even agree in advance on the specific charges. The IPN's second attempt, after six years of preparations, brought indictments against Jaruzelski and nine of his associates, but the trial has been repeatedly delayed because of Jaruzelski's ill health. Now, almost thirty years after the declaration of martial law, the IPN is again gearing up the system. Professor Dudek insists there must be a reckoning. If the general ordered the killings, he should not be allowed to retire in comfort. The fact that he voluntarily ceded power to Solidarity and its chosen few perhaps convinced *them* that he is a patriot, but Professor Dudek will remain unconvinced until a real trial is held and a judge or judges determine Jaruzelski's guilt or innocence.

GAZETA WYBORCZA'S Jarosław Kurski is suspicious of the IPN's passion for finding ex-Communists. His tidy, spacious office is in the steel and glass building that is now home to the former revolutionary daily, the first newspaper to emerge after Poland's transition to almost democratic elections.

Kurski is about forty years old, blond, with a big smile and a journalist's inquisitive, critical approach to our meeting. He says that Dudek's "people believe that our entire society is permeated by former Communists. The great paradox of the place is that the IPN trusts the testimonies of the old political police: the words of the very people they wish to discredit. How can you form a new national memory on such a corrupt base?"

A recent IPN book purports to reveal that Solidarity hero Lech Wałęsa was an informer for the state police. This is the man who came to the world's attention when he climbed the wall of Gdańsk's Lenin Shipyards to head the strike that brought Poland's Communist government to its knees.

Public reaction was fast and furious. Why would the IPN choose to besmirch the good name of a national icon? Wałęsa's rebuttal was a book of his own.

Dudek admits he voted against publication, but he remains unapologetic. The truth, no matter how painful, should be out in the open, he says. It tends to clear the air. Forgiveness is beside the point.

A REVERSAL OF FORTUNE

I visited General Jaruzelski in September 2009. Once he had been among the most feared men in Europe; a general in the second-largest Communist army—second only to the Soviet Union's Red Army; a leader in the Warsaw Pact's invasion of Czechoslovakia ending Dubček's experiment of "socialism with a human face." He was Poland's defence minister during the 1967–68 Jewish purges, eighth prime minister of the People's Republic of Poland and the man who declared martial law on Sunday, December 13, 1981. Now he occupies a modest office in an elderly army building on Jerozo-limskie Avenue, close to Warsaw's main railway station and the much-derided Palace of Culture and Science—a remnant, rather like Wojciech Jaruzelski himself, of Communist times in the middle of this modern city.

Once he would have been closely guarded. Now there is one desultory guard and a single blond secretary who confesses that her schedule is not overly busy.

He is tall, spare, erect in his immaculate grey suit. His hair is thinning, his face impassive, and he still wears his trademark dark glasses. They have lost some of their menace since I read that they hide a weakness caused by the intense Siberian light. His hand is outstretched when we meet. There is the Old World formality of an almost hand-kiss, his thin lips brushing my fingers for a fraction of an uncomfortable second. Apart from the bandage on his right cheek, he looks like he has stepped out of a picture of ancient Polish nobility, polite, cool, a tad superior.

The cool does not last more than the first few minutes. When the general notices that I am not recording this Polish interview, he is furious. He keeps glancing at my notes and complains that I don't write fast enough, that I may have missed something that he has no intention of repeating. He is, of course, entitled to be irritable. He is eighty-seven years old and enduring the latest of a series of trials for acts "against the Polish nation."

When I mention that Article 123 of the Criminal Code, treason, was one of the 1991 charges against him, he leaps from his chair and shouts "Never that!" as if the charge had not existed. "After five years of hearings and dozens of witnesses, I was found not guilty. Furthermore, Parliament agreed that martial law had been necessary, indeed essential, for us to avoid being invaded by the Soviet army."

In March 1981, Jaruzelski was ordered by KGB boss Yuri Andropov to attend a meeting in a railway car near Brest, on the Soviet side of the Polish border. "He wanted to discuss how I would deal with Solidarity," he says. "I knew that [Czechoslovak president] Husák, [East German leader] Honecker and even [Romania's] Ceauşescu were pushing him to attack Poland. He accused me of being unable to control the situation." Jaruzelski insisted he could deal with it if they gave him time. When the meeting was over, Jaruzelski thought they might take him to Moscow. Perhaps there would be a trial.

Of course he wasn't afraid, he yells at me. "I was a soldier. I was shot twice during the war." He was also gambling that the Soviets were not keen on a second war after getting bogged down in Afghanistan.

Solidarity, the protest union of Polish workers, had ten million members in 1981; the Kremlin could not allow it to triumph. Twenty divisions of the Red Army had gathered along the eastern borders, and Jaruzelski was sure they would not be able to enter Poland, as they did in Czechoslovakia in 1968, without a fight. The Poles, as the Hungarians, he tells me, are fighters. "The Polish army," says Jaruzelski, "would have resisted. There would have been a sea of blood."

As it was, *only* a hundred or so strikers were shot. Three days after the declaration of martial law, miners went on strike at the Katowice mines. Police responded with water cannons, tanks and guns.

The new charges laid by the Institute of National Remembrance are under Article 258 of the Criminal Code: "directing a criminal organization"—a reference to the Military Council of National

Salvation, which imposed and ran martial law. This is, however, a strange legal device that would normally be used against criminal gangs. If convicted, Jaruzelski faces a ten-year jail sentence. "They can't try me again for the same supposed crimes," Jaruzelski shouts, "and they can't use the same documents. So, after ten years, a government-sponsored institute is trying me again, with no new evidence and no new witnesses."

Former British prime minister Thatcher and former Soviet president Gorbachev have both written to protest the charges. These were "Communist" crimes, Gorbachev said. Let the general rest.

Jaruzelski's testimony forms part of his newest, and last, book. "It is my statement to the court," he says. "It will be there long after I am gone. My first-hand account. A record of my contribution to history."

He peers impatiently at my writing. The interpreter is nervous about asking him to clarify. He explains that in his statement to the court, he talks of the Soviet army threat, of the Kremlin's conviction that Poland was "an island of heresy" in a uniform world. "Here, culture and science were almost free. The Church was allowed to gather its faithful, there was some private property. Later Gorbachev told me, our Polish reforms had been a laboratory for his perestroika."

"History is always infected with politics," says the general. "It is never objective. But I am not idealizing my life. When I see how others abuse history, I am determined to provide the truth. My truth. I am reaching the end of my life—I have nothing to fear from the truth." He cannot allow the Institute's "infected" history to be the only version left after his death.

He had, of course, been ambitious once. No man could have climbed so high in the ranks of Communist apparatchiks without burning ambition, but he is no longer interested in those things. Nor in discussing them with me. He is less reticent about his early life.

Wojciech Jaruzelski was born into a well-to-do rural family, Polish land-owning gentry who had fought the Russians in 1920 and paid the price with confiscations of property and imprisonment. In 1939, after the Soviet invasion ("We were victims of the Molotov-Ribbentrop treaty," Jaruzelski says), the family, along with hundreds of thousands of other Poles, was transported to Siberia as slave labourers. It's where his father died. Jaruzelski made the coffin by hand and buried him. His mother and sister made a simple cross. "I will always be grateful to Putin for allowing me to visit my father's grave," he says. "And to Gorbachev for placing a stone over his remains next to a memorial to all those Poles who perished there." He does not mention that, as an enthusiastic cadre in the Polish section of the Red Army, he watched the destruction of Warsaw in 1944, nor will he talk about what he thought of the thousands of Poles who were deported to the Soviet Union when the war was over. Most of them perished from the cold, lack of food and sheer despair. Jaruzelski was a survivor.

He tells me he joined the Communist Party with a genuine conviction that the Communist idea was workable, a young man's dream of a just society to replace what he had seen of poverty and degradation. He never forgot the abject deprivation of the poor even in his ancestral home, their lack of shoes in the winter, their gratitude for the smallest handouts. "*The Communist Manifesto* is about equality, social justice; it is ethical, moral, a beautiful idea; but it turned out to be utopian," he tells me.

In the interests of the "greater good," he was willing to overlook the failures of Soviet machinery. "In Poland we didn't use the word 'Communism,'" he announces, "We had 'socialism.' State property. No unemployment. No contrast between rich and poor. But it proved to be economically ineffective, and was burdened with a lack of individual freedoms." While all that has changed, democracy has its downsides. He spreads his hands, palms up, as if to indicate that some people now have nothing.

"I have no expectations now," he declares. "The worst that can happen to a person is death, and I am there. I merely hope that the next generation will understand my role in the context of my time, being in Siberia, then a front-line soldier, my twelve years as head of the army, and that while I am the one who declared martial law, I am also the one who sat at the 'round table' and negotiated democracy." Jaruzelski had, indeed, sat down with Solidarity leaders in 1989 to discuss an orderly transition to democratic elections.

"Solidarity, you know"—he tries for another smile—"wasn't a company of angels. Wałęsa and the Church were realists. They were willing to wait. But there were some 'pyromaniacs' in their midst; in

1981 they rejected my offers to reach an agreement. Just like my people. Some like me and Kiszczak [former interior minister and prime minister, on trial with Jaruzelski] were progressives, but there were others, dogmatic conservatives. Troglodytes. Like Honecker and Husák. I was pressured to do more than declare martial law." It was, he still believes, the best solution to a volatile situation. No, martial law was the only solution and, faced with the same options, he would make the same decision today.

Contrary to Jaruzelski's statements, the Soviet leadership did not want to risk a costly incursion into Poland. As recently revealed transcripts indicate, Andropov had determined that there would be no military action "even if Poland comes under the rule of Solidarity."[14] The Politburo agreed that such an action would be "catastrophic." Is it possible that Jaruzelski misunderstood the Soviets' intentions when he mobilized 80,000 Polish soldiers, 1,600 tanks and 1,800 armoured cars against Solidarity?

He tells me to read "his" chapters in Gorbachev's memoirs. The Institute accusers should read them as well. "They were not there," he says. "They never suffered, they didn't go to prison, yet they scream the loudest. Michnik, who went to prison, understands."

In the *Memoirs*, Gorbachev does talk of Warsaw Pact troops both inside Poland and at its borders and praises Jaruzelski: "He followed his own course, calculated to calm the situation, placate the nation, and gradually transform the political system." Moreover, Gorbachev writes of Jaruzelski's successful promotion of a joint commission of historians who would finally deal with the Katyń massacre. Although the KGB had already destroyed many of the relevant files, Gorbachev was still able to hand some documents directly to Jaruzelski in April 1990 when he apologized for the Soviet leadership's role in the killings.

"We understand each other," Jaruzelski says of Adam Michnik, one of this country's celebrity intellectuals, editor-in-chief of *Gazeta Wyborcza*. Michnik was a prisoner of conscience under Communist rule, yet he has become a friend of the man who had ordered him jailed. Michnik penned the introduction to Jaruzelski's memoirs and interviewed him on television. The book was a national bestseller.

Jaruzelski's second book, published just a few weeks before our meeting, is a regrettable flop—regrettable because he is sure that he has set the record straight. Yet the timely, flattering review in *Gazeta* also didn't happen. The last time, people lined up for his autograph. This time, nobody came.

Like many authors, Jaruzelski is complaining about lack of reviews and poor sales. Why aren't more people interested?

"It's biology," he says. "Those who remember are dying and the young are brainwashed by black and white versions of history, bite-sized, digestible bits." He is right, of course: life rarely presents itself in a made-for-television format and few people's pasts fit into easily identifiable boxes.

"History," says Jaruzelski, "is multicoloured, like life."

History often becomes a political tool to be wielded when needed, distorted when convenient and hidden when harmful to one's cause. Twenty years after the end of autocracy in Poland, the debate about the former Communists continues. As George Orwell predicted, whoever controls the present controls the past, and whoever controls the past controls the future.[15]

THE DISSIDENT HERO

The battle over history raged on in Powązki Cemetery's Alley of the Meritorious on July 21, 2008. The occasion was Bronisław Geremek's funeral, attended by most of Poland's post-'89 political elite. Adam Michnik delivered a blistering eulogy praising Geremek for attacking the IPN's "remembrance forgers" and the Kaczyńskis' "unconstitutional vetting procedures" of public figures. Geremek, a Warsaw Ghetto survivor and medieval history professor, had been at the forefront of the intelligentsia's support for Solidarity, a leader in Poland's 1990 transformation over more than forty years to the first non-Communist government in the Soviet Bloc.

Michnik read from one of Geremek's last letters:

"It is difficult to understand the intentions of the people and institutions who have now launched a campaign of accusations and libel against Lech Wałęsa. The Institute of National Remembrance, supposed to protect national memory, is today engaging in activities that destroy this memory. Today's memory police resort to the hateful methods of the communist secret services and direct them at a victim of this very secret service. These policemen violate the truth and fundamental ethical principles. They do harm to Poland."

WYBORCZA'S FAMOUS editor-in-chief, Adam Michnik, is vociferous in his insistence that the past must be left behind, that the colossal files of Communist wrongdoings should be left for the historians to tackle.

While I admire Michnik's argument, I am with those who wish to see justice done. Historians come too late to provide even a whiff of fairness for those who fought for democracy, suffered violent reprisals and now watch their former jailers drive expensive cars. As the Polish poet Zbigniew Herbert wrote, "truly it is not in our power to forgive / In the name of those who were betrayed at dawn."

Still, it is difficult to argue the point with a man who spent six years in prison.

Michnik is one of the legendary figures of the resistance. His parents, Ozjasz Szechter and Helena Michnik, had been members of the Polish United Workers' Party, pre-war Communists, devotees of Marx and the Bolshevik Revolution, exiles during World War II in the Soviet Union, where Ozjasz joined the army. He had been imprisoned and tortured by the Polish police. The Bolshevik Revolution had offered a hope of building a better world. Later, Ozjasz was a witness to Stalin's bloody purges of his devoted Polish Communists. Michnik remembers being confused by his father's lack of emotion during the national mourning that followed Stalin's death in 1953. It was only later that he learnt of Ojasz's disillusionment with Stalin's paranoid xenophobia.

Both Michnik's parents were Jews. His great-grandfather had been a shochet—a ritual butcher—and his grandparents had spoken Yiddish at home. His parents, however, spoke only Polish to each other and their children. Their rejection of all religion was so complete that they refused to be married in a Jewish ceremony. A Catholic ceremony was out of the question, and no civil ceremonies were available in 1946, when Helena was pregnant, so Ozjasz and Helena chose not to get married. Adam was born in October 1946, a year after his parents returned to Poland from the Ukraine. He carries his mother's name.

Of their extended families, only two people survived the Holocaust. Yet Adam never heard his parents talk of the Shoah. They both
remained in the Party, but Ozjasz had become a critic of its authoritarian ways. It was, after all, not all that different from Poland's own
nationalistic, anti-Semitic, ultra-Catholic parties after the unification. One day, when fourteen-year-old Adam returned home from a
demonstration at the U.S. embassy condemning America's attempted
coup in Cuba, his father told him he should also demonstrate at the
USSR embassy to protest the 1956 Soviet invasion of Hungary.[16]

As a sixteen-year-old history student, Adam was already an outspoken opponent of autocracy. In 1964, he distributed an open letter
to the United Workers' Party proposing ways to reform the political system, criticizing its leaders. "I was not afraid of Communism,"
Michnik says in his *Letters*, "because I thought it was my own system. I was not afraid to criticize the government because it was my
own government." He believed then that the system belonged to him
and his classmates, that criticism would be effective.

It wasn't. He was suspended, and a year later he was barred from
publishing letters or articles. Undeterred, he continued to write
under various pseudonyms. The 1960s culminated in the "anti-
Zionist" purge of 1968. The official pretext was the 1967 Arab-Israeli
Six-Day War. Moscow, an early backer of Israel, had changed sides
and the satellite countries had to follow suit. There was a jocular Polish saying in those days: "Our Jews have beaten their Arabs," as if
Israeli victory over the larger Arab armies in the Middle East had
been, in a way, a defeat of the Soviet Union itself.

Mieczysław Moczar, head of the government's most powerful
ministry, Internal Affairs, sponsored nationwide newspaper articles
blaming a Zionist conspiracy for the student unrest. The scripted
articles singled out students with Jewish-sounding names, labelling
them "anti-Socialist troublemakers,"[17] accusing activists of being
in cahoots with Israeli intelligence. Władysław Gomułka, boss of
the Communist Party, perhaps worried about his own power base,
jumped on the bandwagon, stating that Polish Jews might be a "fifth
column." A slogan asserting that no man can be loyal to two nations
became a rallying cry of the Party, denouncing Jews as a major threat
to the stability of Poland.

Michnik's participation in the March 1968 student protests earned him a prison term, and he was forbidden to complete his studies.

After a two-year stint as a welder, he left for Paris but found exile unbearable and returned home. He edited a variety of underground newspapers and worked with KOR, the Workers' Defence Committee. He was imprisoned again in December 1981 under Jaruzelski's martial law. His last prison term, of three years, was cut short by the 1986 general amnesty. He continued to write and speak about the need for resistance. In 1989, he was at the "round table" discussing democracy with the Communist Party's bosses.

He remembers climbing the steps of Warsaw's Viceroy Palace toward General Czesław Kiszczak, the man who had been in charge of the state security police, looking at the outstretched hand of the man he had learned to hate during his years of imprisonment and wondering what he would do when they were face to face. In the end, what they did was shake hands.

Michnik, who has always preferred to comment on politics in Poland rather than conduct them, nevertheless became a member of parliament from 1989 till 1991.

Gazeta Wyborcza's first issue had declared that there could be "no liberty without Solidarity." Its masthead proudly displayed the Solidarity logo and the paper remained closely tied to the Solidarity movement and its candidates for elections. *Wyborcza* means "electoral," and Lech Wałęsa had taken it for granted that Michnik's newspaper would continue to support his forays into politics. It did not. Michnik and Wałęsa fell out over their different understandings of the concept of a free press. In Michnik's concept, the editor sets the tone and journalists determine content. In Wałęsa's, a Solidarity newspaper has an obligation to support certain politicians. Michnik accused Wałęsa of a complete lack of understanding of how democracy works. Wałęsa ordered the Solidarity logo removed from *Gazeta Wyborcza*'s masthead. Michnik complied.

Today, at sixty-four, Michnik's newspaper is part of Agora, Poland's largest media group. In addition to the national daily, Agora owns a string of local *Metro* papers, regional weeklies, thirty radio stations, an outdoor advertising agency and a bevy of magazines, and it publishes books. In September 2009, it launched a new Internet business portal, Wyborcza.biz. I was with the business editor that day, enjoying the excitement that warmed the floor with old-style journalists—most of them in their thirties and still in awe of electrical devices delivering "content."

Wyborcza, with a daily circulation of over 700,000, giant presses, lucrative advertising contracts and other sidelines, has become highly profitable and much envied by less successful publications. Agora's revenues for 2008 were more than one billion PLN (over 350 million dollars), and while 2009 was hard for the company, Agora weathered the recession that year with only a 30 per cent drop in net profits, and the business editor predicted a quick turnaround in 2010. Not bad for a little paper that began with 150,000 copies only twenty years ago.

While the newspaper's overall tone, I am informed by some regular readers, has remained ironic and loudly critical of those the paper considers detrimental to its notion of liberal ideas, *Wyborcza* has begun to take itself seriously. And, paradoxically, it is in the vanguard of Poland's capitalist transformation.

Its spacious foyer is full of expensive self-regard: big-screen TV sets, walls of colour-filled publications and a front desk manned by officious guards. All this reminds me of Czesław Miłosz's warmly expressed wish that this, the newfound wealth, the material advantages that capitalism offered, was surely not what the Poles had fought for. But what were the alternatives?

Adam Michnik, who rarely gives interviews these days and has a reputation for being gruff and dismissive, turns out to be a sprightly, soft-spoken, painstakingly polite man with impeccable manners, right down to the casual hand-kiss, reminiscent of Paris circa 1920, in contrast to Jaruzelski's courtly, Habsburg Central Europe style. He has sandy hair, a wide, high-cheek-boned open face, inquisitive eyes, a ready smile and a slight stutter. His clothes, while not quite dishevelled, are decisively casual.

His office, on the fourth floor of *Wyborcza,* feels immediately comfortable and familiar. There are hundreds of books, magazines and newspapers and, on one wall, a somewhat incongruous picture of a nude woman in a stark landscape.

He settles into his low chair, arms comfortably at rest, and looks at me, appraising the sort of answers he would give to an unknown foreign author. He speaks fluent French but chooses to address most of his remarks to the interpreter in Polish. It is not until some months later, when he visits Toronto, that I realize he understands English reasonably well and speaks it when he needs to. While listening, he often tilts his head to one side. Sometimes he laughs at his own words.

When he talks about racism in Poland, he speaks of it as a Jew, but he is quite clear in his self-description as a Pole of Jewish descent rather than as a Jew who is Polish. Though some of his countrymen fail to notice this, there is a difference. He sees himself as a loyal Pole, though without the jingoistic mawkishness that many attach to the species. The fact that he is a Jew is secondary, though in Europe unforgettable. He believes that the persistence of anti-Semitism in Poland is rooted in Poles' suspicions of Europeanism or cosmopolitanism—such ideas are suspected of being unpatriotic. He rejects the frequent slur that Poland is a nation of anti-Semites: "To smear a nation that, in 1939, was the first to say 'no' to Nazism is unfair as is the resulting image of the country as backward and hate-filled."

While Michnik has had his share of anti-Semitic attacks, he is inclined to shrug them off as unimportant. When his newspaper was accused of being anti-Polish and, in a reference to Michnik's Jewishness, anti-*goyish*, he viewed the matter as merely stupid.

He is optimistic about the future of a tolerant, cheerful, "socially just" Poland. There is an old Russian joke about the challenges of establishing "civil society" after it has been destroyed by forty-five years of Communism: "We know you can turn an aquarium into fish soup. Question is, can you turn fish soup into an aquarium?" Well, despite the naysayers, in Poland, he says, you can come and see the fish. The transformation has succeeded. It is unfortunate that the working class that so successfully toppled Communism was capitalism's first victim. It was, sadly, inevitable. In an October 2009 article for *Der Spiegel,* Michnik wrote of this paradox of democracy: the Gdańsk shipyards that had once been Solidarity's stronghold could not reform and headed, inevitably, into bankruptcy.

Unfortunately, the assumption that Central Europeans, having suffered under totalitarianism for more than forty years, would arrive with a vision of a "third way" between capitalism and socialism was, at best, naive.

"The third way leads directly to the Third World," Michnik says, though he admits that the idea had once appealed to him. "My heart is on the left. But my wallet is on the right." No one has successfully implemented a compromise between market capitalism and socialist controls.

"Capitalism is neither fair nor equitable, but no one has found another system that works better," he says, echoing Winston Churchill's famous remark that democracy is the worst possible system, apart from all the others that have been tried. "Democracy," Michnik says with a smile, "offers a daily referendum on whether we wish to defend it or not. I sometimes think that our political elite is playing with fire."

"Poland has not had it so good for over three hundred years," he told a packed auditorium in Toronto in October 2009. Nor have the other former Iron Curtain countries. Yet despite the country's amazing success, or perhaps because of it, Poles are angry. "I used to think it was just us," he said in Toronto, "but now, having travelled to Budapest and Prague and Bratislava, I have discovered they are all like the Poles. Furious."

What had they expected? No system is perfect and there will always be winners and losers. People in the satellite countries were used to the idea that the state would take care of them; but the corollary of that fine expectation was that the state owned you. It no longer does. Perhaps the hope was for freedom without obligation. Now there is this strange nostalgia for Communism. "I call it the prisoner syndrome," Michnik said in Toronto. "In jail you dream of freedom. Once you are out of jail, you need to provide your own food and somewhere to sleep. You remember the free food and board and long for the security of your old jail cell."

Poland's future is, he thinks, as part of a united Europe firmly allied with the United States. He has had to repeat this amid an atmosphere of recriminations about Iraq and the financial crisis that began in the United States. The temptation to blame Americans for the failures of Europe's banks and major companies is inevitable. But it is not the Americans who went awry; it is the system. Blaming America is merely a convenient method of passing the buck.

"There is no more faithful friend to the United States in Europe than Poland," Michnik tells me. In 2003, when various European leaders accused him of having abandoned morality by supporting the U.S.-led invasion of Iraq, he was quick to point out that "a world without Saddam is better than a world with him." He accused the French and Germans of knee-jerk anti-Americanism. "I asked my French and German friends," he says, "'Are you afraid that tomorrow Bush will bomb the Louvre? If not, then which side are you on?'"[18]

When talking about his views on President Bush's replacement, he does not share the welcoming wild-eyed enthusiasm of Western Europeans. Poland remained a Bush supporter till the end. "Obama's presidency came with great hopes and promises," he said in 2009. "The problem is that, as with all hopes and promises, there will be disappointments along the way. Nevertheless, for Poland, the only choice is to remain steadfast and reliable as a U.S. friend." By early 2010 the disappointments were real even in the United States.

Michnik is inclined to take a charitable view of Russia's leadership. "Putin's is the language of great, historic Russian imperialism," he said. "He needs to rebuild Russia, to create order out of chaos. When my Russian friends warned me about his KGB mind, I did not believe them," he added. "But he is also a practical man and we have a chance to effect change even in Russia."

His father, Ozjasz, used to tell him that it was important to know that you can never own the whole truth, that you should always try to "put yourself behind the other person's desk, see the world through his eyes."[19] This is useful advice for a journalist, and it has served his son well.

As for General Jaruzelski, Michnik wrote as early as 1983 that "perhaps it will turn out one day that those people whose names are now inscribed in blackest ink on the pages of Polish history actually saved Poland from Soviet invasion."[20] In this context, the general is a hero, and if those who are busily indicting him for offences against the state had done their research, they would understand that the threat was real. Michnik believes that Colonel Ryszard Kukliński's reports have confirmed that Jaruzelski's fears were well founded. Kukliński, as an officer liaison between the Polish and the Soviet armies, would have known what the plans were for a Soviet military incursion into Poland.[21] The general has paid dearly for his choice of allegiances: the long trial, the many humiliations, the lack of tangible rewards for his service. Let the past be. An old man in ill health, forced to stand trial for Communist crimes, "a baseless persecution," Gorbachev said. Let the general rest.

Michnik and Jaruzelski meet for coffee and share stories. Each man mentioned to me that he was looking forward to seeing the other.

THE MAGIC OF SOLIDARITY

What everyone remembers about the end of the Cold War is the breathless, televised jubilation of East and West Germans embracing and dancing on top of the Berlin Wall—the seemingly impenetrable dividing line between "us" and "them," between the lands of super-highways, shiny cars and fancy shops and the lands of rusted toilets and bad teeth.

But where it all began, really, is not Berlin but the Free Hanseatic City of Gdańsk, on the Baltic Sea facing the pragmatic Scandinavians, its back to the rest of the continent with its cauldron of troubles. The new airport is named after Gdańsk's most famous citizen, Lech Wałęsa, The double highway to town is dotted with new developments, an IKEA factory, a supermarket, giant cranes hovering over pale blue and yellow building sites.

Gdańsk has endured a great deal of history. It was a small harbour town in the thirteenth century; in 1358 it joined the legendary Hanseatic League as Danzig, a free trading city that had relations with other trade centres like Bruges, Lisbon and Seville. It was, briefly, a much-fought-over stronghold of the Teutonic Knights, then Kasimir IV of Poland granted it autonomy. In 1734, the Russians laid siege to and conquered the city, and in 1793 the Prussian king annexed it. It was free once more under Napoleon, from 1807 to 1812, and again from 1918 to 1939, then occupied by Germany at the beginning of the war.

Gdańsk had always retained its independent spirit as a free city state, an international trading centre, partly German, partly Polish; its buildings exhibited a comfortable merchant life that did not share in the nationalist inclinations of the nineteenth century. The Free City had its own constitution and its own government.

In 1945, the city was systematically destroyed by the Red Army. Its buildings were buried under two million cubic metres of rubble.[22] Many residents fled the bombardment; the rest of the Germans were expelled when the war was over. Resettled Poles from the east, fleeing Lithuanian persecution and Ukrainian ethnic cleansing, replaced them. Gdańsk became a Polish working-man's town, natural birthplace of the independent labour union movement that challenged the entrenched Communist leadership: Solidarity.

Katherine, my local guide, is proud of her family's long association with the city—four or five generations at least, she tells me. Every year she takes tourists to the reconstructed Teutonic fort at Malbork, a short drive from the city. She talks of the battle of Grunwald and the Polish victory over the Knights in 1410; her description is almost as evocative as Matejko's painting in the National Gallery. She is pleased to show the rebuilt old town of Danzig with its interlocking market squares, the Cloth Hall, the seventeenth-century Golden Gate, the Gothic Rathaus and the massive St. Mary's Church (Bazylikę Mariacką), once the largest Gothic church in Europe. She takes me to the tourist heart of the city, the rows of shops with brilliant displays of amber. "We are now the amber capital of the world," she says, and I believe her. But I am here to follow the course of Solidarity.

THE ROADS to Freedom exhibition is in a wartime bunker, its entrance hemmed in by two freestanding brick walls and an armoured car. One wall was carved out of the two-metre-high brick barrier that used to surround the shipyard; the other is a piece of the Berlin Wall presented to Gdańsk by the mayor of Berlin.

Underground, the first two exhibits remind me of my Hungarian childhood: a nasty-looking, rusty toilet with newspaper wipes and a grocery-store counter without groceries. The first anti-government riots were over food stamps and the rising price of bread and meat, which could be purchased only on specific days. Long lines would form before dawn and often there would be nothing left for half the people waiting. Katherine tells me the average wait for a new pair of shoes was a year, even for growing children; the crowded, miserable flats had only sporadic cold running water. There were strikes in 1956, 1968 and 1970, all put down by the government's anti-riot militia; hundreds were killed, thousands jailed, but the protests continued.

The museum shows a film of the militia's armoured cars and tanks plowing into crowds of unarmed civilians. The riot police, the loathed ZOMO (Zmotoryzowane Odwody Milicji Obywatelskiej, or Motorized Reserves of the Citizens' Militia), beat demonstrators with rubber truncheons. Some died during the beatings. Here, in room #5, there is a menacing lineup of cardboard ZOMO, all clad in black with hard plastic face guards and shields proudly displaying the word *milicja*. One of their victims was a fifteen-year-old boy on his way home from school.

Solidarity surfaced in 1980 with a series of nationwide strikes that culminated at the Lenin Shipyards in Gdańsk.[23] There were student demonstrations, violent reprisals in mining towns in the east and west, but this time the strikes spread across the country. For the first time, intellectuals, who had been punished by the government for their role in the 1968 protests, were openly supporting the workers with KOR.

Senator Bogdan Borusewicz, who looks remarkably like a Kaczyński, used to belong to KOR. When we met in his white parliamentary chambers, he talked of hiding in basements, evading police curfews, using a variety of disguises. He went to his own wedding dressed as a woman. In 1970, in Gdynia, his best friend was shot by the ZOMO. "After that, I did not want people to forget what had happened."

He said KOR had wanted Lech Wałęsa to be the leader of the revolution because he was best person for an impossibly tough job.

The thirty-seven-year-old, out-of-work Gdańsk electrician had been fired by management for being too free with his opinions. He had little education but a great voice and ideas for providing a better world for his several children. A short, stocky man with thick hands, a wide face, longish hair, thick moustache and a wide, closed-mouthed smile, he was energetic, quick-witted, a passionate speaker who could inspire crowds with his straight-from-the-heart delivery and his apparent lack of pretension.

The union's initial conditions for returning to work were simple enough: higher wages, improved working conditions, restitution of workers fired after earlier strikes, the release of political prisoners. Solidarity added the right to organize, the right to strike and a loosening of the government's hold on the news media. The twenty-one demands, written on a wooden plank in red and black ink, are displayed in the museum's third room, together with the glassed-in pen Lech Wałęsa used to sign the final agreements with the government and the shipyard.

Ironically, the government, like all Communist governments, had always claimed the mantle of worker leadership for itself. Now the workers it professed to represent questioned its legitimacy. How could the People's Republic be for the proletariat if the proletariat wanted new representation?

By the end of 1980, Solidarity had over ten million members across the country, and its power was undisputed when the government agreed to legalize its existence. Now even Party members could line up for their Solidarity membership cards.

Wałęsa's final deal with the government included the right to raise a monument to the victims of the 1970 strike demonstrations massacred by the militia.

The massive steel Memorial to the Fallen Shipyard Workers looms over gate #2 of the old Lenin Shipyards. It was erected in 1980, as part of Solidarity's negotiations with the government. Its three crosses stand forty-two metres tall, gigantic towers that Wałęsa compared to harpoons driven into the indifferent body of the Communist whale. Behind the crosses, on the outside wall of the former shipyard, a series of uneven plaques commemorate the dead. The largest, near the gate, dedicates the site to "the remembrance of those slaughtered. A warning to rulers that no social conflict in our country can be resolved by force. A sign of hope for fellow citizens that evil need not prevail."

At the end of October 1981, the first national congress of Solidarity leaders was held in Gdańsk. The sea of people overflowed outside the hall. Jacek Kuroń was greeted with a standing ovation. It was like a wild celebration; everyone was happy. The euphoria did not last.

Late in the evening of December 12, 1981, all phones, radio and television were cut off. The next morning, General Jaruzelski's government declared martial law, banned Solidarity, imprisoned its leadership and instituted a nationwide ten o'clock curfew. Three days later, when Solidarity-linked miners went on strike at the Wujek coal mine in Katowice, riot police responded with tanks and water cannons. The massacre was one of the most horrific moments of the Jaruzelski regime and would come back to haunt the perpetrators after 1989.

Solidarity, like the erstwhile Polish Home Army, went underground and continued to fight. But unlike the Polish army, Solidarity persisted. Lech Wałęsa graced the covers of *Newsweek, Time* magazine and *The Economist* and the front pages of every Western newspaper. In 1983, he was awarded the Nobel Peace Prize. But food shortages continued, the price of bread skyrocketed and no amount of propaganda could convince the population that the socialist system would recover.

My publisher, Zbigniew Garwacki, wrote for several underground newspapers and remembers driving to Gdańsk to join the strike committee. "At the time there seemed to be no choice," he says, smiling. People kept being arrested, some disappeared, some drowned—apparent suicides.

A plaque on the wall of Gdańsk's St. Brygida Church reminds tourists that this was once the meeting place of Solidarity members. The authorities rarely risked invading the sanctuary of a church. They recognized that the Church had power and authority. To oppose it would have meant armed revolt, and neither the local Communist government nor its masters in Moscow were willing to risk that. Here, after he was released from prison, Wałęsa could keep an office next to the sacristy.

On a Monday afternoon in January 2009, the church is empty and dark except for the candles lit in supplication to the Virgin Mary and in front of the sad brass memorial showing the broken figure of the martyred priest Father Jerzy Popiełuszko, murdered by security police in 1984.

At Katherine's request, the sacristan lights up the altar to show us the spectacular cascade of amber and bronze, the glitter that will greet the faithful when they arrive for evensong. The nearby brass sculpture of woven dates glows in the refracted light. It is a memorial to Poland's significant dates, starting with 966, when Poles accepted Christianity.

Behind the Memorial to the Fallen Shipyard Workers, the main gates of the shipyard are open. Inside, the place looks abandoned, a couple of people walking slowly through the mud toward the only area here where ships are still being built. When I was last here, it was owned by ISD Poland, the local branch of a Ukrainian conglomerate. The rest of the place was desolate. The rail line is still unused. The cranes near the water are still.

The Solidarity Centre is in a low-slung rust-coloured building with a dead tree outside. Father Maciej Zięba, who splits his time between the Centre and St. Nicholas Church in the Old Town, is the director. Though you wouldn't know it from his casual outfit, he is a Dominican priest. In a country where religion and politics are often intertwined, it is not particularly unusual that a priest should also have a civilian job. Zięba had been a student member of KOR; he, like others, had become accustomed to being followed and interrogated by state security agents. The police, he tells me, had the right to deal with you as they wished. They could beat you, imprison you, threaten your family. There was no authority you could appeal to. "Every day," he recalls, "I explained to myself why I had to continue to support Solidarity: we needed to live without lies." Under martial law he worked with Tadeusz Mazowiecki publishing over fifty thousand clandestine copies of *Solidarity Weekly*.

Solidarity re-emerged with nationwide strikes protesting the government's inability to deal with food shortages. The national debt had soared; the large industrial complexes were running at a loss; the lines for food grew longer.

In 1989, the seemingly implacable Party gave way. General Czesław Kiszczak invited a group of Solidarity members to meet with representatives of the government. Kiszczak, as minister of the interior from 1980 till 1983, had been responsible for the protection of the state from all anti-state activity—in other words, the activities of all those he would now be meeting. He had been Prime Minister Jaruzelski's right-hand man during martial law.

They met in February 1989, amid rumours of armed Soviet intervention, seated at an Arthurian round table[24] so no one would have pride of place—fifty-seven people around a table twenty-eight feet wide (the joke of the day was that it was designed to be three feet wider than the world spitting record).

The Solidarity team included three men whom Jeffrey Sachs, the young, Harvard-trained economist, would later refer to as the "three wise men" of Poland's future. Their reputations were clean, and they had all served time in Communist jails. They were also all students of history.

At fifty-seven, Bronisław Geremek was the oldest. He had specialized in medieval society, studied in Paris and lectured at the Sorbonne and had a post-doctoral degree from the Polish Academy of Sciences. A well-dressed, dapper man with thick grey hair and a moustache, he seemed to be the least likely figure to have become involved with the workers' protest movement, yet in 1980 that was what he had done.

Jacek Kuroń was fifty-five years old. As a young Communist student he had criticized the oppressive methods of the Party bureaucracy in an open letter that demanded more rights for workers. In 1968, he helped organize student protests. He, too, joined Solidarity, as an adviser to Lech Wałęsa.

The youngest of the trio was Adam Michnik.

The round table agreed to semi-free elections[25] with the Communist Party holding the balance of power, to be followed, within a year, by free elections.

That day, it seemed, the totalitarian government had conceded defeat. Yet Poland was still a long way from democracy. The very notion of human rights, civil rights, a multi-party system, freedom of speech, representative government—all new ideas for the ruling party—had to be introduced and agreed on. There would have to be a new constitution, new rules for elections and an emergency fix for the economy.

"The formal appointment of Tadeusz Mazowiecki to the post of prime minister was handled by President Jeruzelski," Zięba says, "the same man who, only eight years earlier, had ordered his arrest and imprisonment." Mazowiecki, scion of an old Polish family with strong ties to the Catholic Church, had been Wałęsa's choice for the job.

"Two days after he became prime minister, Mazowiecki invited me to his office," Zięba recalls. Zięba waited outside while Mazowiecki finished a meeting with the head of the KGB in Poland. "I never asked what they had talked about," he says, but he remembers praying that if he were sent to Siberia, he would be allowed to wear his white cassock.

The Warsaw Pact was still in force. There were armed Soviet troops inside the country and along the border, and in everyone's minds the belief that all Solidarity leaders would end up in the Gulag.

Mazowiecki announced that a thick line would be drawn between the past and the future. The government would be too busy with the problems posed by the future to deal with crimes of the past. But there was more to it than that: there was also the fear that all this was a mirage, that the ZOMO and the tanks could reappear at any moment, this time backed by Soviet troops.

At the time, for the sake of stability, the three wise men thought it prudent for the old Communist officials and bureaucrats to be left in place as executive agents.[26] Wałęsa did not believe the time was right for settling old scores. History, he said, should hold those who had mismanaged the country responsible.[27]

In 1990, Wałęsa still had the trust of the people. For the June elections, all the candidates were personally selected by him,[28] and it was a clean sweep for the Solidarity team.

IN 2011, the Roads to Freedom exhibition is due to move out of its bunker and into the shipyards. The muddy grounds will be cleaned up and a new shopping mall and conference centre will be built behind the gates where democracy began. Katherine, who was once an interpreter for Wałęsa, tries to hide her disgust at the prospect. "This is a place where people died," she says.

We are treading on holy ground.

SHOCK THERAPY

Bringing in "shock therapy" proponent Jeffrey Sachs and his "big bang" approach to economic reform to Poland was a high-risk manoeuvre in 1989. Sachs, a thirty-four-year-old wunderkind with floppy brown hair and sharp features, was a Harvard-trained professor of economics at Cambridge University. He had distinguished himself by advising the governments of Bolivia, Brazil and Argentina on how to end hyperinflation and energize a collapsed economy. Before accepting his assignment to Bolivia, he told a stunned South American delegation that he could stop hyperinflation in a day and that he would bring the International Monetary Fund to their rescue once they adopted his "therapy." After forty years of Communist central planning, Poland's economic situation was worse than Bolivia's.

Sachs, who had always liked a challenge, viewed the situation of the East European countries as a "pressure cooker," and he was the man to relieve the pressure. Here was a society desperately in need of change, one that was ready for his experiment in quick transformations. Here was a country whose economy was geared to massive industrial giants producing shoddy products no one needed and selling them at a loss to the Soviet Union. The few desultory shops were mostly empty, and huge lineups greeted the arrivals of such daily necessities as bread and milk.

He arrived in Warsaw on April 5, 1989, the day that the "round table" agreement was signed, and was met by the three wise men of the Solidarity movement. Sachs, in a later interview, described the trio as "legends," "men of unbelievable stature, courage, conviction, and knowledge." They had Wałęsa's trust. Wałęsa, in turn, had their belief that only he could unite Poland at a time when the government would need the support of the people.

Never one who enjoyed long meetings and all-night discussions, Wałęsa had the wisdom to absent himself from the exhaustive hours spent with Sachs. Kuroń, Michnik and Geremek confessed to Sachs that they were terrified that when they came into power they would not be able to make enough of a difference in the desperation of people's lives, and the national debt, already at $40 billion, would grow. They believed that if they tried to control the situation, they would be held responsible for the crisis. People would starve. Inflation was at 600 per cent. The IMF had refused even a transitional loan, and although the U.S. had been in the habit of congratulating all attempts to overthrow Moscow's control, it had offered only a minor loan. The country could be bankrupt. Their only hope was that the high-powered young academic would change the IMF's mind—that his theories would translate into practical solutions. Sachs convinced them that the foreign debt could be cancelled or lowered and that there would be new investment in the economy if they took his bitter pill, quickly liberalizing markets.

By the time Sachs went to Gdańsk to meet Wałęsa, the die had been cast. Sachs and David Lipton, an economist with the IMF, presented their fifteen-page shock-therapy prescription for almost overnight change, approved by the wise men. Wałęsa agreed to it.

The method of an instant turn to capitalism was named in honour of the new finance minister: the Balcerowicz Plan. Leszek Balcerowicz, an economist personally chosen by Wałęsa to oversee the reforms, shared Sachs's admiration for Milton Friedman's views of the opportunity for a fast free-market package when conditions were right. Friedman, an American economist and former adviser to U.S. president Ronald Reagan, was a firm believer in deregulation, open markets, free-floating currency rates and tight money supplies to battle inflation—all measures that would make the average man's life more difficult in the short run but would put Poland's financial house in order.

The Institute of Public Affairs's Lena Kolarska-Bobińska remembers the late-night call from Balcerowicz. He asked her how long it would take the new government to effect a complete change of the state-controlled Communist system. He was worried that "Homo sovieticus," the typical product of the Soviet system, lacking in initiative and suspicious of Western democracies, would revolt against the notion of capitalism. For four decades the bogeyman of free markets had been taught at every school, every university, spouted by Party officials at workers' meetings, and now they were going to invite them all to meet the devil. "I told him that if he wanted success," says Lena, "he had to move quickly. There would be no second chances." For a few months, maybe a year, the people would not oppose him. "There was this small window of complete trust, but it would not last." The very nature of democracy is for people to question everything the government does.

"If the reforms were painful," she says, "it was because they had to be. You can't have a major operation without some pain. And we were lucky. Balcerowicz was not interested in his own political future. He did not want to be a politician."

The Balcerowicz Plan went into effect on January 1, 1990. Starting in February, the government removed price controls, tightened credit, cut subsidies, pushed productivity, sold off many of the government's assets and, as Sachs had predicted, ended hyperinflation. Retribution for Communist apparatchiks and their henchmen stayed off the agenda.

In 1991, when the pope called Sachs for an update on the Polish economy, Sachs was able to reassure the Holy Father that "Poland had turned the corner decisively."[29] Foreign debt, he said, would be paid off that year, and foreign investment was growing with the confidence that the changes inspired. By then, Sachs had succeeded in convincing the IMF to come through with a loan of $725 million.

In Polish homes, the plan's victory felt hollow. Food subsidies disappeared overnight. Farming subsidies were denied. The terrible '80s became a cheerful memory for those who could not afford even the bare necessities of life. During the Communist era, the stores had been vacant. Now the stores were full of choice foodstuffs and beautifully made Western garb, but no one could afford to buy. Contrary to Sachs's promise to Solidarity leaders, the standard of living failed to rise.

Within two years, the public lost patience. There had been too much hardship for the underprivileged. The plan, its critics said, had been unreasonably fast, without regard for the welfare of those who had backed Solidarity. The former prisoners of conscience turned out to be ineffectual administrators. Solidarity itself had splintered into opposing camps; their public squabbling, while perhaps predictable in a democracy, was shocking. Two of Solidarity's best-known stars, Wałęsa and Michnik, had a very public falling-out, as did Wałęsa and Mazowiecki. By 1993, unemployment had hit 25 per cent in the industrial sector and young people were flooding out of the country in search of jobs in the U.K. and Germany. Poverty and hunger in former Solidarity strongholds and in the farming countryside led to a desire for the former security of state-controlled enterprises. More than seven thousand protests were held throughout the country.

As president from December 1990 until the end of 1995, Wałęsa failed to soothe rising tempers. His enemies—many of whom were his erstwhile friends—accused him of exhibiting an erratic, abrasive, dictatorial style ill suited to the times. In Gdańsk, Maciej Zięba told me that at this stage Wałęsa had no friends, only admirers and detractors.

In the event, Wałęsa's performance as president failed to pour salve on his people's wounds. The public had grown weary of national heroes running their country.

Wałęsa lost the 1995 presidential election to Aleksander Kwaśniewski, a former Communist functionary. Kwaśniewski had been on Jaruzelski's side of the "round table" discussions but was quick to reinvent himself after the fall of the regime. His public image was now honed in support of pluralistic democracy, the European Union and even membership in NATO. Unlike Wałęsa, he was well groomed, wore expensive suits, had excellent diction and handled television debates like a man born to the medium. Wałęsa chose to focus on his opponent's murky past, while the former Communist talked of the future and changes that could improve people's lives.

Unlike Wałęsa's supporters, the Communists had the old structures at their disposal: many of the former regime's ubiquitous *nomenklatura* had hung on to their jobs. By 1980, there were over 500,000 such positions in the country, all comfortable, none looking for change and resisting when it threatened their own livelihoods and privileges. These networks of well-paid civil servants continued in power in the provinces. And given their local and often specialized knowledge, they remained in place.

Wałęsa had only his past credentials.

He no longer made television viewers tear up. People could be forgiven for switching to another of the now numerous TV channels.

Bickering among the former Solidarity leaders kept them out of power and at one another's throats for the balance of the '90s and into the new century. Michnik accused Wałęsa of assuming the habits of a dictator. Wałęsa accused Balczerowicz of turning privatization into kleptocracy.

When Poland joined the EU in May 2004, historian Tony Judt wrote in *Postwar: A History of Europe since 1945,* the feeling in Poland was of still "being at the periphery of someone else's centre, of being second class outside the core of Europe." This consciousness of still being second-class helped hand the 2005 elections to the xenophobic Law and Justice party's Kaczyński twins. For two years the former child stars made the country a laughing stock of European Union meetings. Lech Kaczyński's vituperative outbursts against Germany and Russia provided months of fence-mending work for Poland's next government: the centre-right Civic Platform party. Civic Platform won the 2007 elections, but the presidential post went to Lech Kaczyński. His tragic death in April 2010 offered a rare opportunity for his long-time opponents to highlight Kaczyński's admirable side.

Prime Minister Putin personally took charge of investigating the cause of the plane crash. German chancellor Angela Merkel, whose country had been roundly criticized by Kaczyński, said, "I knew that he dedicated his whole life to Poland's and Europe's freedom." Polish prime minister Donald Tusk, choking back tears, said that "the world has never seen such a tragedy." Even Adam Michnik, who disagreed with Kaczyński about most political matters, stated that "he was a great patriot," and *Gazeta Wyborcza*'s website was all black for a day of national mourning.

TWENTY YEARS AFTER THE END OF COMMUNISM IN POLAND

Czesław Miłosz once described the difference between Western and Eastern Europe as between respectable upstanding members of a family and a set of embarrassing, slightly annoying, always importuning relations. Well, all that has changed. Now, after the economic disaster of the first decade of the twenty-first century, the Greeks and Icelanders appear to be more embarrassing than their new EU cousins to the East.

When the borders opened in 1989, Poles left by the thousands to find jobs in Germany, the U.K. and Ireland (remember the Polish plumber jokes?). But by 2008 they had started to return home: the U.K.'s Institute for Public Policy Research reported at the time that more than half a million Poles had already left. In late 2008, the zloty was strong; inflation in Poland appeared to be in check at below 4 per cent. Only four years after joining the European Union, the country's economy was looking good; a 5.3 per cent growth of GDP, shrinking debt, the promise of flatter income tax and less bureaucracy the next year, lower inflation and reduced unemployment meant that Poland was at the leading edge of Central Europe's transformation into a euro-friendly, hard-working country. With 67 billion euros offered by the European Union as additional incentive for building infrastructure and public-private partnerships, the potential was there for fast development over the next several years.

Then came 2009, the failure of the U.S. financial system, the real estate disaster, the sinking banks, falling markets and countries no longer able to pay their debts.

There were strikes and protests, revelations of business corruption and bribery of judges and government officials. Capitalism, it seemed, had not delivered the panacea its proponents promised. Or had it? PricewaterhouseCoopers's report on "hard landing" for Central and Eastern Europe revealed that Poland was one of the strongest economies in the region and highlighted the country's stability and high credit rating.

I ASKED Jeffrey Sachs whether he still thought the outcome for Poland was worth the gamble. He said, with considerable confidence, that "if you take the broad, historical perspective, the changes since 1989 have been positive and lasting." The benefits of a more productive, more open society, perhaps even a more "boring country" were worth achieving. In 2010, Sachs is director of the Earth Institute at

Columbia University and is committed to persuading the world of the need to focus on climate change, rather than economic change. He is fifty-five years old now, still with the slender build, the thick hair and the intense gaze of his younger self, but he has the wrinkles to go with his many international bestsellers, new recipes to end poverty and global inequality and the wear and tear of the lecture circuits. Still, his opinions about Central Europe have not changed.

He sees the dangers of populism, broad-based corruption, institutions that do not work and safety nets with gaping holes, but these are not surprising in countries with such legacies of wars, violence and dictatorships.

"The special feature of Poland," he said in a telephone interview in April 2009, "was its overarching ambition to become part of the European Union. It had to be done fast and therefore it was painful, and with great risks, but by and large, it was successful." Twenty years and many countries later, he does not see how the change could have been done better. "Now Poland can take part in the debate about the future of Europe. It is no longer an outsider."

JAROSŁAW SROKA is director of corporate communications for Kulczyk Investments, one of Poland's largest and most profitable corporations, with offices in Luxemberg, London, Dubai, Kiev and, of course, Warsaw. As of 2010, Kulczyk has US$3 billion invested worldwide, though it is focussed mainly on "emerging markets." It is, according to its website, in oil and gas, minerals, infrastructure, power generation, gas distribution and a range of other businesses. Sroka looks like a young man on the move—well-cut grey suit, high white collars on a handmade shirt, long cuffs—someone who would seem comfortable in any U.S. or German boardroom. He speaks four languages fluently, including, of course, Russian. It may be thought by some to be a language of the past, but Jarosław Sroka thinks it is a language of the future. There is a great deal of money and power in Russia, he says. The Russians want to play a key role in Europe, and who can blame them? They have bought into several Western European companies, though mostly in energy or energy-related fields. In addition to Gazprom's Nord Stream, they are going ahead with the

$15-billion South Stream pipeline, bringing gas under the Black Sea to Central Europe.

"Of course," Sroka says, "Putin is using the old KGB network. It's still there and he knows he can trust it." But Putin also offers Russians a new pride in themselves. This is what they crave since their humiliating loss of empire. "In this modern world we can create new relationships," Sroka says. "There will be no more wars in Europe." He sounds both confident and reassuring, as if he is trying to convince both of us.

Sroka's boss, Jan Kulczyk, is one of those who profited greatly from the shock-therapy reforms, picking up formerly state-owned companies and using the new banking system for the loans that gave him the initial down payments. He reinvented himself as a millionaire (later billionaire) businessman in the 1990s while most of his fellow Poles had to make do with less. No one, except the likes of Jan Kulczyk, had been at the right place at the right moment and had been smart enough to believe in the Jeffrey Sachs capitalist future. Kulczyk Investments holds, among other things, a private highway, the biggest brewery in a beer-loving country and the exclusive licences for Volkswagen, Audi and Škoda.

Kulczyk's Warsaw offices, decorated with eye-popping Polish art, are a testimonial to Jan Kulczyk's faith in the country's ability to meet its challenges with unemployment (still at around 15 per cent, though not in Warsaw), too-early retirement, the growing black market and the long drawn-out saga of health care reform. Sroka's father is a retired miner from Silesia. Sroka, nevertheless, decries the cushy deal the miners now have: after only twenty-five years of work, the government takes care of them for the rest of their lives. "If you tried to change that," he tells me, "there would be violent protests again."

Since the end of 1989, there have been hundreds of strikes in every sector of the economy: health care and postal workers, teachers, miners—all demanding more of their piece of the new life and most of them succeeding with another slice for themselves. Yet, at the end of 2009, Poland's economy displayed extraordinary resilience.

The stylish Hotel Rialto is decked out with new art deco furniture and minimalist paintings. The old Polonia Palace Hotel has a shiny new interior and double windows that keep out the noise of late-night revellers along Aleje Jerozolimskie.

Across the wide avenue, the gigantic Stalinist-era Palace of Culture and Science, an enduring symbol of Soviet rule that once lorded it over the city, has been spruced up for the new era. Its Soviet architect boasted of its 3,288 rooms. Unhappy ghosts haunt a few of the empty meeting rooms and, as the elevator attendant mentions, some nights you can hear screaming from the basement, but the upper levels are open for schoolkids and sightseers. There is a pool, a concert hall and a theatre. Although it is forty-three storeys, 231 metres, high, its massive tower does not seem particularly out of place across from the Intercontinental and Marriott towers.

The grey, grim Warsaw I remembered from the 1970s has receded into history. This city looks like many other European cities. Gone are the war-scarred buildings of the '70s; new towers dominate the skyline. There are martini bars and late-night parties in clubs guarded by wide-shouldered bouncers who talk into their headsets. The Paparazzi bar along Mazowiecka Street is described in the Warsaw guide as "the place where city traders ruthlessly advance their careers over expensive account drinks and Escada clad bimbos hunt for foreign sugar daddies." Apart from the lack of political correctness, this would suit several bars I have visited in New York, Boston and Berlin.

Marek and Iza, two students at Warsaw University, take me to a lovely new café-bar on Nowi Świat, the refurbished pedestrian boulevard, and talk about their recent trips to the United States. "Travel feels normal now," Marek says, though he had never experienced the previous abnormal, when a Polish passport would have aroused suspicion at U.S. airports. His memory of those times is gleaned from his parents, both of them journalists under the old regime. Their friends prefer computers, sex, rock concerts, American movies and romantic comedies to serious Polish films. Their favourite bands: Kult, Ti Love and Republika.

It is great, he admits, to be able to take all this for granted.

The Gold Terraces (Złote Tarasy) shopping centre is as well stocked with high-end labels—MAC, Monetti, Sephora, Esprit, Swarovski, Samsonite, Sisley, Zara—as any other European mall, and its translucent undulating ceiling is more inventive than most. Prices in the cafés and boutiques are about the same as in London or Paris.

Nearby, at 44 Złota Street, the most luxurious apartment building in Poland is rising to reshape Warsaw's skyline. At forty-five storeys, 192 metres, high, with an indoor pool, fitness floor and sun terrace, it's been designed by the internationally renowned architect Daniel Libeskind. Libeskind was born in Łódź, an old centre of Jewish learning that became the site of a notorious ghetto, most of whose emaciated inhabitants were murdered at Chełmno and Auschwitz.

As Libeskind describes it, "the building embraces the complex history of the site and the aspirations of Warsaw."

A DEEPLY CATHOLIC COUNTRY

The cream-coloured, high-spired Stanisław Kostka Church, in a residential area of Warsaw, has become the memorial site for the martyred Father Jerzy Popiełuszko, abducted, beaten, tortured and murdered by the secret police in 1984. Popiełuszko had offended the authorities by celebrating special masses for "the homeland" that drew tens of thousands of worshippers, packing the church and the surrounding streets. He was a great orator and remained a friend of Solidarity after the movement was banned. Ignoring clear warnings from the state police, he visited Lech Wałęsa. His sermons warned that Poles must not become slaves to a lie, that silence only encourages the lies. In one of his last sermons he said, "Solidarity had received a wound that continues to bleed, but one which was not mortal because one cannot murder hopes." But, as it turned out, one can murder priests.

On October 19, 1984, Father Popiełuszko disappeared. Four days later, his mangled body was found floating in the Vistula River Reservoir.

Lech Wałęsa spoke at Father Popiełuszko's funeral: "We say farewell to you, Servant of God, promising we will never bow to force, we will be sound in the service of our country, we shall reply to falsehood with truth, to evil with good..." It was a profoundly Christian speech, before an audience of over 300,000—both a confirmation of Wałęsa's own faith and a prayer to Poland's Mother, the Black Madonna,[30] for justice.

On December 19, 2009, Pope Benedict XVI approved the beatification of Father Popiełuszko.

The Stanisław Kostka Church still celebrates mass three times on Sundays for a zealous crowd of the faithful. Here, in this church, their faith and their patriotism coincide with flags of the Polish Home Army, of Solidarity, of honour, and flags with some of the "big" dates: 1569, the formation of the great Polish-Lithuanian Commonwealth, last bulwark of Christianity against the Tatars; 1830, the war against the Russians; 1939, the German and Russian attacks; 1970, the government's reprisals against striking workers.

Wałęsa had always worn a badge with the image of the Black Madonna on his lapel. He believed, as do millions of Poles, that the icon at the Jasna Góra monastery in Częstochowa can perform miracles for her favourite people. Legend has it that the dark wood-painting of the Virgin Mary, guarded by the Paulist monks since 1430, has held the monastery safe during wars and invasions.

Millions of pilgrims still flock to the site each day, overwhelming the meagre facilities. Many approach the Madonna on their knees, as Wałęsa did when he came as a petitioner for the favour of continuing his battle for civil rights and popular sovereignty.

Jasna Góra may be an ostentatious display of faith in Poland, but equally devout gatherings can be found in churches from Gdańsk to Poznań. I saw it in the churches of Kraków, Lvov and Warsaw. Unlike the great cathedrals of France and Italy that have become mere tourist attractions, Poland's churches are for prayers. Kraków's famous seventeenth-century baroque Church of St. Peter and St. Paul is full of worshippers on Sundays and Friday evenings, and there is a crowd for evensong at the Basilica of the Virgin Mary on Grand Square. On Sunday mornings, the churches are so full that young people kneel in the aisles—older worshippers occupy the seats—following the lessons and bending their heads to the sacraments. As the pope said, it is impossible to understand the Poles without recognizing their intense attachment to their Catholic faith.

When Karol Józef Wojtyła, the former archbishop of Kraków, was elected pope by the Vatican Council in 1978, Poland celebrated with a passion that foretold the victory of its Church over the godlessness of Communism. Church bells rejoiced throughout the country. Some believed that the Black Madonna was sending a message to her people.

In 1979, during the pope's first, historic return to his homeland, he spoke to a sea of people filling Victory Square, and all the streets that converge on it. He must have chosen this site for its size but perhaps also for the history it conjures for Poles.

In 1807, this was Saski Square, named after the imposing Saski Palace later levelled by the Germans. In 1921, it was renamed after Józef Piłsudski, who had successfully cobbled together a country from the pieces Poland was awarded at Versailles. Piłsudski was chief of state from November 1918 until 1922, commander of Poland's forces in the successful Polish-Soviet War. When mentioning Piłsudski, Poles tend to focus on his heroic past rather than his later dictatorial tendencies. In 1939, the square was renamed Adolf Hitler Platz, and in 1945 Victory Square, in honour of the Red Army's victory over Fascism. Not surprisingly, it is now Piłsudski Square again, and a small plaque and pots of red and white flowers mark the place where John Paul II stood. When he said "There can be no just Europe without an independent Poland," a million people erupted in spontaneous applause.

The day he celebrated mass at the baroque Holy Cross Church, you could hear a pin drop. Frédéric Chopin's heart is buried in one of the church's baroque pillars, and a ceremonial urn glows red in his honour. Celebrated both as a great composer and an ardent nationalist, Chopin left Poland on November 2, 1830, before the suppression of the November 1830 uprising against Imperial Russia—a fact that gave his music additional sparkle during the Soviet era.

In front of the Holy Cross Church, the bent stone figure of Christ carries a giant cross. The relentless German bombing did not destroy the statue, though the massive figure had been blown off its pedestal and lay in the rubble, the cross raised in silent supplication. To the right of the entrance, there is a side altar with a sad little metal and paint portrait of the Virgin (she appears to be crying) and Child, a memorial to those killed at Katyń. Fresh flowers and rosaries surround the picture. There is also a shrine to Karol Wojtyła—"Let us pray for the beatification of John Paul II"—and fresh candles are lit in his honour each day. The main altar was named by John Paul II as "the altar of Poland—our motherland."

There was no doubt on whose behalf the pope invoked the Madonna's assistance. When he told his millions of listeners that day "Do not be afraid," he was sharing his own strength and belief in the justice of Solidarity's cause.

Wałęsa believed that the Church had been one of the chief reasons for his success. It was churches that offered space for Solidarity to meet when their meetings were forbidden. Lech Wałęsa's St. Brygida Church had given him sanctuary and a chance to speak from the pulpit. The state authorities, even the militia, respected the sanctuary of churches, though they could forcibly disperse gatherings of more than three people elsewhere. In 1981, the pope used his authority with General Jaruzelski (an atheist), entreating him not to order more bloodshed. That was the same year the pope invited Lech Wałęsa to the Vatican for a private meeting. In 1983, at Jasna Góra, the pope declared himself to be "a son of this nation" and told the cheering millions that he shared their aspirations and "desire to live in truth, liberty, justice and solidarity."

In 1987, the pope visited the memorial to the shipyard victims in Gdańsk. He was allowed to walk up to the massive steel structure, but the crowds were kept back by the police. Polish television was to show him, walking alone, with no one nearby to watch him lay a wreath or hear his speech over the dead. "There must have been a hundred thousand people here," Katherine tells me. In his autobiography,[31] Wałęsa credits the pope with keeping the Solidarity fires burning during the most difficult times. In many of Poland's churches, there are petitions for Rome to canonize the Polish pope and mark his place in the ranks of saints.

IN 2010, at least one branch of the Church still supports the flagrantly anti-Semitic Radio Maryja, whose founding president is Tadeusz Rydzyk, a Catholic priest. As a religious institution, the station pays no taxes, though it is the most successful commercial radio venture in Poland. The fact that Radio Maryja collects money at public meetings has fattened its coffers to such an extent that it had considered buying the Gdańsk shipyards for 100 million zlotys ($35 million). According to *Gazeta Wyborcza*'s Jarosław Kurski, it influences millions of people. Radio Maryja is one of only two radio stations that is heard all over Poland. Stanisław Krajewski, co-chair of the Polish Council of Christians and Jews, is more dismissive of the station's influence: "It has prayers, music, stuff about the family— only about 10 per cent of its programming is offensive." That would compare quite favourably with a handful of far-right radio stations in the United States.

Like several U.S. preachers in recent years, Father Rydzyk has also shown remarkable success as a businessman; his latest venture: mobile phones.

I asked Zbigniew Nosowski, editor-in-chief of the influential Catholic monthly *Wiez* ("The Bond"), why Rydzyk is allowed to use the airwaves to promote right-wing extremist causes, why the Church remained silent even when Father Rydzyk ridiculed an African priest for being black. Nosowski, a quiet, grey-haired sociologist-theologian, treats my question with the gentle patience one might accord a boringly troublesome child. It is not the first time he has been asked, and won't be the last. The Church, he explains, is a democratic institution in Poland. Several bishops have criticized Rydzyk, but he pays no attention. He does not have to. No individual, other than the head of his own order, can tell him to desist, and his order has chosen to ignore him. "Rydzyk is a radical fundamentalist with a small following," he says, "and fewer than 2 per cent of Poles listen to him. His audience is declining every year."

Nowoski is proud of the Church's leadership in attacking anti-Semitism. He is co-chair, with Stanisław Krajewski, of the Polish Council of Christians and Jews. Pope John Paul II advised that the Church had to make an examination of conscience, and the Church has complied. Thousands participate in the Church's Day of Judaism. But perhaps the most important achievement is that Poles did not evade the difficult questions, such as the Kielce pogrom and the crime at Jedwabne.

Adam Michnik identifies two Catholic churches in Poland. One is the Church of John Paul II, a church that called for respect for human dignity, a church that provided solace during the terrible times of oppression, led by a man who feared no one and spoke of freedom for all. The other emerged after Communism faltered. It was bent on retrieving property and reselling it for profit. It waded into democratic elections with its own propaganda and directed parishioners' votes. It was a great enthusiast for lustration—at least until an archbishop was revealed to have been a collaborator. It is a church that tolerates Radio Maryja's brand of xenophobia and hatred. It is contemptuous of debate. It holds to the old Catholic belief that there is only one truth and "they own it."

Michnik says, "Radio Maryja and I agree on everything, except agrarian matters: it wants me to be underground."

Radio Maryja provides a platform for the disaffected, those who have lost their jobs in the fast-changing environment of global markets, those terrified of the changes, of becoming part of an uncaring Europe ruled by foreigners, of poverty and uncertainty, of Western pornography and flagrant prostitution, of the erosion of Christian values. Intellectuals, the nationalist demagogues claim, are predominantly Jewish and, as Wałęsa told an interviewer in 1995, "Jews play too large a part in Polish affairs."

THE CATASTROPHE

... the dead don't forgive so easily. The dead have long memories. Unlike the living.—ELIE WIESEL, *The Time of the Uprooted*

Inside Stanisław Kostka Church are memorials to those killed at Treblinka, Majdanek, Sobibór, Bełżec, Chełmno, Auschwitz—place names that resonate with memories of the Holocaust. Here, however, it is not the Jewish tragedy that is being commemorated but the Polish tragedy that happened over the same years with almost as much brutality as the one that annihilated six million Jews. No other country saw as sustained barbarity as Poland, and none lost as large a percentage of its population during World War II: six million Poles were killed (including three million Polish Jews)—20 per cent of the population, compared to 2.2 per cent in Holland, for example. After the devastation of the war, there was no interest here in the fact that 90 per cent of the Jews who had lived here had been murdered.

It was in Poland that the worst atrocities of World War II were perpetrated, with full knowledge of a traumatized population, both witnesses to and victims of bouts of brutal mockery, massacres in town squares, sadism, humiliation, unrestrained horror inflicted upon the non-Christian minority that had lived close to the Catholic majority for several hundred peaceful years. Poland had the largest Jewish population in Europe, and it was here, renamed by Germans the *Generalgouvernment,* that the Final Solution was played out. This is where the locked boxcars from the rest of Europe arrived and disgorged their human cargo, some already dead or dying, and this where most of those who arrived alive were murdered in gas chambers and burnt in furnaces built for the express purpose of turning human beings into ash.

There are remnants of concentration camps throughout Poland, but only Auschwitz has remained relatively intact. The postwar Communists preserved the site but ignored the truth of what had happened here. The museum plaques listed the victims by nationality only. "Monument to the Martyrdom and Struggle of the Polish Nation and Other Nations," went the tagline at Auschwitz. The fact that more than 90 per cent of them were Jews was unimportant.

Until the early 1980s, scant public attention was paid to the Holocaust, no effort made by the educational authorities to single out the Jewish tragedy as separate from the Polish tragedy of the war years. The subject did not suit the curriculum's focus on the great Soviet army sweeping over the Nazis, nor Moscow's philosophy of class warfare. The Holocaust had nothing to do with class. Besides, East Germany had become a faithful ally, a bulwark against capitalism. The truths about the Holocaust were further complicated by the Communist Party's anti-Semitic campaign of the late '60s, during which time Jews were forced out of high positions in the army and government, many were interrogated, some expelled, others jailed. Ultimately, about fifteen thousand Jews were encouraged to emigrate. All those who did so lost their citizenship.

It was not until the 2001 publication of Jan T. Gross's *Neighbors* that the subject of Polish complicity in the murder of some Polish Jews became a matter for widespread public discourse. Jan Tomasz Gross, a Polish-born historian at Princeton University, told the story of how one day in July 1941, part of the population in the small town of Jedwabne, in eastern Poland, killed another part of the population. Some 1,600 men, women and children were beaten, stabbed, drowned in the river, and the remnants were herded into a barn and burned alive. As Gross pointed out, there was a cursory trial in 1949. Twelve people were sentenced; most were soon released. There was never a full inquiry into the role of the mayor who led the massacre, the local priest who refused to help the victims or those who walked off with the Jews' belongings or occupied their homes.

To this day, Gross claimed, descendents of the perpetrators lived in houses they had taken by force, and the one war memorial in the village celebrated Poles who suffered and were killed by the Nazis; it made no mention of what befell the 1,600 Jews who had shared this space with their neighbours. This theme of theft, murder and denial carries over into Gross's next book, *Fear: Anti-Semitism in Poland after Auschwitz*—a full, detailed account of the Kielce pogrom of 1946, when some returning concentration camp survivors were killed by their fellow citizens. It is Gross's belief that those who had stolen their neighbours' goods, occupied their homes and enjoyed these rewards were unwilling to admit to any wrongdoing. In fact, he argues that one of the chief reasons for incidents of Polish complicity in the Holocaust, as well as the subsequent pogroms that greeted the survivors, was avarice.

Fierce and acrimonious debates followed the publications of *Neighbors*. Both of the large daily newspapers waded into the issues. *Gazeta Wyborcza* extolled Gross's views and urged readers to begin dealing with their country's own "dark past,"[32] proclaiming the need to explore collective memory, no matter how shameful, and the importance of integrating the regrettable with the heroic—the two should not be mutually exclusive. The more conservative voice of *Rzeczpospolita* accused Gross of unfairness, citing the situation in Poland during the years he writes about in *Neighbors*. The Soviets had occupied eastern Poland as part of the Hitler-Stalin Pact. The Jews had supported the Communists, who welcomed the Soviet troops that brutalized the population. When the Germans drove the Soviets out in 1941, villages and towns in the area, including Jedwabne, exacted revenge on the Jews under orders from Nazi soldiers.

In an interview, Gross said that there could be no return of Polish history until Jewish history is absorbed into national memory and people can confront their own prejudice.

The Institute of National Remembrance commissioned its own studies of Kielce and Jedwabne. It held a press conference on December 19, 2001, where several experts announced that there was no reason to believe that what had happened at Jedwabne was anything other than a made-in-Poland pogrom. A few historians, however, were quick to point out that there were German bullets in the Jedwabne barn and that the partial exhumation in May 2001 of bodies proved there had been German participation in the massacre. In an unfortunate radio interview, Lech Wałęsa weighed in with his referral to Gross as "a mediocre writer... a Jew who tries to make money."

Some apologists claimed that all the Jews killed had been Communists, or were believed to have been Communists, which somehow justified their murders. There was even a conspiracy theory that Gross's book was the latest example of the Jew-promoted U.S. campaign to besmirch Poland's good name.

The IPN followed Gross's *Fear* with the Polish-language publication of Marek Jan Chodakiewicz's book *After the Holocaust: Polish-Jewish Conflict in the Wake of World War II*. Chodakiewicz suggests that the Jews were, at least to some degree, responsible for their own misfortune because of their record of serving the Bolshevik cause before and immediately after the war. The general belief that a disproportionate number of Jews served in the state's security service has been largely refuted by the IPN's own statistics. That there was no opportunity to discuss "Jewish participation in the Communist movement"[33] allowed people to continue believing what they wished. *Gazeta Wyborcza* itself was attacked for publicizing Gross's findings as was Agnieszka Arnold's documentary about the Jedwabne massacre, *Where Is My Older Brother, Cain?*

That Chodakiewicz has been serving on the United States Holocaust Memorial Council adds to the bizarre nature of his attack on Gross's scholarship and his success with blaming the victims. Like many convinced nationalists, he saw Gross's book as an attack on Poland's good name, a tactic that he said "eerily recalls Stalinist propaganda."

When I meet Paweł Lisicki, editor of the conservative *Rzeczpos-polita,* he rubs his fingers together as if to try to wash them of the whole Jedwabne issue. The book, he says, did not shed a helpful light on the complex relationship between Jews and gentiles in Poland. This unresolved past remains an open wound in the soul of the country, but Poles are not a rapacious and barbarous lot, as characterized by Gross. And if they were, there would be no point in his publishing such a book. In an article Lisicki wrote on November 1, 2008, he says that Gross's picture of Poles as a "bloodthirsty, savage, greedy, thick-headed, sly rabble" is close to the Nazis' categorization of them as "subhumans." Gross, says Lisicki, is not interested in history; he is motivated by revenge.

Gross disagrees. "In order to reclaim its past, Poland will have to tell its past anew," he writes. "How can the wiping out of one third of its urban population be anything other than a central issue of Poland's history?"

Catholic bishops of Poland waded into the *Neighbors* controversy with a pastoral letter. They addressed "the Jewish nation" as if the Jews who had suffered and died had not also been Poles. Their listing of the Polish trees along the Avenue of the Righteous in Jerusalem does not deal with the centuries-long Church-inspired anti-Semitism, the persistent use of the phrase "Christ-killers" that encouraged uneducated villagers of places like Jedwabne to kill. The Church has made no effort to apologize for its role in propagating stories of blood-filled matzos and an international Jewish conspiracy.

Despite worldwide protests, Poland's Catholic primate, Cardinal Józef Glemp, insisted on supporting the building of a Carmelite convent at Auschwitz, at the grave of a million Jews. In a clumsy counterattack on his critics, Cardinal Glemp claimed that some Jews had tried to kill the Carmelite nuns.[34] He went on to accuse Jews of collaboration with the Soviets against Poland.

The convent has now been moved a respectable half mile to a new location, but an eight-metre-high giant cross still stands over the gravel pit where Pope John Paul II made his Auschwitz speech in 1979.

When Polish President Kwaśniewski, in a ceremony of national apology at Jedwabne, asked the Jews of Poland for forgiveness of

behalf of the ordinary Poles who had murdered their Jewish neighbours or stood by while others did the killings, the parish priest of
Jedwabne stayed away, claiming that the Jews were entitled to their
stories and "we are entitled to ours." Neither Cardinal Glemp nor any
of the Polish bishops attended.[35]

In Jedwabne today, there are still two stone monuments commemorating the war. One of them states that 1,600 Jews were killed
here by the Nazis. The other, erected in 1990, reads: "To the memory
of about 180 people including two priests who were murdered in the
territory of Jedwabne district in the years 1939–1946 by the NKVD,[36]
the Nazis and the secret police." Neither makes an effort to come to
terms with what happened here on that July day in 1941.

BETWEEN OBLIVION AND REMEMBRANCE

Andrzej Żbikowski, deputy director of the Jewish History Institute,
participated in *Rzeczpospolita*'s March 2001 round-table discussion
about Jedwabne. He said that Jedwabne "must be the tip of a pyramid. At the base of the pyramid, Polish-Jewish relations spread out
on other levels." It is, he said, indifference to Jewish suffering that
informs the Polish response to the Holocaust. "The heroism of Żegota
is just a drop in the bucket." Żegota was a Polish organization whose
sole purpose was to save Jews during the German occupation. No
such Christian group existed in any other German-occupied country.

Żbikowski, a jovial middle-aged man, works on the ground floor
of the Institute. On the second floor is a display of heartbreaking
photographs of the Warsaw Ghetto, where over 100,000 people perished of hunger and disease. The ghetto was established in October
1940, with 440,000 Jews, about 30 per cent of Warsaw's population, trapped inside an area of 4.5 per cent of the city, seven to eight
people to a room. It was walled in to isolate it from the rest of the
city. Thousands more Jews were brought in from the countryside. In
a small auditorium at the Institute you can watch a pitiful documentary film of starvation and cruelty, of piles of bodies, of little children begging along the corpse-infested sidewalks.

Mass deportations from the ghetto to the Treblinka death camp
began on July 22, 1942, and continued until September 1942. Three

hundred thousand people were gassed upon arrival. About 790,000 were murdered later in Treblinka. Then there was that brief respite of resistance: the Warsaw Ghetto Uprising. A small contingent of fewer than 1,000 poorly armed men and women held out against the German army from April 19 until May 16, 1943.

In 1946, on the third anniversary of the Uprising, a red sandstone disc was placed on the ground near what had once been the ghetto's gate. The words on the disc are still legible today, though the gate and almost all remnants of the ghetto have been razed: "To the memory of those who died in unparalleled and heroic struggle for the dignity and freedom of the Jewish nation, for free Poland, and for the liberation of mankind—*the Jews of Poland*."

Not far from here is the stark Monument to the Ghetto Heroes, erected some forty years later. A group of dark, defiant figures converge in the narrow space in the centre of the stone structure. December 7, 2010, will be the fortieth anniversary of the moment when German chancellor Willy Brandt fell to his knees in front of this memorial in an act of grief, obeisance and, possibly, political derring-do. While his spontaneous action had a significant moment in German-Jewish relations, Brandt's visit was an even more significant moment in his efforts to defrost relations between the two Germanies and reach across the Iron Curtain to Moscow.

Across from the Warsaw Ghetto Uprising Memorial, where the post office and later the designated Judenrat building had been, work has begun on the new multimedia Museum of the History of Polish Jews from the earliest times to today—a history in which the Holocaust is a terrible part, but only one part of the one-thousand-year-long Jewish presence in Poland. The museum's budget of over $70 million is supported by the city of Warsaw, the Polish government and a list of donors from all over the world.

"It's a long history, rich in detail and adventure," Piotr Ogrodziński, former Polish ambassador to Canada, told me. "It is time to give the past its due. Our history was stolen from us—we want it back. All of it, not only the wretched bits." He was working to raise funds for the new museum. His father had been a member of Żegota. It is well to remember, he said, that there are more trees planted in honour of Poles along Jerusalem's the Avenue of the Righteous than for any other nation.

The new museum, which will open in 2012, will focus on the culture of Europe's largest Jewish civilization, which flourished here and extended into Lithuania, Belarus, Latvia, Russia, Estonia and Ukraine. For several centuries, most of the world's Jews lived here. Barbara Kirshenblatt-Gimblett, the leader of the exhibition team, tells me the museum will honour those who died by remembering those who lived. "It is," she says, "important to know them not only in the time of their deaths. They are an integral part of our story."

"What we lost is the Jewish part of our lives."

IF THE Museum of the History of Polish Jews is a most profound act of commemoration, then the most bizarre must be Warsaw's annual Singer Festival,[37] named after Isaac Bashevis Singer, who might have been a famous Polish writer except that he wrote in Yiddish. He was born not far from where the festival is celebrated, and temporary mementos of his life and times appear along a path in the park that connects the Jewish Theatre with the area dressed up for the occasion.

I was there for the sixth festival, in September 2009. In the middle of what used to be the ghetto, Próżna Street was trying to look like a thoroughfare in an old town, with organ grinders and sidewalk hawkers selling beads, costume jewellery, used books and discs, framed black and white photos of Jewish men and women (extra for the frames) and small carved figurines in traditional Jewish garb, including a little black-clad fellow clutching a money bag. I was told that touching him would bring me luck.

In front of the Jewish Theatre—yes, it does mount Yiddish plays—on the small concrete square, tables and benches had been set up for those who liked to eat outside in the vague sunshine. An enterprising barbeque stall sold thick Polish bread with pork fat and pork sausages.

There were Jewish sweets and sandwiches on unleavened bread, a bunch of actors dressed in some bits of Hasidic garb, balloons and wildly joyful klezmer bands on two competing stages, where amplified songs bellowed about the sadness of somebody's mother or lover or both, and an energetic Polish performer who mingled with the crowd urging it to sing and dance along. There must have been at least three hundred people packed along the street, most of them dancing, or at least waving their arms in the air, with not nearly enough space to do justice to the performer's expectations of some kind of Hasidic dance.

On the second day, Mandy Cahan, from Israel, appeared, to the general delight of the expectant audience. He wore shiny black pants and vest with a three-quarter-length coat and matching fez and intoned lively selections from his new album. At the end of the street, above the stage where Cahan sang, a huge canvas showed what the rest of this street may have looked like before the ghetto was destroyed. At dusk a motley band with flashing lights started to compete with the lone Israeli singer and his two-man backup. As I pushed my way through the crowd, now grown to a couple of thousand happy people of all ages, clapping and hooting, the band was playing klezmer hip hop.

"Contrary to what you may think," Stanisław Krajewski tells me as we make our way through this lively scene, "there are no Jews here." All those dressed as old-fashioned village, or shtetl, Jews, selling fake Jewish knick-knacks, singing and waving, were not Jews. Nor were they tourists. Perhaps the locals were trying to recapture the Jewish part of their souls?

Krajewski teaches logic and mathematics at the Institute of Philosophy, but he has not searched for logic in Poles' desire to rediscover their missing Jewish selves. "The challenge we face is very simple," he wrote in *The Bond of Memory*.[38] "We have a choice between oblivion or remembrance. Can anyone have any doubts about which is preferable?"

He is a tall man with a short beard, wearing a cap and a raincoat over a checked work shirt. He had been resisting the idea of drinking coffee in one of the fake sidewalk cafés but relented because there was no other option. I had met him at the Nożyk Synagogue on Twarda Street, part of the festival's area but not a place with cafés and restaurants. A consultant to the Jewish History Museum who takes his Jewishness seriously, Krajewski seemed unamused by the festival atmosphere.

"Sometime during the '80s, it had become 'cool' to be Jewish," he told me. "Back then, I was working for the underground press, often in churches, and I felt that they needed, really needed, Jewish partners. I mean that Jews had been part of Polish life for so many centuries." His parents were ideological Communists; there was no mention of religion at home. In 1979, he joined a Jewish self-instruction group. By the early '80s, new courses in Jewish history had sprung up in several Polish universities, teaching the Jewish contribution to the culture of the country.

As if by some strange magic, young people who had neither known nor cared about Jewishness now wished to discover the Jewish side of their selves. Now many with Jewish or mixed ancestry wish to identify themselves as Jews. They are learning in revived Jewish schools and joining synagogues.

His story is similar that of Konstanty Gebert—another of the children of Jewish Communists who took part in the democratic opposition to totalitarian rule. Solidarity, with their help, triumphed over the system their parents helped build. During the 1970s, both Gebert and Krajewski joined an independent discussion group of students, many of whom had shared the same "guilty secret, best kept private," of being Jews—"shipwrecked," as Gebert wrote in *Living in the Land of Ashes.* They all came from assimilated backgrounds, and they had all started to ask questions about history and identity. Gebert and Krajewski have both become religious. "Seemed silly not to, when so many of my *mishpoche* [family] were," says Gebert. We met in his book-filled apartment in Warsaw. He has become Orthodox and sent his children to Jewish school. "And so the cycle closes." Or a new age begins.

THE SPECTACULARLY restored Nożyk Synagogue, behind the Jewish Theatre, is the only synagogue in Poland to have survived the war relatively unscathed. I visited late on a Saturday. The chief rabbi of Poland, Michael Schudrich, was fresh from celebrating the Sabbath service. Contrary to international opinion, he thinks, there are more than twenty thousand Jews in Poland, though many of them are still struggling with accepting who they are. He talks of "the glorious past" of the Jews here, their legacy and the need to help the young who seek him out for advice.

Ewa Junczyk-Ziomecka, a former director of the Jewish History Museum, now Polish consul in New York, tells me that being Jewish is still in vogue in Poland. It's as if, long after it's amputated, a man feels pain in his phantom arm. How do you explain, then, that the word "Jew" is still derogatory in Poland? That "Jewish courage" still means cowardice and "Jewish honesty" is dishonesty, that to label someone a Jew is to express dislike, as when football fans yell *"Jude, Jude"* at the opposing team? Or, as someone told me, in Poland "a Jew is not the enemy; the enemy is a Jew."

Perhaps old habits die hard.

THE RESTITUTION DEBATE

Jan Cienski is still waiting for something to fall from the tree of Poland's new Europeanization. He is proud of his ancestors, and rather amused by their sacking of Moscow, as my cab driver was. "Bunch of marauding freebooters," he tells me. We are sitting in a café near the Polonia Palace Hotel surrounded by a lunchtime crowd of nibblers and talkers. They are young and noisy, their voices loud over the ringing of cellphones and the shouted orders for toasted sandwiches.

Cienski is tall and relaxed, in a rangy, long-limbed, casual way— floppy hair, wrists reaching out of his shirt sleeves. He, too, looks the part of Polish nobility (ideally, I think, he should have a white horse), which is what he says he is. While stationed in Warsaw by the *Financial Times,* he has tried to lay claim to the family's lands, some of which happen to be in the middle of the city. He is sure there will be an accommodation for people who can prove they are the direct descendents of former owners. Even if it's only 20 per cent of the value,[39] it is still a significant amount for a young man like Cienski, who would never have dreamed of such a windfall before 1989.

"Not a chance for returning all the lost property," Piotr Pasz-kowski says. He is Foreign Minister Radek Sikorski's spokesman, friendly parliamentary assistant and all-around policy man. "It would bankrupt the state," he adds. "Besides, it is impossible to unravel all the ownerships of the past." Owners were supplanted by new owners with each passing era. The Nazis looted. The German army destroyed most of Warsaw. The Soviet army treated whatever they liberated as war booty. The Communist state nationalized and rebuilt, and after 1989 the former apparatchiks grabbed what they could out of the privatizations at ludicrous prices. A home could have had as many as ten or fifteen claimants since 1938.

The *nomenklatura* took over whole industries and banks. Before new laws could be drafted, there was wholesale embezzlement and the new owners fled to other countries.The Habsburg family sued the government to reclaim its famous brewery and real estate in Żywiec and settled in 2005 for a fraction of the property's value. The Catholic Church claimed its old properties as early as the round-table discussions, and sold many of them at considerable profit.

And then there is the question of Jewish property. After the German occupation, gentiles occupied the newly vacated Jewish homes. Many of these new owners lost their homes with the Communist takeover. Jewish businesses were claimed by gentiles and later confiscated by the state. How do you compensate? With most of Jews murdered by the Nazis, how do their descendants lay claims to lands and homes?

"I believe, in a quasi-Millsian, utilitarian way, that the sum total of justice (injustice) should be greater (lesser) after restitution than before," Paszkowski wrote to me. "Because of the complexities of all post-war (and also pre-war) history, I have grave doubts if that can be achieved . . . People not only lost, they also gained, not only in real estate but other assets as well, stayed sharing the deprivations or emigrated, benefited from the new system or were given a hard deal . . . living in cellars, clearing the rubble . . . My feeling is that it would be best to say: yes, injustice was done, but it is in the nature of things that not all injustices can be redressed, compensated."

Chief Rabbi Michael Schudrich views the failure to effectively deal with former Jewish property as an obstacle to Polish-Jewish reconciliation, not to mention a "major moral sin."

However much Piotr Paszkowski would like to see this reconciliation, there will be questions of how to value the rebuilding from the rubble that was left at the end of the war. How to deduct the value of the rebuilding from the cost of the land?

Sikorski suggests going to the courts for determining each case on its own merits. It would be interesting to see how the U.S. government would deal with its embassy in Warsaw. Prince Czetwertyński owned the building from 1900 until it was confiscated. The wartime owner lost it in the 1940s. It was leased by the pre-democracy socialist government to the United States for an embassy, then, on the signing of an eighty-year lease, levelled to make way for the massive new building (more like a large bunker than like the original chateau). There have been renovations, additions, beautifications. Are the Americans willing to give it back to the original owners' descendents?

Konstanty Gebert predicts an avalanche of lawsuits to clog up every court in the country if the government leaves the matter unresolved. But he is more interested in the case of the dispossessed Jews than in that of the deported Germans.

About 3.3 million German civilians (a large part of the over 12 million from Eastern Europe) fled or were expelled from their homes after the war, when the Allies assigned the eastern part of Germany to Poland. Given the extent of German atrocities, it was little wonder that the Polish government, after assuming its position under Soviet control, showed no compunction in deciding to expel Germans from its reclaimed western territories. Besides, it needed a place to settle Poles who had lived in the eastern part of the country, annexed in 1945 by the Soviets.[40] Effectively, the Allies moved Poland's borders westward by 150 miles.

The West German government passed a number of laws recognizing the rights of the expellees as German citizens. The powerful Federation of Expellees—close to 20 per cent of the Federal Republic's population had been expelled from the East—never agreed, however, to give up property claims even after differences between the Polish and German governments were resolved in 1990, when Germany formally accepted the frontiers of the Oder and Neisse rivers laid down by the winners of World War II. The treaty, signed in Moscow on September 12, 1990, opened the door to German reunification in October 1990. It is yet to be seen whether all members of the Federation—including Sudeten, Slovak, Swabian and Saxon organizations—will renounce their aspirations to reclaim their ancestral homes.

In 2008, while laying the foundations of a new hotel in the old Teutonic fortress town of Malbork, near Gdańsk, workmen discovered the bones of more than two thousand people believed to have been German civilians from this area who had not managed to escape in 1945. Setting aside mutual recriminations, the Germans were buried in a mass grave at the foot of the reconstructed castle in August 2009, but grievances still await some resolution. What kind of commemoration is due the dispossessed ethnic Germans and the grandchildren of the murdered Jews?

THE NEW POLAND

Radek (Radosław) Sikorski is one of the most intelligent and charismatic young men in any parliament in Europe, and he is fully aware of it. Tall, muscular, energetic, casually well dressed, a former student activist in the Solidarity movement, an Oxford graduate, author of four books, war correspondent, adviser to Rupert Murdoch and erstwhile fellow of the American Enterprise Institute in Washington, he inhabits the world with considerable self-assurance. Born in 1963, he was just five years old when the students first protested in Warsaw. Though he was involved in protests in the late '70s, he has no personal experience of jail cells or beatings by militia or secret police. He studied philosophy, economics and political science at Oxford and joined the influential, conservative, all-male Bullingdon Club, then went on to a youthful stint in freelance journalism.

Like many Polish intellectuals, he returned from self-imposed exile after the collapse of Communism in 1989, but unlike most of them, he almost immediately entered political life. As deputy defence minister and later as minister of national defence in the Law and Justice party's coalition government, he dazzled journalists with his quick wit. He quit his post over a tiff with one of the Kaczyński twins.

Between these two high-profile appointments, he returned to Washington as a resident fellow of the American Enterprise Institute, a conservative think tank and enthusiastic supporter of the second Bush administration. Paul Wolfowitz, former U.S. secretary of defence, Lynne Cheney, wife of former U.S. vice president Dick Cheney, and Newt Gingrich, prominent Republican Speaker of the House of Representatives, have all been fellows of American Enterprise. Yet the thought of continuing to enjoy the financial rewards of working in Washington, Sikorski says, never occurred to him. He had always planned to come "home." Home, as it happens, is a traditional Polish manor house that he and his wife, American Pulitzer Prize–winning author-journalist Anne Applebaum,[41] have restored to something resembling its former pre-war glory. In his book *The Polish House*, he talks about his personal commitment to living in an old house of the kind that he believed was central to Polishness.

He ran as a Civic Platform candidate and, when the centre-right Civic Platform won, was named foreign minister. He seems to have a friendly relationship with Prime Minister Donald Tusk and tried not to see too much of President Lech Kaczyński. The presidency is a rather more powerful function in the Polish constitution than in some other European parliamentary systems, so this pleasant state of cool civility was unlikely to last. As one of his duties, the president gets to approve all ambassadorial appointments. As another, he is allowed to make statements on behalf of the country. With the first of these responsibilities, Lech Kaczyński practised glacial progress; with the second, he was astonishingly eager to express himself, frequently in direct opposition to the governing party's views.

Both times I met Sikorski, it was in one of the designated meeting rooms in the Foreign Ministry—a stark, pillared, grey building with a massive marble entrance hall with a winding staircase and formal rooms with uncomfortable gilt-backed chairs. Photographs of grim-faced former foreign ministers line the walls on the first floor leading to the meeting room.

Sikorski is the new generation of Polish politician. He manages to be at once a nationalist and a pan-European for whom "civil society" can be achieved only by espousing democratic principles. Assuming responsibility in an atmosphere Adam Michnik describes as replete with "envy, intrigue, greed, suspicion, and the urge for revenge" must have seemed an easy choice. It is, after all, democracy.

While Sikorski is interested in history, he does not necessarily wish to institutionalize it. The Institute of National Remembrance, he believes, should let the air in, open all of its files to the public and thus put an end to the debates about the files and their uses and abuses. It does not matter that some of the files will cause embarrassment. Governments should treat their citizens as grown-ups: the citizens can discount suspect testimonies and moderate indiscretions. Nevertheless, at the beginning of 2010, his government slashed the pensions of the secret police.

Sikorski is more engaged by current affairs than with the past, by the difficulties of being a businesslike customer of Russia and a friendly ally of the United States and by fairly representing Poland's interests in Europe. The past two years have provided him with ample opportunity to prove his mettle.

In May 2008, when Russia installed Dmitry Medvedev as its new president in a gold-and-incense ceremony complete with Orthodox patriarch, redolent of Russia's lost empires, the minister managed to express cheerful optimism. He viewed the symbolic handover of power from Putin to Medvedev as "a hopeful development . . . because he is the first Russian leader who doesn't come from the Communist party or the security services." But he cautioned that so long as Russia remains nostalgic about its past, it continues to be dangerous.

The facts are that, under Putin's leadership, Russia has updated its nuclear arsenal—at last count, at least sixteen thousand warheads[42]—and increased its military spending on fighter jets, helicopters and submarines. Its soldiers, who only a decade ago were bartering handguns and fur hats for food, are now a million strong and well equipped. All Medvedev has done to burnish his own image is to announce a desire to "modernize" Russia. He waxed eloquent about Russia's creativity, praised innovation and promised an overhaul of the antiquated educational system. Medvedev's term expires in 2012, but starting that year, the Russian presidential term will extend from four to six years and Putin would legally be allowed to serve two more terms.

Former KGB officer Putin has reawakened in Russians the golem of world dominance. He has referred to the end of the Soviet Union as the greatest geopolitical catastrophe of the twentieth century, has revived the Soviet national anthem and seems bent on restoring Russian pride. Putin has summoned the old devils of "patriotism," and he has found a receptive audience.

Sikorski, always the diplomat, told the *Financial Times*' Jan Cienski, "we have to deal with the Russia we have, not with the one we wish for." Indeed, since Civic Platform's majority election in September 2007, Russia has lifted its ban on Polish meat imports and, once more, assumed a role as one of Poland's preferred customers for farm products. "We do 17 billion euros in trade with Russia," Sikorski told the BBC on April 29, 2009. As for the issue of oil and gas, Sikorski says, smiling, that these are not geopolitical tools but commodities like any other.

He shares with other Central European leaders the unenviable task of ensuring a continuous supply of both. As Russia has not been exempt from the worldwide economic crisis, 2009 was a good year to negotiate a new deal with Gazprom. In January 2010, Poland won a reduced price for gas from Russia in exchange for more favourable terms on transit fees to Germany.

When president Lech Kaczyński took off for Tbilisi to reassure the Georgians of Polish support against Russia, Sikorski was left to hope that the Russian ambassador had a sense of humour about the president's antics. Tusk's government is ready to lay to rest the old ghosts. It will not risk angering Russia unless the risk is worthwhile. "Last week I asked the Russian chief of staff not to threaten us with nuclear annihilation more often than once a quarter," Sikorski said with an open grin, though for Poles the Russians have rarely been a joking matter.

As for whether Georgia represents a worthwhile risk: "Georgia allowed itself to be provoked," according to Sikorski, "but the Russian response was disproportionate." When the European Union finally opined on the Georgian crisis, it concluded much the same but in more elaborate language.

Seeing Russian armed forces bombing civilian targets would be terrifying for anyone who has grown up with a fear of Russia, and Sikorski is only too aware of Poland's unequal strength in a potential military engagement with its neighbour. Perhaps this is why he signed the deal with Condoleezza Rice for the installation of a U.S. missile defence system in Poland. True to form, Russia's foreign minister announced that Poland was "playing a dangerous game." Sikorski was quick to respond that nothing would please Poland more than a strategic alliance with Russia.

Putin's Letter to the Poles pointed out that "it is impossible to set up an efficient system of collective security without involvement of all countries of the continent, including Russia"—no doubt a reference to the missile defence system. The U.S. missile shield, Sikorski thought, could provide additional security to back up NATO's commitment of one for all and all for one.

On September 17, 2009, the Obama presidency postponed the U.S. government's missile defence agreements with both Poland and the Czech Republic. It was an interesting choice of timing: the seventieth anniversary of the Soviet invasion of Poland, coinciding with Hitler's devastating attack on the country, the day of commemoration at Westerplatte. Perhaps inadvertently, the message the U.S. sent to the Poles was that this part of the world is no longer on its agenda. That message was reinforced by the absence of both President Obama and Hillary Clinton from the Westerplatte ceremonies.

It is no doubt due to Sikorski's careful handling of the United States that a battery of American Patriot missiles arrived in Poland in March 2010.

Poland, said Sikorski, has been the most pro-U.S. country in Europe. Despite Russian opposition, Polish troops had been part of the U.S.-sponsored war in Iraq. That's not because of the eight million Poles in the U.S. or Ronald Reagan's unstinting support for Solidarity, but because of what U.S. democracy has represented to the Soviet-repressed Poles. That said, U.S. influence and esteem have diminished. Poland may be the only European country that preferred President Bush to President Obama.

Although Sikorski wants to move beyond history, he has found it useful to frequently remind Poland's Western allies of how they had ignored the country's plight during World War II. The British declared war on Germany when it invaded Poland, but their army did not arrive to help defend the country. This time, should they be needed, Sikorski wants to see "boots on the ground."

He is also clear about Poland's commitment to NATO. Being part of the NATO force in Afghanistan is a sign of that commitment. But sending armed men, he is quick to point out, is not enough to secure the region's future. There must be long-term investments, assistance for the Afghan people to create their own democratic process. Sikorski knows the terrain better than most. He travelled through Soviet-occupied Afghanistan with a group of mujahedeen in 1987. According to his book *Dust of the Saints*, he helped transport arms to the "warriors of Islam." He witnessed Soviet attacks on villages and shared memories with Afghans of the Soviet occupation of his own homeland.

IN 2008, Adam Daniel Rotfeld, former minister of foreign affairs, now member of the UN's Advisory Board on Disarmament Matters, was appointed special envoy for dealing with Russia. He seems in too much of a hurry to sit while we meet. He has a plane to catch, a lecture to give and a paper to deliver. A small, immaculately attired man, wearing the grey pin-striped suit of an Old World diplomat, he is most comfortable when he is talking about major issues. Adam Rotfeld's family, including both his parents, were murdered in the Holocaust. But this seems to be one of the subjects the distinguished scholar has no time to dwell on.

He places Poland at the heart of "a historical and eternal dilemma of being caught between Germany and Russia. All its efforts for balance between the two rivals for territory have been doomed to failure."[43]

He complains about how little credit Poland receives both for its wartime contribution and for its battle to end Communism. In a June 2009 article in the German magazine *Der Spiegel,* he complained that European history textbooks contain little about Polish history: "Poles fought on all fronts against the Nazis, from the first to the last day of the war... [T]his was the largest army apart from those of the Soviet Union, the United States and Britain. Poles consider the widespread ignorance of Polish history as contempt for, or even falsification of, their past."

There are few ghosts of past horrors that make Poles more uneasy than a potential Russian-German pact. The 2005 deal to build the Nord Stream pipeline to transport Russian gas under the Baltic Sea directly to Germany is precisely such an agreement. It is a joint project, but although there are smaller partners in Scandinavia and Holland, the dominant figures are Russian and German: Russian energy giant Gazprom and the German corporations BASF/Wintershall Holding AG and E.ON Ruhrgas AG. Sweden and Finland, having expressed their environmental concerns, gave their seal of approval at the end of 2009. The chairman of the new consortium is none other than Germany's former chancellor Gerhard Schröder.

Unlike Sikorski, Rotfeld does not see Putin as another czar, an empire builder, but as a man faced with the impenetrable "problem of how to effect change while keeping stability in a volatile land." He hailed Putin's invitation to Tusk for a joint commemoration of the Katyń massacres as a vital step "in the normalization of Polish-Russian relations."[44]

Both Sikorski and Rotfeld have mentioned Poland's massive coal supplies raising the possibility of delaying the EU's environmental ruling. Poland has the biggest coal reserves in Europe. Its own electricity needs are fully met. What's missing still are new, clean technologies to appease the EU's climate-change environmentalists. Meanwhile, state-owned PGNiG (Polish Oil and Gas Company) and Gazprom have agreed to increase by about 30 per cent the amount of fuel Poland will buy from Russia.

In 2011, Poland will hold the EU's prestigious rotating presidency. Given the size of its population, its political will and its government's engagement in European affairs, it will be able to exert much more influence in the international sphere. During my last visit to Sikorski's ministry, I noticed Prime Minister Donald Tusk, dodging persistent reporters, dashing up the palatial staircase. It was the day the government announced that Poland's budget deficit would grow to a whopping 27 billion zlotys ($9.5 billion), which would explain Sikorski's bland statement about his country's cautious approach to adopting the euro. Nevertheless, Poland was the only country in the EU to boast of economic growth in 2009.[45] It is one of Europe's biggest economies and, unlike other troubled Central European countries, it can still borrow at reasonable rates. Perhaps by 2011, it will bring the deficit under control and pass into the eurozone without painful repercussions. As the front page of *Warsaw Business Journal* trumpeted, "Poland Rising," "A force to be reckoned with."

In early 2010, Donald Tusk announced that he will not run in the next presidential elections. The betting here was that Radek Sikorski would become Poland's next president, but it was not to be. Fifty-eight-year-old Bronisław Komorowski, Speaker of the Sejm, was voted by the Civic Platform Party as its candidate for the presidency. Komorowski, a member of the anti-Communist resistance during the 1980s, stressed the length of his experience compared to the younger Sikorski. When President Lech Kaczyński died in 2010, Komorowski assumed the role of president.

THE LAST OF

THE GREAT RESISTANCE

INTELLIGENTSIA

BRONISŁAW GEREMEK died in a car accident on Sunday, July 13, 2008. The rest of the world went on with its day of rest, but Poland should have experienced an earthquake of the soul. Geremek was one of the last legendary intellectuals of the twentieth century, opposing the Communist totalitarianism, speaking for the morality of resistance. A quiet, soft-spoken man with an iron will, one of Sachs's "three wise men," he had been Poland's representative to the UN.

In 1980, it was Geremek who drove to Gdańsk to present a statement signed by sixty-four intellectuals in support of the Lenin shipyard workers. The alliance between Geremek and Wałęsa, between the intellectuals and the workers, remained a constant in the negotiations for the beginning of democracy. In its obituary, the Telegraph quoted Geremek's favourite metaphor about the "winds of history" finally blowing in Poland's direction. Geremek had taken part in the discussions with the European Union for Poland's admission and signed the agreement for Poland to take its place in NATO. Yet he was not so naive as to imagine that Western Europe was excited about the spread of democracy. After 1989, as he pointed out, it became obvious that "Western governments to a great extent pursue their own national interests."[1]

He fiercely opposed the Kaczyński twins' attempt to extend lustration to all senior positions in Polish life. He refused to sign a declaration that he had never been in any way involved with the Communist security apparatus. As always, he stood on principle. He accused the twins of trying to create a "kind of ministry of truth—a police of memory" and added that "it makes a citizen defenseless when facing a smear campaign." In the European Parliament he accused the IPN of violating moral principles with its "lustration law."[2]

Geremek had never made a secret of his youthful commitment to Communism in the days after the Second World War. He said it was "sensitivity toward those whom history does not love,"[3] toward the poor and powerless, that had attracted him to Communism. Like Czesław Miłosz, he had once seen Lenin's Party as an antidote to mindless wars protecting nations' financial interests. Like Miłosz, he later rejected the regime that had absorbed so many left-leaning intellectuals.

During the years of totalitarianism, the intelligentsia's task was to keep a light on the truth, to show people that they need not be afraid, that they were part of a great opposition, something ennobling, more potent than any individual life. This is why students and professors, scientists, writers and journalists joined forces with Solidarity to defeat totalitarianism. Historian Timothy Garton Ash, a Western intellectual and recognized authority on Central Europe, talked of the envy he felt when he visited his colleagues in Poland in the 1980s: "Here is a place where people care, passionately, about ideas."[4]

Jacek Kuroń died five years ago. Leszek Kołakowski died in July 2009 and, as the obituaries pointed out, an era was coming to an end. In a September 2009 essay, Tony Judt wrote of the Polish philosopher's intense interest in good and evil, "he took the devil extremely seriously." Unlike his Western contemporaries, Kołakowski was unwilling to cede the middle ground, to consider moral relativism.

Philosopher-politician János Kis, a founding member of Hungary's Alliance of Free Democrats, moved to New York. Few people listen to Hungary's great intellectual George Konrád now, and the much-admired intellectuals of the pre-democracy era have become mere voices in the cacophony that is modern Western dialogue. "The republic of literature as a body of normative spiritual values is a thing of the past," he wrote in his essay "Something Is Over."

"Once we won, we lost whatever power we thought we had," Konrád told me. "There are still intellectuals here, but there is no longer an intelligentsia." Later, he added rather sadly that "technocracy has won." The mindless pursuits of the West leave little time for reflection. Questions of good and evil are no longer of vital interest to the public, and in an era of moral relativism, an era that wishes to be inclusive of many points of view, the devil is just another player.

AS RYSZARD KAPUŚCIŃSKI asked in *The Soccer War,* what would happen if one day—one beautiful day—Poland regained its political life? "Would the churches be deserted? Would poetry become—as it does in untroubled countries—food for a bored handful of experts, and film one branch of commercialized entertainment?" Well, one answer to his question of what would follow was the publication of a critical biography of Kapuściński's own life and work. Artur Domosławski's book *Kapuściński Non-Fiction,* published in February 2010, posits that the great Polish journalist's work should be reclassified as fiction and that he traded his privileges of travel for work as a Communist spy.

When Communism collapsed, intellectuals became ministers, government appointees, deputies, ambassadors. Their ideas were no longer of vital interest to their countrymen. They became observers, commentators, spectators, rather than participants in the making of history.

And what is the future of a country's individual culture in a world where American cultural products and global media rule? Under Communism, books and ideas were treasured by the public, often because they were banned. Intellectuals, who saw themselves as the conscience of their nations, were persecuted and jailed for continuing to seek an audience for their ideas and forbidden ideologies. Their countrymen, including the Communist government's functionaries and their security police, saw them as the torchbearers of truth. Now that everyone can publish what they want, what is the role of the intellectuals? Have they lost their authority?

Has the age of ideas passed?

In a speech about the role of intellectuals, former dissident Václav Havel argued that "intellectuals have a responsibility to engage in politics in the broadest sense of the word,"[5] that they must remain involved in events affecting their countries yet stay out of politics itself. By their very nature, he argued, politicians will look at only one side of an issue. Intellectuals, on the other hand, must look at all sides and engage in public discussion of policies. They cannot and should not pursue political power. Yet Havel accepted the role of president of Czechoslovakia and, after the split with the Slovaks, of the Czech Republic.

László Szigeti, founder and president of the publishing house Kalligram in Bratislava, has talked of the café meetings where intellectuals in Bratislava found common ground and talked of the future of their countries. He was with Havel in Washington when the Czech leader told the American Senate that that the "best we can offer you is our experience with fascism and communism, and what we have learnt." Szigeti wondered, even then, whether such experience is transferable. How to put a human face on the greatest atrocities in our history? As leading intellectuals, all they can offer is thier best efforts. He publishes in both Slovak and Hungarian, offering mirror images of two formerly warring peoples to each other, in hopes that they will recognize the common features rather than points of difference.

"The role of the intelligentsia, in a normal democracy," Adam Michnik said to me, "is to defend liberal values, liberty, freedom of expression, pluralism, tolerance for others' views." He has remained optimistic that unique Polish voices, Polish culture, will survive, though he admits that it will need brilliant cultural policies to support it. American books and movies, video games and quiz shows are what the young seek out in Poland, as in the rest of Europe. For Michnik, this is not a threat but a breath of fresh air. He views American culture not as monolithic, but as rich and varied, like European culture.

Miłosz talked of how irritating American consumerism is for the Eastern intellectual. Coming from a country where the intelligentsia had assumed the role of moral integrity, a permanent reminder to the "people" and the state that not everyone could be threatened or bribed into silence, he found it particularly difficult to exist in a society where there was no intelligentsia.[6] Here, in America, "the triumph of the individual had wrought an inner sterility. They had souls of shiny plastic."[7]

Most movie theatres in Central Europe are now showing the same Hollywood films that you can see in London or Munich or New York. A quick walk through a Warsaw bookstore reveals J.K. Rowling, Stephen King, John Grisham and a slew of pink and mauve romances. More than a hundred and fifty years ago, in his famous book about democracy, Alexis de Tocqueville warned of the dangers of "the tyranny of the majority," the worship of uniformity, the loss of respect for excellence. Would there be room for the heroes of the resistance to Communist tyranny in this new world where all ideas are equal?

In October 2009, Havel spoke of the pressures of twenty-first-century consumer society: "On the one hand everything is getting better—a new generation of mobile phones is being released every week. But in order to make use of them, you need to follow new instructions. So you end up reading instruction manuals instead of books and in your free time you watch TV where handsome tanned guys scream from advertisements about how happy they are to have new swimming trunks...The new consumer society is accomplished by a growing number of people who do not create anything of value."

Andrzej Olszewski of Poland's Centre for Public Opinion Research told me in 2008 that his surveys show the young have no time for ideas. They are not interested in moral values or political issues. Family, even friendship, seems of fleeting importance to them. They are not engaged in trying to change the world. They care about instant gratification. Mass culture has come to Central Europe, and the free market is rarely kind to ideals.

THE CZECH REPUBLIC

"THE POWER OF THE POWERLESS"[1]

DRIVING TO Prague from the airport on a clear day, there is a moment, as you start your descent from the hills, when the domes and rooftops of the golden city present themselves to the visitor and you know you have arrived at the heart of Europe. In that first glimpse of the cupolas and towers, the river, a medieval church spire, the sun glinting off the slate rooftops, you are grateful for the magic of a city preserved from the general destruction meted out to most of its neighbouring capitals. And as you pass some army barracks, what could be more Czech than a small platoon of cheerfully chatting army cadres, the boys in spic-and-span regulation khakis, the girls looking chic in their uniforms of mid-thigh skirts and knee-high boots? I am trying to imagine how they fare in NATO. Or Afghanistan.

But no need to worry about that: the Czechs have returned home. "I do not think we have fought a war with enthusiasm," Josef Škvorecký, the famous Czech novelist, told me, "since the one with Jan Hus against the Habsburgs." He has forgotten the famed Czechoslovak Legions of some fifty thousand who fought with the

Bolsheviks in 1917, then against them when they met with a Hungarian army as the Czechs tried to march westward.[2]

My hotel on Wenceslas Square, in the New Town, is irredeemably ugly but with a Czech flair for making the most of a bad situation. In the Triton Restaurant bar, a huge mermaid hovers under the ceiling, and the cellar restaurant's walls feature mythical sea creatures—an underwater werewolf, scantily dressed sprites with fins and an old man in diapers and glasses leering at the table settings. The food is eminently forgettable but quickly served. It is February 2009, and I am the only guest interrupting a vigorous soccer game on the kitchen TV set.

It is Wenceslas Square that drew me to this location—its great moments of history such as Prague Spring of 1968 and the mass demonstrations of the 1980s that demanded freedom and forced this stronghold of totalitarianism to capitulate.

Wenceslas Square is not really a square but a long, broad boulevard with a concrete divide in the centre—a natural location for bars and restaurants, clubs, music and T-shirt stores for the tourists. Even in February, the locals come here for a good time. It's a noisy Saturday-night place with loud music and young people looking for friends or would-be friends. The massive equestrian statue of St. Wenceslas (briefly king of Bohemia and dead since 935), surrounded by barely remembered saints, has been a magnet for Czechs ever since his canonization as their patron saint. In February the saint is green with algae, and his high pedestal, once home to student protestors, posters, candles, announcements, is bare except for a couple of irreverent graffiti.

At the south end of the square, in front of the National Museum, is a small memorial to the victims of Communism. A bronze cross is embedded in the pavement at the spot where Jan Palach, a twenty-year-old student, set fire to himself on January 16, 1969, to protest the 1968 Soviet invasion of Czechoslovakia and the crushing of the tentative reforms attempted by the Dubček regime. Communist Party secretary Alexander Dubček had announced some softening of the government's rigid opposition to freedom of speech, freedom of the press and citizens' right to travel. The Kremlin bosses were not interested in seeing Dubček's "Socialism with a human face."

Palach died of his wounds three days later. His funeral was attended by thousands of students and faculty from the university, proving that, at least for a while, Palach's countrymen could be shocked out of their apathy. For the next two decades of hardline Communism, this was where the young came to remember and resent. It's also where the ruling regime felt most vulnerable and most determined to stop any signs of grieving, let alone repeats of Palach's sacrifice. Despite the authorities' best efforts, two more students soon committed suicide by fire in commemoration of Jan Palach's ideals and his death.

Tomáš Halík, a student friend of Jan Palach's, helped organize the requiem for his funeral. During that night he placed Palach's death mask over the face of the Lenin statue that had once dominated the square now named after the '68 martyr.

Halík remembers the empty square, the silent streets. "It was a winter night, and I had a sort of conversation with Jan about life and death and what it all means. We were both very young. We had both been philosophy students under our terrifying professor Jan Patočka, one of the most famous European philosophers of the twentieth century. I knew then that it is not enough to live my life only for myself and my family. I must use it for something more worthwhile." He decided to become a priest.

To prevent Jan Palach's grave in Olšany Cemetery from becoming a flashpoint for protests, the Czechoslovak secret police (Státní Bezpečnost, commonly referred to as the StB) exhumed and cremated his remains. His mother received the ashes in an unmarked box, which she was not allowed to deposit in the cemetery until 1974.

WHILE JÁNOS KÁDÁR was experimenting with "goulash Communism" in Hungary, declaring that "those not against us are with us," and the Poles were allowed to gather in their churches to praise their lost country, the Czechoslovak Communist Party invented "normalization"—as if it were normal to pretend that the country had been invaded for its own good by Soviet and Warsaw Pact forces in 1968. The attempts at mild liberalization under Communist leader Alexander Dubček were demolished and about half a million Party members expelled, forced to resign or simply "deleted."[3] More than 100,000 trade unionists were expelled; diplomats were replaced; bank managers were removed; teachers were disqualified from teaching.[4] Not only were people prevented from publicly expressing even the mildest forms of disagreement with their government, but punishment for evading the strict rules of conduct was fast and fierce.

In Milan Kundera's novel *The Joke,* young Ludvik, an otherwise devoted Party member, tries to win a girl's love by his wit and insouciance. As a joke, a desperate attempt to gain her admiration, he is dismissive of her bug-eyed enthusiasm for the Party. The authorities, however, have no sense of humour, and Ludvik loses his Party card, his education, his girl, his hopes and his future. His efforts to be reinstated are rebuffed, despite his genuine and heartfelt admiration of the Party and his overwhelming desire to belong again.

Jan Urban, a prominent former Czech dissident, characterized that time: "We had to prove our loyalty by humiliating ourselves. If you didn't do it, if you didn't accept their normalization, you could not continue your education. Even if you could accept that your own career would be over, could you accept it on behalf of your children? Would you deny them an education? Would you subject them to being targets for the StB?"

Urban is a tall, slender man with short-cut grey hair, a creased face that manages to seem both seriously focussed and amused at the same time. He wears soft corduroys, long arms stretching past his jacket sleeves. We talked under the mermaid in the bar, the barman pretending not to listen.

"It was no different from the Nazi occupation. My father was in the Czech resistance, a partisan in Eastern Bohemia, a hero of the Communist Party, ambassador to Finland after the war, but in '68 he, too, had to go through the vetting process. The StB did not trust him. He was too strong, too confident, and he believed in the system's promises. He would not sign their paper supporting the Warsaw Pact's invasion of Czechoslovakia. Instead of a deputy minister, he became a night watchman. His heart gave out after his third interrogation."

After 1968, authorities were too busy purging the professors at Charles University to bother with Jan, who was quietly studying philosophy. The dismissed professors were replaced by faithful Party members who would do anything for the larger salaries, the better apartments—anything, that is, except teach. They simply lacked the right qualifications. There was an unwritten rule, a "social contract," that allowed for the survival of the least principled and the expulsion of the fittest. Displaced academics who chose to make their way to the West knew that the punishment for their escape was borne by their families.

The totalitarian government's chief aim was to preserve its place of privilege. To achieve that, it had to silence all opposition.

Urban got a teaching job in Southern Bohemia. "Our predominant activity was to avoid trouble, to look grey," he told me. But they did notice him once he refused to denounce Charter 77, the 1977 declaration signed by 243 people (by 1989, almost two thousand people had signed), from all walks of life, who were brave enough to protest the government's failure to abide by the United Nations' 1975 Helsinki covenants on human (political, civil, economic and cultural) rights, which Czechoslovakia had signed.[5]

Members of the Charter described themselves as "a free, informal, open community of people of different convictions, different faiths and different professions united by the will to strive individually and collectively for the respect of civil and human rights in our own country and throughout the world . . . It does not form the basis of any oppositional activity."[6] Its chief spokesperson was scholar and author Jan Patočka (martyr Jan Palach's professor). Banned from teaching since 1972, Patočka continued to write, give free lectures at night and meet with his many Western admirers who came to Prague to have a chance to be in his company. He died in March 1977 after an eleven-hour interrogation by the StB. He was sixty-eight years old. His books and articles continued to be published in *samizdat* and circulated among his many admirers.[7]

Jan Urban was brought out of the school by armed police, interrogated and barred from teaching. As a bricklayer he thought he was safe from the StB's attentions, but they continued to take him in for further interrogations, arrested his pregnant wife, terrified his little daughters. "Of course, she lost the baby," Jan says, his voice hushed, hands flying over his face, covering his eyes.

"I lost twenty years of my life because I would not sign a document denouncing Charter 77. You learn to live without expectations, you live in the moment, pray for one more day to pass without pain."

IT WAS Václav Havel who drafted Charter 77's self-defining statements. Of course, Urban knew of Havel long before that. Everyone in the resistance knew of Havel. Already in the '60s he was a popular playwright. *The Garden Party* was first performed at Prague's Theatre on the Balustrade in 1963; its central character is an ambitious young man so transformed by the mindless system he inhabits that not even his own parents recognize him. It was followed by *The Memorandum*, whose characters attempt to deal with a bureaucratic non-language imposed on them by an unnamed powerful entity who employs them all. In 1968, Havel reported on the Warsaw Pact invasion for Radio Free Czechoslovakia. Not surprisingly, his work was banned as part of "normalization." His plays could no longer be performed and his writing could not be published. He got a menial job in a brewery and continued to write.

Havel's seminal essay, "Power of the Powerless," was published in '78, in Czech in *samizdat* and in translation in Germany and the U.K. It talked about internal exile, about living within the state without being part of its apparatus. Writing on either one of these subjects would have been sufficient reason for Havel to be tried for treason or betrayal of the proletariat or merely subversion of the state.

His plays found dedicated audiences on secret stages where the performers and crowd melted into a single group of protestors against the rigidly controlled Communist system. When he was not in one of its jails, the government's agents harassed him and his wife, Olga. They cut off his phone, barred his friends from visiting him, prevented him from buying gasoline for his car and from attempting to leave home. Never one for easy compromises, Havel co-founded the Committee for the Defense of the Unjustly Persecuted, an offshoot of Charter 77, just prior to his longest incarceration. In prison he continued to write essays as well as open letters to government leaders. The tamed Czechoslovak press continued its attacks on him and his friends, at home and abroad, while his international reputation grew. His four-and-a-half-year jail term—June 1979 to January 1984—ended while he was hospitalized with pleurisy and the government was anxious to get rid of him before his death was laid at their doorstep.[8]

THE 1980S brought widespread discontent as the Party's planned economy faltered. Central planning had created a handful of giant industries whose products were unsaleable in the West and unprofitable to sell below cost to the Soviet Union. A tacit agreement with the majority of the people meant that they would pretend to work and the authorities would pretend not to notice the large-scale workplace theft, so long as people went along with the system. By the mid-'80s, that deal seemed to have come apart.

The demonstrations that ended twenty years of Communist Party rule culminated here on Wenceslas Square. They were not particularly well organized, nor well planned, though some of the occasional leaders were the children of dissidents who had slipped through the controls that should have denied them an education. From mid-1988, the size and vigour of the demonstrations grew, as did their frequency. Neither water cannons nor attack dogs nor brutal beatings seemed to deter the young students from marching to Wenceslas Square shouting slogans about freedom, which none of them had ever tasted. The government's speedy imprisonment of leading dissidents seemed to have the opposite effect to the one intended.

Finally, in 1989, the young refused to be intimidated. In January of that year, students commemorated Jan Palach's death by a mass demonstration on Wenceslas Square.

November 17 was the fiftieth anniversary of the bloody suppression of student resistance to the German occupation. On this day in 1939, nine student leaders had been executed, 1,200 transported to Sachsenhausen concentration camp and all Czech universities closed. The government could hardly object to an occasion commemorating resistance to the Nazis, even though it knew that the event could lead to demands for freedom from the current oppression. The Berlin Wall had been breached more than a week before, and even the most vociferous Communist leaders realized that the best they could hope for was to stem the tide a little longer.

The crowd of more than fifteen thousand young people carried candles and carnations, their banners reading, "Who if not Us, When if not Now!" "Democracy and Law!" "Academic Freedom!" They had planned to march past St. Wenceslas's statue, close to the National Museum, but helmeted, shield-bearing police barred the entrances to the square.

By the time the crowd reached the river Vltava, it had swelled to fifty thousand and the shouting for free elections gave way to "abolish the Communist Party." Someone draped a flag between the front line of students and the armed policemen. A few students offered them carnations; others placed candles at the policemen's feet. It is worthwhile to note, in hindsight, that the policemen who stood stone faced, as they had been trained, and the students who sang the national anthem and "We Shall Overcome" were about the same age and were all afraid.

The demonstrators jangled keys to denote that they felt jailed. When the police waded into the seated protesters, kicking them and beating them with their truncheons, no one in the back of the crowd believed what they thought they heard. The police brought in a black armoured car with barbed wire around its hood and reinforcements from the Ministry of the Interior's anti-terrorist shock troops, the Red Berets. Now all exits were blocked except a narrow alleyway along National (Národni) Avenue, with room for only one person at a time, easy prey for the truncheons. The Red Berets were trained in hand-to-hand combat and martial arts, unlike the unarmed civilians, who fell by the hundreds and were brutally battered where they lay. The oldest victim was a man of eighty-three, the youngest about seven.

The next day, the world learned of the brutality of the Czechoslovak government, and no amount of sanctioned local media reports about unruly demonstrators and restoring the peace could soften the nation's disgust.

The dissidents, Václav Havel and Jan Urban among them, started to return to the city.

There is a small plaque on National Avenue to remind visitors of November 17, 1989. Even on a cold winter day, a tiny bunch of flowers lay under it. Perhaps the person who recently laid a wreath on the monument to the victims of Communism on Wenceslas Square had been here, too.

JAN URBAN never imagined that the Communists could be defeated. When his Polish dissident hero, Adam Michnik, called him in July of 1989—"It was the day the StB searched my apartment and took my wife and children for interrogation"—to say that it was over, that he, Adam, was part of the new government in Poland, Jan did not believe him. "Adam arrived at three AM, after an eight-hour search at the border, and we went down to Wenceslas Square to stand in front of St. Wenceslas's statue. There were StB men on every corner watching us and listening. Adam pointed at the big neon 'Hail Communism' signs hanging from the surrounding buildings and he said, 'I bet you there will not be one of those red stars on those lampposts a year from now.'"

Jan's silver spoon clanked inside his coffee cup, as he said, grinning, "In four months we were forming the government."

REINVENTING THE COUNTRY

The disgust with the police actions of November 17 brought out more and more demonstrators—150,000 in Wenceslas Square on November 20, over 200,000 on November 23—carrying banners, chanting slogans, and convoys of truck drivers honking their horns near the National Museum.[9] On November 25, before a gathering of close to a million people in Letná Square, economist Miloš Zeman announced that Czechoslovakia had been reduced to the status of a Third World country and everybody cheered.

On a balcony about midway along Wenceslas Square, Václav Havel spoke for the first time about Civic Forum, an informal organization of citizens who would negotiate with the Communist Party on behalf of both Czechs and Slovaks. The Charter 77 group, other dissidents and their most faithful observer, historian-journalist Timothy Garton Ash, assembled daily in the auditorium and on the main stage of the old Laterna Magika ("Magic Lantern") theatre,[10] at the corner of National and Jungmann streets, a few steps from Wenceslas Square. There Havel assembled the dissidents who would form the core of his first democratic government. Timothy Garton Ash described the mirror-lined grand foyer and the small backstage rooms smelling "of cigarette smoke, sweat, damp coats, and revolution." It is only in Prague that theatres became launch pads for the protest movement, only in Prague that a playwright would become the spokesman for a lost generation.

It was a heady time for those running in and out of the theatre on missions to shore up support, meet with government officials, plan a future for the country and their own place in it. Some had been victims of the Communist regime; some had lost positions for signing Charter 77; many had been banned, harassed, barred from their professions. Tomáš Halík, having kept his promise to his dead friend Jan Palach, had been ordained a Catholic priest. Miloš Zeman had just been dismissed from a job for being too outspoken about the country's economic malaise. Rock singer Michael Kocáb, whose music had been banned by the government, became an unofficial go-between to Ladislav Adamec, the last Communist prime minister of Czechoslovakia. Martin Simecka, who could not be granted a university education because of his father Milan's opposition to the regime, would become editor of the liberal daily SME. Martin Palouš, another Charter 77 signatory and former student of Jan Patočka, who had been forced to accept work as a stoker in medical clinics, would become Czech ambassador to the United Nations. Martin Bútora, the Slovak sociologist and founding member of Slovakia's Public Against Violence, a sister group of Havel's Civic Forum, was to become Slovakia's ambassador to the United States.

Slovak philosopher Miroslav Kusý decided to take on the job of dealing with the press on behalf of Civic Forum. Oldřich Černý, an English literature graduate considered "unemployable" after turning down an opportunity to spy for the StB, was there to help translate from Czech into English. He would become Havel's security chief. And economist Václav Klaus, who would become Civic Forum's first minister of finance on December 10, 1989, was just embarking on a political career that would lead to the prime minister's office.[11] There, in partnership with Slovakia's Vladimir Mečiar, he would orchestrate the breakup of Czechoslovakia.

Civic Forum's demands included the resignation of the Communist leadership and the immediate release of all "prisoners of conscience." To make sure that the authorities took them seriously, the Civic Forum announced its support for a national general strike.

The general secretary of the Czech Communist Party, Miloš Jakeš, resigned on the evening of November 24, 1989. The Czechoslovak round table, which included members of the Communist Party and the newly invented Civic Forum, continued to meet to attempt to find a mutually acceptable way forward. Martin Palouš described the bizarre scene of a group of randomly selected individuals with no political experience facing their "well-trained opponents who were backed by the repressive organs of the state, still ready to intervene in its defence." The unlikely revolutionaries had to feel their way in uncharted waters, never entirely sure how far they could push before their opponents called for armed backup.

On December 29, 1989, Havel was elected president by a unanimous vote of the Federal Assembly. It was a surprising decision by a man who had always insisted that he was not interested in politics. "I am a writer," he said, "and I have always understood my mission to be to speak the truth about the world we live in, to bear witness to its terrors and its miseries—in other words, to warn rather than hand out prescriptions for change."[12] The "Velvet Revolution," as the Western media called these astonishing events in Czechoslovakia, had been won.

In June 1990, Jan Urban led Civic Forum to victory in the first free elections in Czechoslovakia since 1948. One day after his victory and the end of Communism in Czechoslovakia, he resigned from his political positions, to resume his career as a journalist.

ROCK 'N' ROLL

It's not only in Czechoslovakia that music became a part of the protest movement, but here the government itself felt threatened by music. As early as the 1950s, Communist Party bosses had recognized music as a voice of dissent. Then it was jazz, both American and Czech, that kindled their fear of the uncontrollable. Josef Škvorecký, a lifelong jazz fan, wrote of the shock of realizing that the Communist Party viewed jazz in much the same way as the German occupiers had viewed it: "'perverted,' 'decadent,' 'base,' 'lying,' 'degenerate'... 'the music of cannibals,'"[13] Jazz, by its very nature is free-wheeling, and authoritarianism, by its very nature, needs to have all things confined by rules. In the 1960s, it was rock 'n' roll, a latecomer from the West, complete with hippies, psychedelic lighting and a range of bands that played to young audiences much like their Western counterparts. They, too, were disaffected with society's mores, dressed badly, wore their hair long and talked of love. In the warm glow of Prague Spring, rock bands filled halls all over Czechoslovakia.

PAUL WILSON came to Prague almost by accident. It was 1967. He had been studying in London, living in pubs, the theatre, the museums and the British Library's fusty old Reading Room, poring over Henry Miller's fiction and everything by George Orwell. It may have been Miloš Forman's *Loves of a Blonde,* or Karel and Josef Čapek's *The Insect Play;* however it came about, he became interested in how Communism thrived where it was at home, and jumped at the opportunity to take a teaching job in Czechoslovakia. He loved it. "Prague lives in full highs and lows; people go off the deep end so easily," he said. "There was, then, all that excitement about a new beginning, a bubbling feeling like porridge coming to the boil." With Dubček everyone thought it was possible to change the system from the inside. In the euphoria of that time, it was easy to make friends, and Paul met "everyone"—writers, poets, painters, philosophers, musicians. Even then the musicians were the rebels. They didn't wish to belong to any movement. They were truly "outside the system"; they ignored its existence, and they continued to do so after the Warsaw Pact's tanks rolled in and "normalization" began.

Paul played guitar and sang in a band that called itself the Plastic People of the Universe, after Frank Zappa's song of the same name. They were wild about the Velvet Underground, the "big beat," the Beach Boys, Bob Dylan, the new American scene and the Beatles.

The secret police noticed the Plastic People of the Universe, tried to change them then coerce some of its members and eventually deprived them of their "professional status," without which they could not play at official venues. When the band defied the rules, their instruments were confiscated, their music was banned and some of their members were arrested, tried and convicted of "disturbing the peace," an offence that called for prison terms.

Paul's first encounter with Václav Havel's writing was an essay he read in 1976, in the form of a letter to Czechoslovakia's Communist leader Gustáv Husák. It talked of the system's "lethal principle" of reducing everything to "a state of dull, inert uniformity," and warned that people's life force could not be suppressed forever.

Václav Havel, who had attended the Plastic People's 1976 trial, wrote of his disgust with the state's display of naked tyranny, that the prosecution had become "the symbol of an inflated, narrow-minded power, persecuting everything that does not fit into its sterile notions of life, everything unusual, risky, self-taught, unbribable... everything that is different from itself." [14] Strangely, in a world where such words were dangerous, this letter was signed "Václav Havel, Writer."

Paul Wilson was expelled from Czechoslovakia and returned to London, where he met Tom Stoppard for the first time. Stoppard had been born Tomáš Straussler in Zlín, Czechoslovakia; his family fled to Singapore with other Jews in 1939. He was educated as British in India and had already become a well-known playwright by the time he met Paul and persuaded him to start translating Havel and Škvorecký into English. They also talked about the Plastic People and their odd, stubborn bravery. But it was not till 2005 that Stoppard called Paul to tell him that he was thinking about writing a play about that rock band and the times it had inhabited. After that, Stoppard called often, seeking details, memories, songs, place names and personal stories. *Rock 'n' Roll*, the play, opened in London and New York in 2006. It tried to capture a time and a state of mind that was as foreign to audiences in those cities as it is today to audiences of young Czechs for whom rock is just another form of music.

Paul is seventy years old now, living near Lake Huron in Ontario. He still has the smile of an optimist and long grey-blond hair that he does not bother to control. In many ways, he is still a '60s kind of guy—curious, witty, laid-back, engaging—he still loves to travel to Prague and he still loves rock 'n' roll.

THE MINISTER OF MINORITIES AND HUMAN RIGHTS

Minister Michael Kocáb's office is in Straka Academy,[15] the seat of the Czech government and its administrative offices. It is a massive baroque palace that stretches along the river Vltava, near the Manes Bridge, in the centre of Prague. In its formal entrance foyer there is a marble statue of a young girl holding a cup or Greek amphora. She is larger than life size and completely naked, which may account for the fact that she seems somewhat uncomfortable. The minister seems equally uncomfortable in his vast office on the second floor. In his late fifties, he is tall, loose-limbed, wearing slim-cut blue jeans and a black jacket over a black-collared polo shirt. He has a big handshake and an easy open smile.

Until 1982, when his rock band was forbidden to perform, Kocáb had paid scant attention to politics. But the six-year ban on his music made him think about the regime that ran the world around him and could, with just a thin piece of paper, deprive him of what he most enjoyed in his life. When the band returned with a live televised show in 1988, he grabbed the opportunity to speak his mind from the stage. "Every nation has the government it deserves," Kocáb told the audience. "It is time to return the power to the people." That speech, he thought, was the reason Communist prime minister Ladislav Adamec chose to invite him to his office here at Straka Academy. It was November 1989, the beginning of the Velvet Revolution. He would enter through a side door and be led upstairs by one of the prime minister's trusted men. Nothing had been decided yet, but "we were talking about the handover of government. He still thought there was going to be a role for him. That we would devise something like the Poles did at their round table, that there would be a gradual transition." There wasn't.

"We (the Civic Forum) were meeting at Laterna Magika in the evenings and I came here every morning to visit with Adamec," he says. "It was utterly unreal. My being here, his talking with us as equals, the absence of the secret police." Here was Kocáb conversing with the head of one of the most repressive regimes in the Soviet Bloc, negotiating for democracy that seemed, then, no more than an optimistic dream. "The hard-liners in his party were still urging military action against us," he recalls.

Under Civic Forum, Kocáb also assumed the task of dealing with the army. He remembers going to army headquarters with Václav Klaus and a tense but cordial meeting with Chief of General Staff General Miroslav Vacek. The general agreed that Czech troops would not fire on Czech civilians if the leaders of Civic Forum ensured there would be no mob attacks against soldiers. Given the long years of suppression and the brutal beating of the students just days before in Wenceslas Square, this was a tough demand. But Havel's extraordinary credibility and his humanity were such that violence could not become the response to the state's own violence.

Through it all, Kocáb played rock 'n' roll. When he wrote a letter to USSR president Mikhail Gorbachev demanding the departure of the Soviet army, he was still putting the finishing touches to a movie about his band at the state-owned film studios in the Barrandov buildings, which had once belonged to the Havel family. Minister Kocáb's band, Pražský Výběr, plays hard rock. *Pražský výber* means "Prague selection," a broad, humourous reference to a cheap Czech wine.[16]

I asked the minister when he realized that the old regime was over, that they had won. He contemplates this for so long, I begin to wonder whether he still doubts that the last twenty years are real. Havel used to say that during his years in the presidential castle, he would often wake up during the night, imagining that all that had happened was a dream and when he awoke he would be back in his cell.

Then Kocáb tells me the story of his May 1990 visit to the Kremlin, accompanied by Alexander Dubček, hero of '68, Speaker of the Czechoslovak parliament. They had been charged with engineering the withdrawal of Soviet troops from Czechoslovakia.

All the way to Moscow, Dubček, understandably nervous, was working on his speech to the Supreme Soviet. The last time he had been in the Kremlin was in 1968, after being kidnapped by the KGB, kept in solitary confinement, then delivered to the Politburo to be lambasted for his liberal ideas. Soon afterwards, he lost his position as first secretary of the Czechoslovak Communist Party's Central Committee and was sent into political exile.

He had been preparing this speech for weeks but felt that it was still not perfect, that some sentences still needed to be spruced up. This was the first and probably only time that a Slovak had had the opportunity to speak in such a place, and for this Slovak, who had briefly defied the Soviet Union, this was a historic moment.

Alas, when the moment arrived, Dubček was nowhere to be found. Kocáb recalls, "We stood at the entrance to that vast hall—we had all seen it on our TV screens so many times, the very heart of the Soviet empire—and we waited. I went down the hall, searching for Dubček, opening doors, looking into every toilet cubicle... taking my time, still hoping he would turn up. He didn't. We waited some more at the entrance, and finally our Soviet hosts [Kocáb had been talking about music with Eduard Shevardnadze, then Soviet minister of foreign affairs] urged me to go up there instead of the still-missing Dubček. I moved slowly, dying with every step, asking God to rescue me, to make Dubček materialize even at this last second, but suddenly and inevitably, I was standing at the podium where Stalin had once stood, murdering history."

Minister Kocáb's first words were "Hello." A sea of severe, immobile faces looked up at him, every one of them, he imagined, another hostile, disapproving Brezhnev. Then he tried a few tentative sentences and a joke. The interpreter was so terrible that a few of the stone-faced men started to smile. Thus encouraged, Kocáb tried another joke, and the room erupted into laughter...

At the time there were some 200,000 Soviet soldiers in Poland, Czechoslovakia and Hungary. One of the Soviets' top-secret facilities stored nuclear warheads on Czechoslovak territory. Three years later, the facilities had been dismantled and the soldiers had gone home.

THE MEMBERS of Kocáb's band have changed, the staging of their shows has improved, the venues are more professional, as are the

CDs and DVDs, but the sound is the same. They still fill theatres and bring huge audiences to their feet. Indeed, the minister has recently returned from a sold-out gig in Bratislava. He shows me a video of the band and its lead singer: Michael Kocáb, in white wig, black T-shirt, white gloves and his trademark dark glasses. For this video the glasses are heart-shaped and white-rimmed and he is prancing about the stage, waving his naked arms (are those real or temporary tattoos on his upper arms?), shouting the words into the mike as the music thuds and the lights career around the stage and the audience has risen to its feet, screaming the words along with the minister of minorities and human rights.

His ministerial role, however, has been less enjoyable of late. In 2009, far-right extremists paraded through towns with significant Roma populations; someone threw Molotov cocktails through the windows of a Roma family home in Vitkov, near the Moravian-Silesian border, injuring three people. David Duke, the infamous former Klu Klax Klan Grand Wizard, was invited to give a speech in the Czech Republic about the superiority of whites over all others; Prague's Kontingent Press published the Czech translation of his dreadful book *My Awakening*.

There were noisy demonstrations and neo-Nazi gatherings, including one that marched through the town of Ústi nad Laben, to celebrate the 120th anniversary of Adolf Hitler's birth. Uniformed "security brigades" of the xenophobic Workers' Party strutted through Roma housing developments, and, as the financial crisis deepened, the ultranationalists have attracted more of the young who share a sense of frustration and anger with other Central Europeans, along with the belief they are entitled to more out of life and the European Union than their current lot suggests. These times are reminiscent of the years of discontent following the new government's stiff economic measures twenty years ago. Then, too, a 17-year-old Roma boy was killed and Ústi nad Laben erected a wall between its Roma and non-Roma populations.

A sharp rise in the number of Roma seeking asylum in Canada has prompted the Canadian government to impose visa requirements on Czech citizens, along with one on Mexicans trying to flee the murderous battles between drug cartels and the cartels and the police. Even the Czech liberal press has been critical of Roma tax-payer-funded benefits and starting to blame the Roma for using their "excessive free time" to commit petty crimes and irritate their neighbours with noisy parties. Exporting the problem to Canada may have seemed like a happy solution to some, but the minister blames local governments for failing to support their Roma—they should not have to seek support outside the country.

The minister has accused his fellow politicians of marginalizing the Roma by wishing to appeal to the lowest common denominator in the Czech Republic. In Parliament he presented a declaration against all forms of extremism, signed by the leaders of all parties and of both the lower and upper houses as well as by ex-president Václav Havel. While the symbolic all-members' resolution spoke to the Czech middle class, in Bohemia—home of the unfortunately named neo-Nazi groups Hammer Skins and Blood & Honour—there were pitched battles between the police and members of the ultra-nationalist Workers' Party, a party not represented in Parliament.

October 2009 ended with the good news that police had arrested more than thirty individuals suspected of ties to extremist and neo-Nazi groups. In Prague there was a peaceful demonstration of women against racism. The European Union announced a long list of "integration" subsidies, worth 750 million crowns, for towns with significant Roma populations. In December, Parliament approved Minister Kocáb's Roma integration plans.

Kocáb says that sometimes there is a crossover between the two halves of his life. He asked Parliament to vote for a Roma Holocaust memorial at Lety, the site of the Roma internment camp, where, of 1,327 prisoners, more than four hundred died, including all the babies, and five hundred more were transported to Auschwitz to be murdered. When Minister Kocáb's colleagues reminded him that there was an economic crisis, that this was a time for cutbacks for new projects that would cost 120 million krona, he sang them a song about a man who has lost his memory and all he can remember is one song. It worked. The pig farm on the site of the camp will be relocated and a new monument will be built to commemorate the suffering of the Roma.[17]

WE ARE NOT LIKE THEM

Václav Havel announced in his much-quoted 1990 New Year's speech that "we should not forget those who paid for our present freedom." He promised that independent courts would consider the guilt of those responsible.

The newly democratic government of Czechoslovakia determined that it must cleanse "the body politic" of all those who had been connected with the Communist state security apparatus. In February 1990, the StB was ordered to hand in its weapons and thirteen thousand StB officers were dismissed. Both the Czech and Slovak National Assemblies passed a "lustration act" in October. According to the new law, former agents and members of the Communist Party were banned from public office for five years. The law's function was to bar the totalitarian government's satraps and collaborators from certain jobs. A government that uses terror and coercion to govern is, according even to its own avowed rules, acting unlawfully.

But why had it taken so long to tackle the question of how to deal with the archives and personnel of the Party's self-defence apparatus? Why allow them the opportunity to destroy thousands of files? Oldřich Černý, Havel's former security chief, told me that the transition to a new, democratic government took time. The KGB "advisers" didn't leave till just before Christmas and warned that they would be back right after the Russian New Year. "Given the extraordinary speed of the transition," Černý said, "it was impossible to deal faster with the mass of paperwork."

The shredding and burning of files went on throughout the days of the new government of "National Understanding." The delay gave those in charge of the StB a chance to melt into the population, many of them selling their expertise to the new companies and branches of international firms setting up local enterprises. They were, after all, well trained in security matters. Concerns that Havel had agreed to overlook the StB's sins drove Jan Urban away from him in those early days of suspicion.[18]

Pavel Žáček, now director of the Institute for the Study of Totalitarian Regimes, was appointed department head, Security Services Archives, in 2006 and inherited the StB's documents: about twenty kilometres of reports on individuals the Communist regime considered dangerous or useful. Žáček is a young man with an almost unlined face and a small moustache that emphasizes a full mouth he keeps in a permanent scowl, expecting criticism for the work he has done.

He was born one month after the short-lived '68 Prague Spring, and his parents were in the protest movement throughout his childhood. They kept a library of forbidden books behind the titles displayed on their shelves. He was arrested and interrogated three times before he reached the age of twenty. On November 17, 1989, he was one of the students marching along the river toward Wenceslas Square. "I couldn't believe the violence," he recalls. "We were beaten and kicked by the police. My parents came that day and my father's arm was broken along National Street. They beat women who had already fallen; they even assaulted the ABC television crew and some Spaniards who were filming." But he came back to Wenceslas Square on November 20, carrying a large, flapping Czech flag. There were thousands of people and no one was afraid anymore.

Žáček is the right man for the StB files. He attacks the job with a vehemence and dedication rare in these confusing times, when so many would rather forget the sins of the past and focus on the sins of the present: the capitalist manoeuvrings that have landed the country in such uncertainty. He is certain of his task. Three million pages of documents were digitalized in eleven months. "It took them eleven years to assemble these pages," he says, "and a lot more than the two hundred workers who now spend their days at the Institute."

There has been much talk of the small fry whose reports were found in the files and whose lives have been ruined since their complicity was revealed. But not much is written about the men who harassed and persecuted the dissidents, who took thousands of photographs of dissidents and of everyone who talked to them. No one mentions the victims anymore, Žáček tells me, those killed by the system and those killed by these operatives.

One of his interesting "finds," he says, is Lieutenant-Colonel Miroslav Chovanec's diary, with Chovanec's notes about meetings and regular reports to his superiors. "He is a clever man," Žáček says. "Not that different from many others who did it for money, position, easy travel, a good life. He was responsible for surveying dissidents—people like my parents." What irks Žáček is that Chovanec has succeeded in continuing his easy life. He went on to work for a bank or an insurance company.

Major General Alojz Lorenc, the man who ordered the "deployment" against anti-government demonstrations, who advised the regime on how to suppress "agitators," managed to keep his job till the end of December 1989 and was not let off the government's payroll until March 1990, giving him plenty of time to destroy evidence of his rule of terror. Though the Czechoslovak Military Court convicted Lorenc of "abuse of power," he evaded even a modest jail term when Slovakia separated from the Czechs.[19]

Lorenc retired to a quiet life, advising corporations on security, interrupted briefly by a successful tour promoting his memoir.

Žáček believes that whatever harm may come from the misuse of files will never balance the harm done by the StB. Discrediting public figures may cause them a small amount of embarrassment, but that is nothing compared to the pain caused by those who have ruined lives. That Communist Party Secretary (for Prague) Miroslav Stepan, who had approved orders to beat the students on that memorable day in November, had toured the country cheerfully signing his memoirs was far more galling than knowing that a few innocent people got caught in the web of lies that was the state secret service. Stepan had served a short prison sentence that allowed him both the time and the solitude needed to write his book.

Žáček has no sympathy for Milan Kundera, the acclaimed Czech novelist who, documents revealed, had informed on a twenty-two-year-old student who spied for the West. The fact is, according to Žáček, the student suffered more than the embarrassment Kundera endured for his youthful folly.

The event took place in 1950, when both Milan Kundera and Miroslav Dvořáček, the supposed spy, were only twenty years old. According to the reports of StB agents, Kundera volunteered the information that led to Dvořáček's arrest and subsequent fourteen-year prison term. The story was featured prominently in *Respekt*, a highly regarded political-cultural magazine, in late 2008. Kundera's internationally acclaimed novels explore moral issues, a fact that added to the outraged interest in the story.

Žáček, who almost lost his job over the article, has no regrets. The documents were authentic. The researcher who had found them was not planning to sensationalize what he saw. Martin Simecka, *Respekt*'s editor at the time, also has no regrets for commissioning the story.

"In hindsight," Simecka told me, "bringing the truth of that betrayal into the open was the right thing to do, despite the attacks the magazine attracted." And yes, he would do it again. That he tried to reach Kundera and offered him every chance of an explanation but was rebuffed with silence is justification for having run only one side of the story. The truth, in the end, may not be kind, but it is useful. Sometimes it even helps lay ghosts to rest.

Erik Tabery, *Respekt*'s editor in 2009, says, "We felt the story would help people understand the '50s, especially the young who had never experienced the fear and compromises of that era."

At the heart of the debate following the revelations about Kundera's past was the question, why humiliate such a great writer—why pursue a universally admired Czech? "I think," Tabery says, "that you have to know your past to think about your future. The past, no matter how often it's examined, is never black and white. No one was untouched by the system."

Václav Havel might well disagree. In a short essay on the matter in *Salon,* he wrote that "even if Milan Kundera really had gone to the police to report that there was a spy somewhere around, which I do not believe was the case, it is necessary to try, at the very least, to see it through the lens of those days." He ponders why anyone should "spend ten years in a prison camp just for 'knowing and not telling.'" Yet, as everyone knows, Havel did choose to spend time in prison; Kundera did not.

Havel's advice for the young was to "take care when judging history. Otherwise you can do more harm than good."

Czechs, Žáček believes, must face the truth about how they behaved under Communism. There were too many informers. Often a person would inform merely because he or she was sure the authorities already knew about someone else's clandestine activities, such as distributing or reading forbidden books, and failure to report could lead to imprisonment. It is time, Žáček says, to face the small evils everyone took part in while serving a system that was, itself, evil.

Jan Urban thinks that Czechs don't wish to remember the past because memory could mean having to take responsibility. "The mood is to disregard the past," he says. "One of the legacies of Communism is that the past does not matter, that memory is irrelevant. We lost most Czech Jews during the German occupation. Three and a half million Germans who had lived here for centuries were deported after 1945. After that we were occupied by the Soviets... Under both occupations you had to prove your loyalty by humiliating yourself—it was the only sure way to stay alive. We have no sense of continuity."

For every dissident, for every intellectual who was willing to lay bricks or become a stoker, whose children missed out on an education, there were a thousand people who kept quiet, who were afraid not to report on their friends and families, who hoped that they could keep their heads down long enough to evade notice. It is dangerous to take responsibility.

Most of the judges who had condemned resisters to long prison terms were still sitting in judgment after 1989. How, Pavel Žáček asks, can you hope to reform the system if those charged with the upkeep of the law have themselves offended against the laws of humanity?

On June 3, 2008, the Senate of the Parliament of the Czech Republic adopted the Prague Declaration on European Conscience and Communism. The first sentences of the Prague Declaration affirm that "societies that neglect the past have no future. Whereas Europe will not be united unless it is able to reunite its history, recognize Communism and Nazism as a common legacy and bring about an honest and thorough debate on all the totalitarian crimes of the past century." It goes on to acknowledge that "many of the perpetrators committing crimes in the name of Communism have not yet been brought to justice and their victims have yet to be compensated." What the Declaration fails to tackle is the process that would punish and compensate.

JOSEF ŠKVORECKÝ presents another face of the story in his *Two Murders in My Double Life*. In the novel, a renowned writer's wife is accused of having been an StB spy, just as Josef's wife, Zdena Salivarová-Škvorecká, publisher of about three hundred forbidden books under her imprint 68 Publishers, was accused of being an informer. Her name appeared on a list of possible collaborators.

Josef and Zdena left Czechoslovakia in 1968. Josef was already "well known to the police" for writing what they considered subversive literature, a habit he kept up after settling to Canada. His novel *The Cowards*, first published in 1958, was deemed by the censors to be "decadent" and "reactionary" and ordered recalled by the publisher. It continued to be sold under the counter by booksellers willing to risk arrest. It was published again during the late-1960s thaw, and banned again with the rest of Škvorecký's literary works after "normalization."

Zdena's name was included in a list of those in the StB files. In *Two Murders*, the woman *samizdat* publisher receives the "Order of the White Lion" from the "world-renowned playwright, who is now president of the country" for her efforts on behalf of banned Czech writers, including the playwright-president himself. A few days later, "The List" is published and the heroine succumbs "to a deadly depression."

As in real life, "The List" is published by an overzealous group for whom the lustration laws are too little too late. It took years for Zdena to clear her name. She sued the Ministry of the Interior and won, but she believed that her name had not been truly cleared. Once it was on that list, it would be muddied forever. She felt "she would never get rid of the dreadful suspicion; that it was like being hit by a poisonous spittle which, no matter how quickly one rubs it off one's cheek, penetrates instantly... and remains there as an invisible but universally known mark of Cain."

Zdena's health never recovered.

The files had engendered an atmosphere of resentment, hatred, suspicion. Worse, the Lustration Act seems to have spared the real sharks, who destroyed their own incriminating files or hid behind the old cavil of acting within the confines of the existing laws. Yet, despite the pain of false accusations, and despite the Škvoreckýs' personal journey through the Kafkaesque legal system, the conclusion has to be that the past, no matter how disgraceful and no matter whom it hurts, needs to be examined, otherwise the Czechs, like their fellow travellers in the other former satellites, will continually be forced to deal with bits of its nastiness as it oozes out of the ground, one cupful—such as the Kundera revelations—at a time.

THE LIBRARY OF PROHIBITED BOOKS

Jiří Gruntorád is the guardian of Libri Prohibiti—the Library of Prohibited Books—at 2 Senovážné Square. His cramped, dark rooms hold 27,000 different books and 2,200 periodicals, of which 14,000 are *samizdat* publications in Slovak, Czech and Polish. They are novels of all genres: essays, short stories, poetry, philosophy, translations of works by British, American and Russian authors; they have nothing in common except that they were all banned under the Communist regime. Some of the *samizdat* volumes were meticulously typed and typed again, twenty or thirty times, each by an individual who risked his or her freedom for the words on these pages. A few thousand are carbon copies of the old-fashioned kind—ten, fifteen copies on ultra-thin paper, the last copy very hard to read.

Because each version was typed by a different person, some are much better than others. "There were a few excellent typists, many of only average ability, and a few whose enthusiasm far outstripped their manual dexterity," Jiří tells me. "Some left out words, sentences, even whole paragraphs. That's why we have twenty 'editions' of the Czech translation of Orwell's *Animal Farm,* and about twenty of Solzhenitsyn's *Gulag Archipelago.*" There are early works by Bohumil Hrabal, author of such international bestsellers as *Closely Watched Trains.* Hrabal, Gruntorád says, had agreed to censor his own work rather than have it silenced, but this collection displays the novels he did not submit to the state's critics.

There are three very different "editions" of Havel's *The Beggar's Opera.* Havel himself made about two hundred different copies of his books. He was a diligent worker, and signed them all. There is Pavel Kohout in Czech and in translation, Zdenek Urbanek, Jaroslav Seifert's poetry volumes (Seifert was openly published only after his 1984 Nobel Prize for Literature), Ivan Klíma, Arthur Koestler in translation, Czesław Miłosz and Josef Škvorecký, whose books were banned after the success of *The Cowards*. After 1968, Škvorecký's name couldn't be said in public because the government had a rule that no émigrés could be mentioned in the newspapers or on the airwaves. When Miloš Forman's production of *Amadeus* shut down most of downtown Prague, neither the film nor its director could be mentioned, though all of Prague knew that Forman had paid for permission to shoot his Mozart film here. Seifert, one of the early signatories of Charter 77, who had been a Communist in the 1920s and 1930s, could not attend his own Nobel Prize ceremony in 1984.

Even authors such as Mark Twain and Guy de Maupassant ended up on the banned lists because their translators were on the authorities' forbidden authors lists.

Jiří Gruntorád blames his near-blindness on the time he spent editing *samizdat* manuscripts. He blames his bent back and sallow complexion on the four years he spent in prisons. The first two years were tedious, the second two backbreaking work in Minkovice—a forced-labour camp for hardened criminals and intellectuals. There was one poet: a member of the Plastic People of the Universe. "After Minkovice, I knew what hell was like," Gruntorád says, laying his gnarled hands on a table laden with books and manuscripts waiting to be catalogued.

"We had such optimism in 1989," he says with a small smile and a shrug. "Now? One of the wardens at Minkovice who harassed and sometimes beat me became a spokesman for the prison service in the '90s, and another warden was elected to Parliament."

MUSEUM FOR A VANISHED PEOPLE

A tour of Jewish Prague is likely to be on a list of recommended excursions at most hotels in the city today. It will include at least five synagogues and one multi-level graveyard. The synagogues are all within short walking distances from one another, and each one is an architectural gem of its era. The Old-New Synagogue, built in the thirteenth century, is the oldest in Europe. It combines late Gothic and early Renaissance elements, and it has survived several pogroms and occupations and even its questionable fame for housing the body of the Golem in its attic. The famous story of the giant built by a man who could not, in the end, control it was written by Rabbi Judah Loew ben Bezalel and is available in every gift shop and bookstore in a multitude of languages and sizes, with and without illustrations. Our guide pointed eagerly to a high window where a face is said to appear in times of trouble. The tale, published some two hundred years after the rabbi's death, preserves the fame of this Jewish scholar and mystic today.

The Spanish Synagogue is a few steps from 27 Dušní Street, where the Kafkas lived.[20] Jaroslav Róna's extraordinary bronze statue of Kafka straddles the border between Jewish Town and Old Town. A giant, respectably suited, headless, footless and handless man strides toward the intersection, seemingly unconcerned about the small figure of Franz Kafka sitting on his shoulders. At the 2003 unveiling of his work, Róna talked of the era of senseless trials and camps and of "the cruel, self-ironic jibing" that followed the Nazi years. He did not explain his creation but imagined that Czechs who have "Kafka deep inside them" would bring their own meaning to the disturbing monument.

The nearby Maisel Synagogue is a complete and largely unrecognizable reconstruction of its original Renaissance self, now turned into a permanent exhibition of the early history of Jews in the Czech lands. The second part of the exhibition, housed in the Moorish-style Spanish Synagogue, carries the history of the Jews in Bohemia and Moravia to the present.

I have a strange feeling walking through the exhibits of Torah scrolls, shields, bibles, table settings, silver, textiles, prints and books brought to Prague at Hitler's orders, all duly marked and numbered. It is hard to escape the sense in this well-ordered space, this beautifully designed multi-building museum, that this is more or less what Hitler had intended when he said that Prague would become a museum of an extinct race. Though the buildings themselves are expertly maintained, I am told that the rabbi has a real problem collecting ten men for a minyan on Friday evenings. There are simply not enough Jews in Prague.

In the Pinkas Synagogue, a series of white walls display eighty thousand names of the known Czech victims of the Holocaust. "In 1968," our guide says, "the names were whitewashed." The Czechoslovak government was following Soviet policies regarding Jews and their potential threat as allies of Israel. The names have been added to or deleted over the years. Her father's name, for instance, was in the alphabetical list of those murdered. But when he came home after some years as a Soviet prisoner of war, his name was allowed to stand with those of the other victims. Jews who survived German concentration camps were sometimes picked up by Soviet soldiers, eager to fill their quota of captured foreigners, and transported to Siberia.

On the second floor is an exhibition of children's drawings from Terezín, a transit camp for Jews from 1941 till 1945, where inmates—many of them children—awaited transports to extermination camps. Before being deported to Auschwitz, art teacher Friedl Dicker hid two suitcases filled with about 4,500 children's drawings. This is a selection of those drawings. Most of the children were murdered in Auschwitz, and all that remains of their lives are what you see on the second floor of the synagogue. Near the window to the right of the entrance, there are a couple of drawings by Petr Ginz, a young boy whose diary was published by his sister.

It is the saddest book, so heartbreakingly sad that I wanted to put it down almost as soon as I read the introduction, but there is something so charming, so mischievous and boyish, so ordinary about many of the diary entries that I persevered. I wanted to know more about this boy who cheerfully copied his music test so he would not fail, who invented a form of secret writing, made a violin out of tree bark and rubber bands, struggled with difficult homework, coloured in his grandmother's old engravings, ran for class president while his friends and relations kept disappearing into transports to nowhere. He clung to the normalcy of childhood, fought with his friends, found a bit of personal space by a river where he and his buddies could play once Jews were forbidden to be in the parks.

Petr was only eleven years old on March 15, 1939, when the German armies marched into what Hitler called "this rump country" of Czechoslovakia and put the lie to British prime minister Neville Chamberlain's declaration that Britain had gained "peace with honour" when Chamberlain agreed that the country be divided as Hitler wished. Along with the armies came the restrictive anti-Jewish laws that started by denying Jews education and jobs and ended by denying them life.

Petr's first diary entry is dated November 19, 1941: "The weather is foggy. Jews were told to wear a badge." It is a year and a half after German occupation. By this time, some of the previously unthinkable had become commonplace. On October 1 he writes, "It is Yom Kippur, I fasted from Tuesday evening until Wednesday evening... Lots of people were executed for preparing the sabotage..." A few days later a children's race had to be cancelled because "some boy kept throwing stones at us," and one of Petr's friends is warned not to play with Jews. Then a boy he knows "is leaving with the first transport of five thousand Jews to Poland." It's the first transport from Prague to Auschwitz, where, ultimately, most Czech Jews were murdered.

It is this juxtaposition of the ordinary with the unimaginable that kept me reading: Petr goes to a school performance—theatre, music, singing, one of his teachers plays the violin—and on the way home he learns that Jews had been "terribly beaten up... their entire faces broken"; his mother is thrilled with two gift geese for New Year's Eve, and then all Jews have to hand in their cameras, thermometers, mouth organs and all portable musical instruments, woollen undergarments, furs, pullovers; he aces his oral geography test, and the ss begin their bloody reprisals for the May 29 assassination of Obergruppenführer Reinhard Heydrich. Petr's accounts of the daily death toll is more immediate than the sheer numbers: "... in the afternoon at Grandma's. I heard there was a big massacre near Kladno... In the morning at school... In the afternoon I went for a walk... Again they executed 153 people..."

One by one Petr's teachers and the older students are gathered for departure for Terezín, the closest ghetto/concentration camp to

Prague. He is thrilled that his grandmother can see his final exam results—all A's—before she is deported. All his Jewish relatives and friends line up at the deportation centre, suitcases in hand, as ordered, and leave for the camps. At age fourteen, it's Petr's turn.

His last entries are in his sister's introduction to the book: Petr's attempt to comfort his mother, his farewell to his best friend, his selection of what to take on the journey—"a supply of paper, linoleum, small knives for cutting it, the unfinished novel... some leather for binding, a few watercolours..." His father gave him his best shirts and a thick jacket. His parents still had protection papers as his mother was not Jewish, but according to the anti-Jewish laws, Petr was considered a Jew.

At six o'clock on October 22, 1942, Petr boarded the train for Terezín. It was the only camp the Nazis were happy to show foreign visitors, the camp the Red Cross thought was acceptable; but behind the fake facades, it was not much different from other concentration camps—except that there were no gas chambers here. Instead, those destined to be killed were transported to Auschwitz by regular trainloads as the commandant—Hauptsturmführer Alois Burger at that time—ordered.

Petr survived two years in Terezín. Squeezed into a low wooden barrack with no comforts, he continued to write, paint, read and plan for the future.

He was selected for transfer to Auschwitz in late 1944 and murdered mere months before the end of the war, and of the Reich.

THE MORALIST AND THE ECONOMISTS

During the heady days of November–December 1989, so many people were offering to become part of the spanking new Civic Forum that later Václav Havel did not remember meeting Václav Klaus before Klaus's appointment to the finance portfolio. He had, of course, heard of Klaus—they had both been on the editorial board of a literary journal—but even after the appointment, Havel had difficulty recognizing the new minister of finance.

Although no one is sure when Klaus arrived at Laterna Magika, there was general agreement that he seemed to be the best-qualified man for the tough job of improving Czechoslovakia's shaky financial situation. Forty years of central planning had destroyed what had once been a powerful industrial base. Klaus was not only an economics graduate, he had been at Cornell University in the United States, and he had worked at the State Bank of Czechoslovakia and at the strange Prognostics Institute, where economists were forecasting the country's future well into the next century. The Institute's predictions for Czechoslovakia all the way to 2010 were so critical of the country's economy that the government prevented their publication, but after a few chapters were read on Radio Free Europe, the Party allowed some of the papers to be published in *Politická ekonomie*.

While Havel, as president of the Czechoslovak federation, hesitated about making tough decisions on economic reforms, Klaus pushed from the beginning for radical, rapid transition to market reform. The two men also clashed over the shape of the constitution and the importance of keeping the federation together. In 1991, Klaus founded the Civic Democratic Party, mostly from early rightwing supporters of Civic Forum. His party won in the 1992 Czech elections at the same time as Vladimir Mečiar's Movement for a Democratic Slovakia won on the Slovak side of what had already become a great divide between the partners in the federation. Havel's efforts to find common ground, to hold the country together, were all blocked in the federal parliament—by the Slovak deputies as well as many of Klaus's followers. Mečiar believed that an independent Slovakia would give him an ideal base to effect the changes he wished for, and Klaus had begun to see the Slovaks as a liability.

When both Klaus and Mečiar assumed the leadership of their respective geographic areas, the federation was doomed. Still mourned by Havel, Halík, Urban and many of the original Civic Forum—the "elite," as Klaus derisively called them—it fell victim to two men's ambitions and rather similar views on what was good for the future. Masaryk's dream country was divided into two separate entities without a bullet being fired, and Klaus and Mečiar assumed the role of prime minister, respectively, of the Czech Republic and Slovakia. After the "Velvet Revolution" had come the "Velvet Divorce."

During the years that followed, Klaus and Havel continued to clash over a multitude of issues both large and small, ranging from foreign policy to the importance of "civil society" non-governmental organizations in a democracy. Klaus believes that no unelected person or organization should have the right to influence government. Havel is adamant that they are vital to a healthy democracy. Havel apologized for the Czechoslovak treatment of "Sudeten" Germans after the war; Klaus condemned their cooperation with Nazi Germany and resisted all acknowledgment of Czechoslovak wrongdoing. He accused Havel of taking unnecessary risks on behalf of Czechs when the latter invited Salman Rushdie to Prague Castle, the Hrad, in September 1993. They disagreed about the Visegrád Group—Poland, Czech Republic, Slovakia and Hungary, whose Central European location made them ideal allies in Havel's view and quite unnecessary in Klaus's. Klaus opposes making the environment a matter of national concern and speaks derisively of global warming. Havel thinks this is shortsighted and urges each person to take responsibility for the degradation of the world.

They clashed over Havel's wish to decentralize power and over the corruption surrounding Klaus's voucher privatization, which Havel referred to as "gangster privatization."

The voucher system allowed people without cash or securities to buy state enterprises as thousands of companies were privatized. With the brand-newness of all this, some felt safer if they gave their vouchers to "privatization funds" that promised to take care of the new shareholders' interests. Václav Klaus's swift "voucher privatization" led to the fleecing of Czech companies and a level of corruption that Adam Smith would have found astonishing.

The regular Wednesday meetings with Klaus had turned into such dreadful experiences for Havel that he lost sleep each Tuesday night.

Klaus held the job until his party was defeated by Miloš Zeman's in 1997.

I MET Miloš Zeman in his city apartment-cum-office across from the main railway station. It's a traditional building with a large open courtyard, a doorman, a parking space for the Zeman car and a chauffeur who drives him from his village home to Prague once a week.

During Prague Spring, Zeman had joined Alexander Dubček's Communist Party, but he lost his Party card for criticizing the hardliners who supported the Warsaw Pact's invasion. From 1971 till 1984, he was employed as a long-term forecaster by Sportpropag, a sports organization, where he developed a centre to predict future trends. He also produced such astonishing papers as *Immanuel Kant and Sports.* The StB member who listed him as an "enemy person" seemed unaware of the humour. Zeman lost his job. When he joined Civic Forum at the end of 1989, he was quick to point out that unless the country changed direction, it would be bankrupt in a couple of years. He was elected leader of the Social Democratic Party, then prime minister of the Czech Republic from 1998 till 2002.

His secretary, Mr. Gregr, a former member of his 1998 cabinet and a card-carrying Communist Party member before 1989, is a small, rather anxious man who brings wine and coffee, scurries in and out of the room where he placed me to wait, organizes papers in files, checks the phones for messages and pulls chairs into position in what turns out to be Zeman's office. Zeman arrives with a flourish. He is a huge man, towering over me and the secretary, endangering the low coffee table as he shoves past it with a wide-open smile and a handshake that could break more fragile fingers than mine.

He talks with gusto about his effort to transform the failed economy. "In two years, we turned things around. I am a long-time Keynesian, never tempted by Milton Friedman, never interested in trying Jeffrey Sachs's methods." In two years, he told me, his government changed the legal system, established the protections for human rights, privatized banks, the media, all non-public-sector institutions. Unlike the idealist Havel, who may have hoped people would learn to be entrepreneurs with the stroke of a pen, Zeman says he opposed voucher privatization: "Without a legal framework, it offered an opening for thieves."

He is quick to point out that the real enemies in this part of the world are not, no matter what the purists would like us to believe, former Communists. Zeman once belonged to the Communist Youth organization, and he has no time for the men who run the lustration archives.

"They are fanatics, and they know the big fish all disappeared in the final years, as have their files. The anti-Communist manifesto was produced by past Communists. We had a number of them in our first government," he adds with a smile. "There is no critic of ideas as knowledgeable as a man who used to believe in them. Even Russians," he shouts, "are going to give up on their discredited dreams of a proletarian Utopia. Russia will become a member of NATO, as we have. I do not see it as a danger to us or anyone else in the world."

Rather, he says, it's the extremists who threaten the stability of Central Europe. "The real danger, as you must know by now, is Islam. I fully support the United States in its endeavour to fight Islamist terrorism. What I don't understand is why the West decided to support Kosovo. Its current ruler, much like the men the West prosecutes in the Hague, participated in the execution of his opponents. Or do you think that terror is divisible? That good can come out of evil?"

I remember now that Havel had found him to be stubborn, loud-mouthed, but the best orator of all living Czech politicians. Zeman leans across the narrow table, his grey-white hair flopping over his forehead, his eyes narrowed, then he smiles and fills his glass with more wine. "Are you sure you won't try it? Have you ever tried Czech wine?" He laughs a huge closed-eyes, stomach-shaking laugh, then he leans back into the wide settee. "I guarantee it's as good as yours."

I assumed he was referring to Canadian wines, until Gregr saw me out of the building and I realized Zeman had categorized me as a Hungarian. Hungary happens to make some of the best wines in the region.

Strangely enough, Zeman was not the only forecaster to have joined Civic Forum. Václav Klaus, who succeeded Havel as president in March 2003, worked for the Prognostics Institute of the Czechoslovak Academy of Sciences until his decision to become a politician.

THE JOYS OF UNRESTRAINED CAPITALISM

Adam Smith's eighteenth-century classic and perennial bestseller *An Inquiry into the Nature and Causes of the Wealth of Nations* advocates a free-market economy but does not open the way for unbridled greed without obligations. Smith believed that people's behaving in a way that promoted their own interests would also benefit society. However, when he mentioned the "invisible hand" to describe the role of competition in the free market, he did not mean a hand that furtively steals from others. He was a philosopher who believed in our innate ability to form moral judgments, despite our inclination to self-deal.

While Klaus took credit for the Czech "economic miracle," the fast transformation from state to private ownership, he failed to mention his leading role in forcing the privatization of state enterprises before instituting new laws to govern their new owners' behaviour.

The fast-emerging new enterprises drew an increasing number of speculators who used the voucher system to purchase state-owned corporations, siphon their value into privately owned companies and allow the original corporation to subside into bankruptcy. The Czechs even invented their own word for the practice: "tunnelling." Miloš Zeman labelled privatization "the fraud of the century" and predicted that his country would be "the first state that succeeded in almost completely robbing itself."[21] Václav Havel talked of the Mafia-like way in which former Communists exploited the system.

Klaus accused the former Civic Forum members of slowing down his essential reforms. In a 2006 speech recorded in the Cato Institute *Economic Development Bulletin,* he denounced the Communist reformers of the 1960s and the former dissidents for opposing his agenda. By labelling both a self-declared elite group of intellectuals, he wanted all to see that he was a man of the people.

"The world, they reasoned, was supposed to be governed by a chosen few," according to Klaus. "They considered market forces demeaning." Given his proudly displayed degrees and his admiration for the Milton Friedman style of economics, it is difficult to see Klaus as folksy, but that is what he has been striving toward. *The Economist* suggested that Klaus should be labelled "nationalistic populist" instead of Thatcherite, which had been his preference.

That the former *nomenklatura* would emerge the winners in the new capitalist system was not unique to Czechs, but the clever way in which some enterprises were ruined for the sole purpose of private greed, without a chance of prosecution, was a Czech phenomenon.

"You can't produce a thousand brand-new judges overnight," Havel said by way of explanation or excuse.

Several private banks, according to *Respekt*'s Erik Tabery, were complicit in a system of lending money to individuals who would not be able to repay loans, often on the advice of government luminaries. Tabery talks of Investiční a Poštovní Banka (IPB), once the country's third-largest bank, whose chairman and deputy chairmen were eventually charged with illegal business practices, and Agrobanka, eleven of whose senior executives were charged with fraud. IPB had been one of Klaus's favoured banks, a regular large-scale contributor to his political party. Jiří Weigl, long-time Klaus associate, had been a director. According to Tabery, Klaus protected his protegé banks from foreign influence and from meddling in their balance sheets. IPB collapsed, as did Agrobanka, whose remaining assets were finally sold to GE Capital.

George Soros, the American philanthropist billionaire, cancelled his plans to set up his Central European University in Prague because Václav Klaus did not welcome him. Klaus, in Soros's opinion, believes in the "pursuit of self-interest" unalloyed by the need to make sacrifices for the common good. "In my view," Soros says in *Soros on Soros*, "Klaus embodies the worst of the Western democracies, just as the pre-revolutionary Czech regime represented the worst of communism." Soros set up his university in Budapest and, while he has supported numerous causes in Europe, he has stayed out of Prague.

Despite his reservations, though, Soros admits his funds did well with voucher privatization.

OF CHARTER 77, Jan Patočka wrote, "No society, no matter how good its technological foundations can function without a moral foundation, without conviction that has nothing to do with opportunism, circumstances and expected advantage. Man does not define morality according to the caprice of his needs, wishes, tendencies and cravings; it is morality that defines man."[22] Or, he could have added, it is the lack of morality that also defines man.

After 1989, the former Iron Curtain countries were so eager to become Westernized, so willing to accept capitalism as part of the bargain that would allow them to join with the winning side of the ideological wars, that they did not notice that capitalism had become, as Slovak journalist Martin Simecka observed, "emptied of its sense of fairness and responsibility." As the temptations of instant riches overwhelmed former Communist societies, as opportunities for corruption grew, someone should have posted Patočka's statement on bulletin boards throughout the region.

IN 2009, the U.S. and Europe moved to fix their economies, approving direct government involvement in faltering banks, trust companies and the auto sector. Czechs were anxious not be trapped into the "Third World" again. Fortunately, having learned caution during the previous decade, Czech banks remained stable. The currency could still be devalued, and the day of converting to the euro could be postponed. Unemployment rose but not into the disaster zones of other European countries. Czech reliance on exports was hammered by the worldwide recession, but local entrepreneurs were showing remarkable resilience. If only they would curb countrywide corruption and the rise of racism and populist xenophobia, the next few years would be restful.

Martin Palouš, Czech ambassador to the United Nations, said, "History didn't end with the victory of Western liberalism, as Fukuyama claimed." He had been fiercely pacing his spacious New York office, remembering scenes from twenty years ago when he took part in the protests that changed the face of Central Europe. He stopped suddenly and smiled. "We have merely started another chapter."

THE DANGERS OF MEMORY

When I was in Prague in September 2009, Václav Klaus was much too busy to see me. The Czechs were to ascend to the presidency of the EU. In the middle of a worldwide financial crisis, Mirek Topolánek's centre-right government was forced to resign after a no-confidence vote, thus boosting some EU members' jaundiced view of their Eastern members' stability. Topolánek had not been Klaus's first choice for the leadership of his former party. The local press, depending on its appreciation of President Václav Klaus's politics, either gloried in or decried the fact that he was largely responsible for this international embarrassment.

An arrogant, outspoken man, Klaus is a formidable EU skeptic, refusing to endorse closer ties with the rest of Europe. When the Czech Republic joined the European Union in 2004, he did not take part in the celebrations. He went hiking. He has criticized the EU for being overregulated and excessively bureaucratic—a view he shares with his avowed political idol, former British prime minister Margaret Thatcher—but it is equally likely that his suspicions of the EU stem from his Czech nationalism. He has spoken about "the creeping, silent unification of the continent" as a threat to the sovereignty of its member nations.

If Klaus wouldn't see me, then Jiří Weigl, chancellor of the Office of the President, would. *Respekt* editor Erik Tabery had assured me that Weigl agreed with Klaus on every single issue, including what clothes to wear. Havel favours baggy jeans, open shirts, corduroy jackets; Klaus prefers suit, tie and starched white shirt. For our meeting in the Castle, Jiří Weigl was dressed formally, as would befit a man in his august position. He is a dapper, immaculately polite man with thick black eyebrows, well-groomed hair, a small, expertly shaped goatee and the impeccable manners of a diplomat.

Weigl had been one of President Klaus's economics students in the mid-1980s at the Academy of Sciences. When Klaus became minister of finance of the Czech and Slovak Federal Republic, Weigl was one of his advisers, and he took part in planning the far-reaching economic reforms that included the restitution of property to former owners, some small-scale business privatizations and the voucher distribution scheme designed to make citizens into instant shareholders. Klaus took credit for the turnaround of the economy, low unemployment, a reasonable level of inflation and robust growth in the GDP. Weigl followed Klaus to the prime minister's office in the Czech Republic and is now happily ensconced in the president's office, in the ancient seat of the Bohemian kings. Along the way, he has collected two real PhDs (Klaus has dozens of honorary doctorates from a range of universities): one in Oriental languages, the other in economics.

His office is located in the royal palace, the Castle's third courtyard kitty-corner from the magnificent St. Vitus Cathedral. The view from his windows takes in the orange and pink tile roofs of the city and stretches past the river to the Old Town's Gothic spires and baroque domes. The dominant presence in his enormous office—not counting the view—is the life-size painting of Tomáš Garrigue Masaryk, philosopher, statesman, founder of Czechoslovakia, the man who had been responsible for carving a country out of Austria-Hungary after its disastrous loss as Germany's partner in the First World War and convincing the battle-weary Allies that it would become a perfect democracy.

With an obvious reference to the Sudeten Germans and the Slovaks of the 1930s, Weigl suggests that citizens' hopes for a brighter future were dashed on the altars of xenophobia—the Slovaks wanted their own country; the Germans had other plans.

It was the German minority in Czechoslovakia that wished to identify with Hitler's Nazi state. The national trauma of Czechs who know history is still Neville Chamberlain's "peace in our time," the agreement the British prime minister reached in Munich with Hitler in September 1938. Hitler had been agitating on behalf of Sudeten Germans inside Czechoslovakia. At the Munich Conference, while the Czech delegation waited in an anteroom, the French and the British agreed to give Germany the Sudetenland, a part of Czechoslovakia that contained most of its industrial base as well as its fortifications against Germany. The gentlemen who betrayed Czechoslovakia in Munich were inclined to listen to Hitler's argument in the interests of avoiding war.

Chamberlain referred to the Czechoslovak resistance to German might as "a quarrel in a faraway country between people of whom we know nothing." That he called the country "insignificant" and claimed to have trouble finding it on a map still irks Czechs, as does their president's unconditional surrender of a chunk of their country into German hands. Jiří Weigl is no exception.

In Milan Kundera's telling of the familiar story, "at Munich in the autumn of 1938, four great nations, Germany, Italy, France and Great Britain, negotiated the fate of a small country to whom they denied the very right to speak... In a room apart the two Czech diplomats waited all night to be led, the next morning, down long hallways into a room where Chamberlain and Daladier, weary, blasé, yawning, informed them of the death sentence." After that, the Czech lands had been an easy prey to the German armies.

Czechoslovakia barely protested when the Germans marched in a year later. In the summer of 1942, some quarter of a million Czechs swore allegiance to the Third Reich and sang the national anthem in Wenceslas Square.

Weigl showed me the table and chair once occupied by Hitler's henchman, Obergruppenführer Reinhard Heydrich, Hitler's man in Czechoslovakia. "Hangman Heydrich," as he was known in Germany, was shot by Czech commandos on May 29, 1942, and died of his wounds on June 4; 1,331 Czechs, and three thousand Jews were killed (not including the 152 Berlin Jews Göring ordered executed in reprisal, though they never learned of Heydrich's death).

"Because of our experience of foreign domination," Weigl says, "Václav Klaus fights whoever wishes to dominate us. The EU's dominion-making is moving farther and farther from the people the EU pretends to speak for." He puts Klaus in a straight line of descent from Masaryk's idea of a democrat, a believer in the freedom of the individual. "One of the cornerstones of his thinking is the protection of civic freedom, the right of the people to choose their own future."

Klaus was the last to sign the EU's Lisbon Treaty, on November 3, 2009, and he demanded, as a condition of signing, that a clause be added guaranteeing that the deported Sudeten Germans give up all attempts at the restitution of their expropriated pre-war properties. Not surprisingly, given his own brand of populist nationalism, Slovak prime minister Robert Fico followed suit, insisting on a similar rule for his country.

Klaus's move revived memories of the discredited 1940–1945 Beneš decrees—not one of Czechoslovakia's brightest moments—by which about 2.6 million (some documents state 3 million) Germans and several thousand Hungarians were expelled from Czechoslovakia with Stalin's active encouragement. The postwar ethnic cleansing of Czechoslovakia was seen, even then, as collective punishment. The explanation was that the Sudeten German Party had vigorously supported Germany's 1938 claim of the Sudetenland and Hungary was Germany's ally during the war, but the expulsions were brutal, the confiscations of property smacking of revenge. The treatment of women and children as if they had been direct participants in the war was, to say the least, unfair.

The bitterness on both sides of the Sudeten German issue persists.

Perhaps Tomáš Masaryk would have opposed the inhumane deportations and the confiscations of property. Perhaps he would have found another solution to what is often presented as a moral issue. Perhaps. But the Beneš expulsions were, Weigl says, when "looking down the long lens of history, only one of many confiscations. The Habsburgs took from the princes of the old kingdom; the Germans took from the Czechs and the Jews. The Communists took from everyone." Restitution is, simply, impossible.

As one of Klaus's former aides put it in the *Süddeutsche Zeitung,* it was "cheap populism based on panic-mongering."[23] However, the truth is that if the property claims of the dispossessed Sudeten Germans were honoured today, a significant number of Czechs would lose their homes.

As usual, Klaus has hit on a hot button issue for his countrymen: if the West could betray you once, it could, as easily, do so again.

"We shouldn't believe in illusions," says Jiří Weigl, with a glance at the portrait of Masaryk. "Our grandparents believed in illusions, and our parents believed," he says with a sigh. "There was once a hard-fought peace and there was once a Communist paradise."

THE PATRICIAN PHILOSOPHER

In the years after Jan Patočka's death, his good friend Tomáš Halík "discovered that faith gives us the strength to stand the test of the difficult circumstances of persecution."

Halík was ordained a Catholic priest in 1978 in a secret ceremony in East Germany. Given the regime's animosity to the Catholic Church, being ordained in East Germany was still a risk, but not as great a risk as his ordination would have been in Czechoslovakia, where the StB watched his every move. He was regularly investigated, called in for questioning and banned from teaching. He worked as a therapist with alcoholics and drug addicts—a perfectly suitable job for a priest, he thought at the time. After the Velvet Revolution, he was one of Václav Havel's advisers.

Halík is a tall, balding man with a round, well-trimmed dark beard, an open-necked shirt with button-down collar and a frequent smile he offers every time someone stops by to greet him. We met in a student bar near the university where he teaches—he has doctorates in philosophy, theology and sociology—between lecture tours. Judging by the number of people who come by his table, he is well liked.

He talked of his friendships with other dissidents, of the continuing problem of racial intolerance and his determination to find common threads that tie the warring world religions together. He believes in remaining open to new ideas, to the "other," to dialogue. Unlike Zeman, he does not draw the line at Muslims. He is a Central European intellectual of the Václav Havel–Adam Michnik–Bronisław Geremek–George Konrád school.

In 1998, when Havel told the media that Halík would be an ideal candidate to succeed him, Halík declined, because he no longer saw the presidency as a position that can influence ideas and ideals. The presidency here, as everywhere else, has become a contest between political parties and business interests. It is no longer a place for a philosopher.

"To realize the platonic ideal of the 'philosopher king' is unrealistic except in very special occasions," he said, "such as Masaryk after World War I and Havel after the fall of Communism."

Instead, Halík has lectured at universities throughout Europe, chatted with the pope about religious freedom, discussed mutual understanding with Hindus, Muslims and Jews and written over two hundred books and articles, and he still finds time to laugh at himself.

We walk to his church in the dark, dodging around buildings facing narrow alleyways and eager tourists looking for the old town. We skirt the Theatre on the Balustrade (Divadlo Na Zábradlí), a white, three-storey building that offers a mix of drama and comedy. Halík tells me that this is where Havel first staged *The Garden Party,* as part of the Balustrade's Theatre of the Absurd program. For a moment I glimpse the amazing Gothic towers of the Church of Our

Lady before Týn on Old Town Square, when Halík pauses to give me a chance to see it lit up for the evening.

Halík's church is the bulbous-towered St. Salvator, on the Knights of the Cross Square near Charles Bridge. Its long isles, simple nave and altar suit his personality. As the title of one of his recent books, *Patience with God*, suggests, he still has a few things to settle with his God. We say goodbye in the alleyway that leads to the vestry.

When I turn back, I see him in the church. He has put on his cassock and dropped to one knee in front of the altar, made the sign of the cross over his chest; he stays that way for a while, very still, head bent, shoulders forward. When he stands up, his face has become gentler, but somehow more resigned. He prepares for the evening mass as the church fills with mostly young people. "There is a lot of optimism among the young," he told me, "and they are still willing to make sacrifices for the future."

Perhaps the time for idealists such as Tomas Masaryk and Václav Havel, intellectuals who based their politics on morality, is not yet past.

THE CRUSADER

As a journalist, Jan Urban has won two international human rights awards—a Humanitas Human Rights Award in 1991 and an award from Centro Demos in San Salvador in 1995. He travelled extensively in Central America to study the problems of post-conflict societies and the media, and worked as a war correspondent in Bosnia and Herzegovina from 1993 to 1996.

His latest book, however, is about conflicts closer to home: corruption and its beneficiaries versus the moral society Patočka had defined and Havel advocates still.

"It isn't that corruption is any worse here than in neighbouring countries," Jan Urban told me. "It is just that we had expected more of ourselves."

When I last saw him, he was vehemently engaged with the need to expose corruption, especially corrupt politicians, to what he says is a generally indifferent public and, if the political will is not there to fire them, at least to shame them out of office.

He is as intense and restless as he was the last time we met, in my improbable hotel on Wenceslas Square. He has just come from visiting a friend in hiding from some branch of the local mafia, thugs hired by vested interests to prevent him from testifying at a corruption trial. Urban's special interest is the pursuit of politicians who take cash for favours, including his recent spat with one of the largest Czech companies he accused of bribing both of the leading political parties. When he first went after them, six years ago, the radio station that carries his commentaries fired him. He sued and was reinstated, but neither the initial accusations nor the subsequent court case damaged the company or the politicians he sought to expose. Another of his recent targets, Ivana Řápková, mayor of the North Bohemia town of Chomutov, called Urban "raw evil" on a television show, for his attempts to expose her election campaign as racist and financed by those who owe her favours for past gifts of a newspaper and construction business.

He has been waging a lonely battle against the judiciary. "Can you imagine," he asks, eyes wide, "in a Western country, two couples appointed to the highest courts in the land? Two couples? All of them, coincidentally, friends of President Klaus. That's the same president who referred to the wartime Roma camps that led to the extermination of most of Czech Roma as 'labour camps.' Is it any wonder the Roma are trying to escape to Canada?" He asks whether I have followed his story about the "blood plasma" case,[24] and did I know about Viktor Kožený, the disappeared billionaire who siphoned money from shareholders and is evading their ire on a tax-free island?[25]

"I haven't fought against Communism to see my country run by people who have no moral sense. Mobsters," he says, struggling into his rain jacket and striding across the café, his head down, shoulders hunched, glancing about as if he is expecting a blow. Czechs, it seems, were not so indifferent to abuses of power and corruption in business as Jan Urban had feared. The May 2010 parliamentary elections turfed out both ruling parties and replaced them with Prince Karel Schwarzenberg's fiscally conservative-socially liberal reformers who promised to establish the rule of law. Schwarzenberg, an old-fashioned politician and former foreign minister, has long complained about political influence on judges, "tunnellers" flaunting

their unseemly wealth and the destructive effects of pervasive corruption. He has promised to salvage public finances and restore
Czechs' self-respect.

As the venerable House of Schwarzenberg served the Habsburg
empire with distinction for some centuries, there is reason to assume
that the Prince, who does not use his titles, will serve his country
well. Another hopeful sign: the record turn-out of young people to
vote.

THE ANNIVERSARY

Summer Meditations, Václav Havel's political testament, imagined a
bucolic future in an age that is rarely accessible to modern man. "Life
in the towns and villages will have overcome the legacy of greyness,
uniformity, anonymity, and ugliness inherited from the totalitarian era. It will have a genuine human dimension. Every main street
will have at least two bakeries, two sweet shops, two pubs, and many
other small shops, all privately owned and independent..."

When he wrote this, Havel must have been thinking of an era that
was ending, as big-box stores like IKEA and chains like McDonald's
and Starbucks moved into the small towns and began a new march
to uniformity. It was not the forced uniformity that characterized Communist Czechoslovakia but the uniformity of small-town
America, a consumer culture that makes each place much the same
as another, where the cheapest goods, the best deals, fast food and
consumers rule. It is a world that led to the collapse of the quick,
profit-driven American car industry; that allowed giant lenders
to misuse public trust to create nothing but shells of value without
substance.

"It appears that we have a great choice in the supermarket but in
fact it is a variety that is false," Havel told Adam Michnik in a *Gazeta
Wyborcza* interview. "We are losing centres of social self-manage-
ment—such as small shops and pubs. All this goes hand in hand with
the destruction of the environment... I don't see many great moral
or spiritual authorities in our world today."

Now, as Adam Michnik predicted so many years ago, Václav Havel
has retired. "A charismatic leader initially wields almost metaphysi-
cal power," Michnik said. "His entitlement to authority springs from

the past: it is he who worked the miracle, it is he who toppled the dictatorship and brought freedom. But his charisma is apt to fade under democratic conditions... At this stage, the charismatic leader is in danger of becoming a caricature of himself." Turning to Havel, he asked, "Vašek, how will you feel when the clapping stops?"[26] What Havel did in 2003 was to cede the Hrad to his hard-nosed enemy, Václav Klaus, who had once accused him of being in love with power.

I LAST saw Havel at Forum 2000 in September 2009. Since 1997, the Forum 2000 Foundation has organized gatherings in Prague of various personalities from all over the world to discuss topics ranging from religion and human rights to national security, terrorism and conflicts in civilization. The annual gatherings have become central to media, as well as political, intellectual and business, elites and the interested public.

As all Forum 2000 conferences, September 2009 was flawlessly planned by Havel's friend Oldřich Černý. Černý had been head of the intelligence service from January 1993 till the end of 1998, a role, he told me, he was least likely to play with distinction, but how could he refuse when Havel asked? "The good jobs, foreign policy, human rights, ecology had already been taken. Nobody wanted to touch security." Several others had already turned down the job and, well, somebody had to do it!

Černý did not sign Charter 77. "I was afraid," he says with a disarming smile. He is a small, energetic man with sandy hair and very blue eyes. His English is almost flawless. That he had been jobless, considered a pariah by the Communist government, drove him to taking a range of freelance assignments translating English books into Czech. He had been thrilled to get a job at last with a children's book publisher and, later, in a studio dubbing films. His biggest hit: *Lassie Come Home*—hardly suitable training for national security.

The 2009 Forum venue was Prague Crossroads, a conference centre built into the skeleton of an old church—AD 927, says the brochure, and ordered by St. Wenceslas himself—that retains its frescoes, arched glass windows, peeling paint, wooden cross-hatched raft ceiling, even a Romanesque rotunda of somewhat later addition. The church was restored and refurbished by the Dagmar and Václav Havel Foundation VIZE 97, the non-profit organization that holds most of Havel's hundred million crowns received as restitution for the Havel brothers' pre-war property. The windfall included Lucerna, a building in the centre of Prague, and the Barrandov Terraces on the outskirts. In *To the Castle and Back*, Havel acknowledges that his new-found wealth aroused hostility among Czechs who opposed the new laws that created such wealth—"another of our Communist paradoxes," he said.

Dagmar—Dasa, as friends and the tabloids call her—is Havel's second wife (Olga died in 1996), an outspoken actress whose clothes style and past roles in mindless comedies and a vampire movie incited delicious scandals during the first year of their marriage. The scandals have since died down, as has her penchant for revealing clothes and bouffant blond tresses. Some think she has aged into her new role as the famous intellectual's wife, others that she was cowed into this subdued act by her husband's friends and advisers. Havel credits her with saving his life on at least two occasions: once when he needed lung surgery, again when he had a ruptured intestine that no one else had noticed.[27] I thought she still looked beautiful and the long blond curls did not seem ready to give up their theatrical life.

This year's Forum theme was sombre: Peace, Democracy and Human Rights in Asia, with opening remarks by the Dalai Lama, whose country was still under China's control. Despite that—and though no head of state gave him an official welcome here, as none had done in Bratislava, where he was the night before—His Holiness insisted on being his usual cheery self.[28] China's wealth has long arms, even in Central Europe. Whether it was the strangeness of the venue, the incongruity of the name of the conference or his saffron robes and beatific smile, His Holiness seemed to reduce the audience to silence, except for the incessant click of cameras that reaffirmed his renown as an international star.

When Havel took the stage, however, the audience was no longer quiet. It rose to its collective feet, clapped, shouted and wept. The tears were real, if a little distressing as nostalgia for a simpler time. Havel stands for the lost innocence of Prague's 1989 moral high point, when everything seemed possible. For the time when he first entered the Castle and his friends rode his gift scooter down the long corridors recently vacated by the regime that used to consign them to its jail, laughing and talking.

He is a slight man in a dark suit, with unruly hair—a Central European intellectual from Bohemia, quiet, determined, peculiarly unafraid of deprivation. He was born to bourgeois money, the kind of heritage that meant he could not attend university under the Communists' rules. But he read voraciously and almost indiscriminately. He used his work experiences after his plays were banned as material for more plays. He continued to write throughout his life, though he was harassed and imprisoned for his words. In his welcoming remarks, he talked of the necessity for human beings to reflect on their own actions, to be open to learning of the experiences of others, to listen and become aware of worlds beyond their own.

I had the strange sense that at least some aspect of his remarks was addressed to his successor in the Hrad, Václav Klaus. Klaus, who is notoriously arrogant, has rarely shown an interest in other people's points of view.

As the West's favourite symbol of non-violent resistance to Communism's inhumane regimes and its favourite spokesman for democracy, Havel has appeared on too many world stages to welcome one more interview. But he is persuaded by Černý, and we crowd into a tiny, perhaps seven-by-seven-metre, dressing room at stage left. The wide mirror and reflecting light, ideal for an actor about to make a public appearance, make him seem exhausted and lethargic. He had throat surgery early in 2009. He seems frail; his voice is husky.

He talks, briefly, of his new venture, a film he is working on—writing the script, taking part in the casting and directing. He is confident it will be released in March 2011. "The best way," he says with a self-deprecating smile, "to face the dangers of senility is to work. To find a new adventure..."

I wanted to ask him about the recent documentary film *Občan Havel* ("Citizen Havel"), which made its debut in Poland. "Super-Czech on the silver screen," enthused one reviewer, who went on to talk of the man who has become a legend in his own lifetime. I didn't raise the subject because he is impatient with questions about his status as a symbol or a hero. He has always viewed himself as a man who has arrived at his station almost accidentally. He prefers irony and humour to romanticism.

About his hopes for his country, he tells me, at least there are no imminent catastrophes in sight. "We are like Holland, relatively secure, just another democracy. Like the others, we don't know how to face globalization; we are groping our way in the dark. I assume," he shrugs, "it has to be that way. We are banal capitalists, having drawn no lessons from fifty years of the West's own experiences... But at least we have free speech." I assume he means we are all free to criticize our governments. He has made no secret of his opposition to what he sees as the lack of morality in current Czech politics.

In *To the Castle and Back,* Havel said his most important accomplishment as president was the dissolution of the Warsaw Pact. Today he is reluctant to talk of his accomplishments.

On the way out, Černy reminds me that Havel withdrew his candidacy for the Nobel Peace Prize in 1991 so that Burmese democracy leader Aung San Suu Kyi would be sure to get it. "We already have our democracy, you need yours," Havel said at the time.

IN 2009, the Plastic People of the Universe rarely play, and rock is, in any event, a bit passé in Prague. Paul Wilson still translates Havel into English, but they are, he says, both slowing down a bit.

Theatres are no longer platforms for political discussions or spirited debates about society. They produce comedies, drama and musicals similar to those on stages in London, Berlin and Paris. Laterna Magika is now part of the National Theatre and bills itself as the ideal venue for kids of all ages. You can book a seat for a colourful performance of actors, dancers and film in flashy glass and steel building. Saturday evenings the auditorium is full of tourists—as is the rest of the city. Prague has become a favourite destination for all comers, a giant city bazaar of Gothic towers and baroque facades, ostentatious galleries, public sculptures and history. It treats its visitors to church concerts, Mozart nights, rich restaurants and, if you can afford it, trips to the Republic's many exotic spas. And, in the teeth of all dire predictions, the last Czech opinion poll[29] of the first decade of the new century found that most Czechs were "successful in their personal lives" and many expected 2010 to be an even better year than 2009.

While European leaders debated how to deal with the spectre of global warming, Czech president Václav Klaus was promoting his new book, *Blue Planet in Green Shackles,* which denies the existence of global warming. It has been published in twelve languages. (The Russian edition was subsidized by Russian oil giant Lukoil.) A few weeks before the United Nations conference in Copenhagen, Klaus told a Washington audience that the choice for the world was between "carbon capping or prosperity through freedom... productivity and hard work."

Havel said in a 2007 interview that Czechs "got used to the fact that Klaus sometimes got under our skin, and to his capacity for radiating a negative energy, to his brand of irony, to his narcissism, and to his aversion—which he mostly kept well hidden—to the rest of us, whom he had clearly consigned to the same dumpster, with a sign on it saying 'left-wing intellectuals.'" But he added later, "I don't think that modern, post-revolutionary Czech history ought to be seen as the history of the personal relationship between me and Václav Klaus."[30] And yet, twenty years after the beginning of democratic governments in Central Europe, the undisguised mutual dislike between Klaus and Havel remains one of the most talked-of facts in Czech politics.

They both appeared at the ostentatiously billed Debate and Gala Evening to Mark the Twentieth Anniversary of the Political Changes in Czechoslovakia and the End of the Iron Curtain. In a preface to the program, Havel mentioned that he wished to "recall especially the role of music which was an inherent part of the events of those days and accompanied them," and to "raise the issue of whether the ideals of that period were transformed into reality."

Jan Urban was there. So were Martin Bútora from Bratislava, former United States secretary of state Madeleine Albright, Tom Stoppard, Adam Michnik. And, of course, that constant commentator and eyewitness to the ending of totalitarianism in Central Europe,

Timothy Garton Ash. The venue was the splendid old church of Prague Crossroads, the band played the Plastic People's "Magic Night," Lou Reed, Suzanne Vega and Renée Fleming sang. There were video messages from Angela Merkel, Mikhail Gorbachev, Barack Obama and the Dalai Lama. And Havel, of course. He spoke of his simple statement about truth and love prevailing over lies and hatred and how, for twenty years, he has been ridiculed for this simple, unplanned thought that came to him when he was pushed to the balcony of Wenceslas Square the night he made his first speech to the people. Ignoring the laughter, he said there must something in that little sentence if it still annoyed his detractors. He also spoke of the dangers of "prisoner syndrome" and, using his own experience as an example, he recalled the time when all decisions were made for him and the difficulty of having to make his own decisions once he was out of jail. In the world inside everything is certain. In the outside world, nothing is. You have to learn to think for yourself. He warned against accepting easy, ready-made answers and against newly sophisticated methods of manipulating people. Some people cried. Others cheered.

I want to remind him of the end of his book, *To the Castle and Back,* when he asks Dasa about the past twenty years: "Was it not also suspenseful, exciting, exhilarating, and occasionally full of laughter?"

Determined to express optimism about the future, Havel told Adam Michnik, "One day, when new generations, unspoilt by communism and normalization, have grown up, cynicism will lose its power and its practitioners will be forced out of social life. Herein, I hope, lies the chance for a real change."

On April 10, 2010, U.S. president Obama, fresh from signing a nuclear limits treaty with Russian president Dmitry Medvedev, stood in front of the bulbous-towered St. Nicholas Church in Prague and echoed Havel: "We are here today because enough people ignored the voices who told them that the world could not change."

THREE

SLOVAKIA

THE USES OF HISTORY

FOR OVER a thousand years, Bratislava was Pozsony for the Hungarians, Pressburg for the Austrians and Germans, a free royal town under Hungarian rule, then, during the sixteenth and seventeenth centuries, while the Ottoman Turks ruled the lands below, the capital of Hungary.[1] What is now Slovakia was Hungary's Felvidék, or "Upper Lands," an integral part of the Kingdom of Hungary from the tenth century until 1920, when the victorious powers of World War I gave their blessing to the artificial construction of the new country of Czechoslovakia from bits of former empires. The winner of the high-stakes negotiations at the Versailles Peace Treaty was Tomáš Masaryk, with his vision of the new state. The biggest loser by far was the old Kingdom of Hungary. Slovakia, having had only a short interlude of independence during World War II, finally shook off its ties to the Czechs (and vice versa) in January 1993.

Bratislava Castle—huge, hulking, yellow-grey, with its four red-roofed, pointed corner towers that make it look like a giant upturned spider or, as the locals refer to it, an upside-down table—still dominates the city. It is hard to discern its original fifteenth-century design, perhaps because the castle was often rebuilt and overhauled, gentrified and beautified to suit different rulers' personal tastes or the styles of the times. Gothic, then baroque, then mid-Renaissance, it nonetheless retains its original fortress look, and the seven-metre-thick fortifications that might well have withstood a Turkish attack, had the Turks decided to approach Vienna from the north. (They did not. They came from the east and were defeated at the gates of Vienna with the able assistance of Jan III Sobieski, the king of Poland.) Vienna is only sixty kilometres away, a couple of hours on horseback or by rail, as the Viennese used to travel from the Habsburg capital to what they saw as an extension of their own city. For them, Budapest is just down the Danube, the grand river of "Mitteleuropa" that cuts through all three of the cities and adds lustre to Bratislavsky Hrad, the castle, just by being visible from many of its windows.

The interiors of the castle had once been opulent, the walls festooned with silk tapestries and drapery, the furniture decorated with gold leaf. Kings, queens and their retinues lolled about in landscaped gardens and high-ceilinged rooms. This is where the gold-braided Hungarian nobility plotted the overthrow of the Habsburgs once the Turks departed. Their attempts, though undeniably and romantically heroic, were doomed to failure as neither national pride nor exquisite horsemanship made up for the Habsburgs' superior armies.

My Hungarian histories featured heart-rending stories about Prince Ferenc Rákóczi and his lion-hearted mother, the evil Austrians and the brave *kuruc* volunteers who fought unequal battles against the Habsburgs' merciless mercenaries on blood-drenched fields. Although the Rákóczi family castle was in Munkács (today's Munkacevo, Ukraine), there is a Rákóczi house in Bratislava, and the Rákóczi crest is embedded in numerous buildings in Slovakia, including the wall of the fifteenth-century Gothic Cathedral of St. Elizabeth in Košice (the former Kassa), where the prince is buried. Rákóczi's War of Independence (1703–1711) was the last time that large numbers of Slovaks enthusiastically participated in a Hungarian uprising, a genuine war for liberation.

Just down the hill from the castle, St. Martin's Cathedral displays its royal heritage with a gilded copy of the crown of St. Stephen, the

"Holy Crown of Hungary," atop its eighty-five-metre-high Gothic tower. Beethoven's *Missa Solemnis* was first played here. Franz Liszt first conducted his *Hungarian Coronation Mass* here. From St. Martin's all the way to Michalská Street (named after Bratislava's surviving medieval guard tower), brass paving plaques with crown engravings mark the royal parade route of nineteen newly crowned Austrian emperors and Hungarian kings and queens, to be greeted by the nobility. The old town, with its narrow streets, its nineteenth-century buildings formerly owned by the Hungarian nobility, its many church steeples and its long, wide public spaces, still has a sense of Habsburg Europe.

Slovak children read a rather different version of history from the one I learned in Hungary. In their version, Slovaks and their language were suppressed by Hungarian overlords; they were taxed beyond their means to support the cavorting Hungarian gentry, deprived of the best of their livestock and forcibly Magyarized. Lajos (Louis) Kossuth, a formidable Hungarian hero, leader of the 1848 Revolution against Habsburg rule, gave impassioned speeches here about the need to wipe out the use of the Slovak language, close their schools and make Hungarian the only language spoken in "Upper Hungary." Hungarian language laws eliminated teaching in minority languages in an effort to force assimilation.[2] The Hungarian Declaration of Independence makes no mention of the rights of minorities, though in aggregate they were, then, the majority in the Hungarian Kingdom.

The 1848 Manifesto of the Pan-Slav Congress, held in Prague, states: "We Slavs reject and abhor every domination by mere force. We demand, without exception, equality before the law and equal rights and responsibilities for everyone. When one person... is born into oppression, there, true freedom is unknown."[3] When Slovaks joined the Habsburg forces against the Hungarians, they hoped to convince the Habsburgs to grant them what the Hungarians failed to give: collective language rights and some autonomy in majority Slovak areas.

I discovered the work of Professor Stanislav Kirschbaum while I was in a boutique hotel on Bratislava Old Town's main tourist street. The young man at the front desk mentioned that he was writing a thesis with the use of Kirschbaum's best-known work, *A History of Slovakia*. It is the only Slovak history written or published in English.

The book's subtitle, *The Struggle for Survival*, suggests the theme that runs through the book: the unequal battle of the plucky Slovak people to maintain their language and culture against all odds. Kirschbaum traces the story back to the sixth century, before the crippling Hungarian occupation that lasted a thousand years. In the final chapters, he honours the Slovaks' struggle to free themselves from Czech domination. Professor Kirschbaum's father, Jozef, secretary general of the Slovak People's Party and leader of the Slovak World Congress, had also written extensively about Slovak history and culture after he emigrated to Canada at the end of World War II.

Strangely, both the Slovaks and the Hungarians hold somewhat fond memories of the Habsburgs, now that no Habsburg intends to rule here or anywhere else in Europe. For the Hungarians, being part of the empire was a whole lot more satisfactory than their new reality as just another small nation in Central Europe. For the Slovaks, whose national aspirations went unheeded by their Hungarian rulers, Emperor Franz Joseph's 1859 edict that "non-Magyar languages must enjoy adequate facilities under Hungarian rule" was a welcome boost.[4] Near the Danube in Bratislava there used to be a rather flattering Carrera marble equestrian statue of Empress Maria Theresa, the only woman to have ruled the Habsburg dominions, but it was mercilessly smashed in late 1921 after the Habsburg Empire had drawn its last breath. The empress had once been a frequent visitor to Pressburg, to stay with her favourite daughter at the castle.

In the early 1900s, Bratislava was 41 per cent German, 40 per cent Hungarian and only 4 per cent Slovak. Until the late 1930s it remained a cosmopolitan city where nationalities, customs and languages mixed. Conversations in the sidewalk cafés would be in two or three languages. The thriving Jewish community—rooted here for at least five centuries—added Yiddish and a great marble-floored synagogue, demolished in 1967 to make room for the SNP (Slovak National Uprising) Bridge, now the Nový (New) Bridge, adorned by the high-flying UFO Restaurant.

Kossuth Square, where Kossuth addressed his adoring supporters from the balcony of what is today the elegant Radisson Blu Carlton Hotel, is now the great promenade of Hviezdoslavovo Námestie, presided over by Pavol Hviezdoslav's huge, brooding statue. Widely considered to be the greatest Slovak lyric and epic poet, Hviezdoslav translated Shakespeare, Goethe, Schiller, Mickiewicz and other icons of European literature into Slovak.[5] A statue of Hungarian lyric poet Sándor Petőfi used to stand nearby, but after several attempts to destroy it, it was moved to a quiet park where it sometimes loses an arm to vandals but is quickly restored by local Hungarian poetry fans. Ironically, it was Hviezdoslav who first translated Petőfi into Slovak.

Kossuth's statues have all been destroyed. In these parts, he is remembered mainly for his passionate avowal of the superiority of the Magyars to the Slavs and his insistence that the various Slav languages be curtailed in favour of a uniform nation. An ardent Hungarian nationalist, Kossuth had been imprisoned by the Habsburgs for fomenting separation from the empire, became a member of the Hungarian parliament, led a revolution to wrench power from the Austrians and—though the effort, like Rákóczi's, was doomed to failure—is still celebrated by gigantic statues and grand memorials in most larger Hungarian towns.

The fact that Hungarian monuments have been demolished since 1919 is merely a response to the fact that there were no monuments to Slovaks here before then. According to historian Lubomir Liptak, "monumentizing" the Hungarian Kingdom was political and "had the function of marking territory and fixing tradition."[6]

It is impossible for a city to change its history. Memories are in its stones. Still, that hasn't stopped Bratislava from trying to remove itself from its Hungarian orbit. Now, as the capital of Slovakia, its population is 95 per cent Slovak, and the city is at the centre of nationalist pride. It has destroyed over two hundred buildings in the Old Town, removed plaques commemorating the past, raised a modern bridge with a revolving restaurant over the Danube, widened avenues and renamed streets. The cube-shaped UFO Restaurant atop the New Bridge was finished in 1972, in the heyday of Communism, but is a proud reminder that Slovak nationalism is neither new nor fleeting.

Unlike the nationalisms of the surrounding countries, this one is distinguished by not having had borders to redefine, resurrect, move or abolish. For most of its history, Slovakia did not exist as a separate country—it was part of the Kingdom of Hungary. What it had was a language.[7] No one attempted to codify Slovak until the late eighteenth century, and it was not until the middle of the nineteenth that Ľudovít Štúr, poet, philosopher, teacher, leader of a romantic nationalist movement, wrote the Slovak language standard that led to the contemporary Slovak literary language.

Nineteenth-century Europe was awash in a sea of nationalist movements, pining for an idealized, heroic and often bucolic past. Štúr's visit to the massive ruins of Devin Castle at the confluence of the Danube and the Morava, about ten kilometres west of Bratislava, convinced him that the origins of his people were rooted in the tenth-century Great Moravian Empire, a bulwark of civilized, Christian Europe that fell to the marauding, uncultured Asiatic Magyar hordes—ancestors of the Hungarians. Contemporary chronicles described them as "the scourge of Europe," with "hideous appearance" and "blood-curdling battle-yells." Devin Castle's foundations date back to the ninth century. Its many subsequent owners added to and prettified it, but Napoleon's army blew it up in 1809 and it has never recovered.

Like his contemporaries, the British poets Shelley, Keats and Byron and Hungary's Petőfi, Štúr wrote fine lyric poetry. He and Petőfi were soldiers during the 1948 revolution, but they fought on opposite sides, Štúr with other Slovaks in the Habsburg battalions and Petőfi with the Hungarians.

As a politician in the Hungarian parliament in Bratislava, Štúr distinguished himself with his brilliant oratory. He could match Kossuth in eloquence and do so in both Hungarian and Slovak. When today's populist National Party leader, Ján Slota, talks of Magyars as Asiatic, big-cheekboned, bowlegged warriors, he has no less an inspiration for such vitriol than Štúr. Today's anti-Hungarian rhetoric is merely a replay of the Slovaks' nineteenth-century martyrology, now given voice in a nation some fear may still be threatened.

Their national aspiration, with the determination to keep their language alive at its core, has helped create a country, first in 1939, then again in 1992. The March 1939 event occurred under the aegis of Slovakia's own clerical nationalist[8] government, presided over by the controversial Jozef Tiso. Tiso, a Catholic priest, had inherited ideologies and the leadership of the Slovak People's Party from Andrej Hlinka, another Catholic priest. In 1938, after the Munich "Peace with Honour" deal allowed Germany to annex the Sudetenland, Hungary retrieved the southern chunk of Czechoslovakia it had lost at the Versailles (Trianon) Peace Conference, and Tiso declared Slovakia's independence under his own command. Encouraged by Hitler, who had already decided to put an end to Czechoslovakia, he declared the Slovak Republic (under German "protection") on March 14, 1939. On March 15, Germany invaded the remaining Czech lands. Given the times, Slovak independence had been somewhat illusory, but it did last until the Slovak Uprising of October 1944, when German troops occupied the country. Father Tiso remained in his titular office till the end of the war.[9]

Fifty years of Soviet rule had discouraged overt discussion of different nationalities as, in the Marxist view, workers of all nations shared common interests. The governing Communists did ensure, however, that old rivalries were kept alive, if only in the interests of dividing their subjects. Slovaks got a major share in heavy industry and leading roles in the secret police. The Czechs got everything else.

The second and less fraught event has become known as the "Velvet Divorce" of June 1992: the peaceful end of Czechoslovakia, arranged and orchestrated by Vladimir Mečiar with the able assistance of Czech leader Václav Klaus. On January 1, 1993, Klaus would become the Czech Republic's first prime minister and Mečiar would become Slovakia's first premier.

DEMOCRACY EXPERIMENTS

The grey-white Slovak parliament building stands next to Bratislava Castle. It is a solid, straight-lined, parsed-windowed, no-nonsense piece of architecture that seems to mock the ornate castle's elaborate designs. Ľudovít Štúr's imposing marble statue graces the entrance hall. In front of the building, beyond the stone steps that lead to the walkway, is the tall stone figure of Alexander Dubček, shoulders bent, face turned slightly to the left. It is said by many in Bratislava that Dubček's August 1993 car crash was not an accident, that he was murdered by the forces who did not wish to see the federation survive and did not like the prospect of his interfering in a contest for power. Dubček's autobiography is prophetically entitled *Hope Dies Last*.

It was a formal day in the chamber of Slovak National Council and most of the 150 desks were occupied. I was allowed to watch the proceedings from the public gallery above the representatives' hall. It faces the huge Slovak national crest's white double cross on a blue hill against a red background, which looks remarkably like the left half of Hungary's emblem.

Vladimír Mečiar made his way to his desk, amiably chatting with a couple of men in the centre area that his rather diminished party, the HZDS (Movement for a Democratic Slovakia), occupies. He seemed relaxed, playing with his pens, looking at his notes. A couple of weeks before, his former political ally Ivan Gašparovič, a Dubček loyalist, had won his second presidential election. Though Gašparovič had once been his right-hand man,[10] Mečiar uncharacteristically refrained from comment. Perhaps he was still sore from his party's recent losses at the polls.

Former prime minister Mikuláš Dzurinda, leader of the Slovak Democratic and Christian Union (with thirty-one seats out of the Council's 150), was there, as was Miklós Duray, one of the key figures in the Party of the Hungarian Coalition (twenty seats). Ján Slota, leader of the xenophobic Slovak National Party (twenty seats), barely glanced at the Speaker on the high podium. He continued talking with one of his colleagues. My guide told me he rarely bothers to come to these sessions, but today was a special day.

The issue was language rights, vital for the Hungarian minority. But it was a foregone conclusion in this parliament that all street signs, monuments, tombstones and shop signs would be in Slovak and no Hungarian radio program would be allowed unless every word was also broadcast in Slovak translation. Prime Minister Robert Fico (SMER, or Direction–Social Democracy, with fifty seats) arrived late, but not too late for the vote.

Mečiar, Duray and Gašparovič had all supported Alexander Dubček's "socialism with a human face," the grand experiment to reform the Party from within that failed at the end of the Warsaw

Pact's guns. As punishment for his youthful enthusiasm, Mečiar had his Communist Party membership cancelled in 1969. Two decades later, he joined the anti-authoritarian Public Against Violence movement (VPN in Slovak). He was appointed minister of the interior once the Czecho-Slovak government was formed with Havel's Civic Forum on the Czech side. In June 1990, he was elected premier of the Slovak segment of Czechoslovakia (or Czecholovakia, as some preferred to call it) after the first democratic elections.

A brilliant orator, he was Slovakia's most popular politician—a former boxer, a down-to-earth, anti-intellectual man of the people. He sang and danced on video. He wept when he lost an election. He was eager to present himself as ordinary. Mečiar was elected prime minister four times. A self-declared patriot, he accused every critic of his regime of being anti-Slovak.

His opponents criticized his autocratic style, his insistence on the last word for all government appointments, his lack of interest in democratic institutions. But his opposition to the joys of American-style capitalism gained him as much in friends at home as in heavy-handed criticism from abroad. He declared American philanthropist George Soros *persona non grata* in Slovakia for predicting that Mečiar's methods would disqualify Slovakia from membership in the EU. Even today, he stands for people who are anti-capitalist, isolationist and nostalgic for the past.

After his 1994 re-election to the post of prime minister, he changed the existing system of privatization to enable his cronies to buy hotels, resorts and businesses at bargain prices. His friends were able to buy prime properties at a fraction of their value with only 10 per cent down, then resell them at vast personal profit. The obvious favouritism has harmed his political aspirations, but seems not to have landed him in a sea of wealth, except for his luxurious villa, Elektra, in Trenčianske Teplice. He has aggressively ignored the Slovak media's questions about how he could afford a holiday resort worth over US$5 million on the meagre salary of an HZDS politician.

His government tried to muzzle the media, attacked academics and intellectuals who opposed him and cheerfully awarded a journalism prize to an anti-Semitic magazine. His minister of education eliminated whole university departments, and several museum directors were replaced by Mečiar loyalists.[11] Mečiar successfully prevented the country's then president, Michal Kováč, from appearing on public television because he knew the message would be critical of his methods of dealing with the opposition.

Mečiar has made no secret of his disdain for the Hungarian minority (while campaigning in 1997, Mečiar had talked of a Hungarian threat to Slovak territories that had once been part of Hungary and, in a meeting with Hungarian prime minister Gyula Horn, had offered a population transfer of Slovak Hungarians across the border to Hungary in a not-so-veiled reference to the 1945 deportation of some seventy thousand Hungarians[12]), yet he had agreed to meet me in Miklós Duray's office.

After the vote on Hungarian language rights, Mečiar swaggered in, hand outstretched and a big, disarming sideways smile. The two men greeted each other with relentless politeness. At sixty-six and somewhat ballooned in the midriff, Mečiar still seemed to be in fighting shape; his shoulders outflanked his tummy, and his arms bulged aggressively in his tight suit jacket. Adjusting his tie as he settled across from me, he was every bit the people's politician. He seemed pleased with the way the vote had gone.

He announced right away that he has not been giving interviews to the Western press. No point—they have already formed their opinions about his leadership. When I asked him about his own assessment of his contributions to Slovakia, he grew somewhat pensive. He said he would like to be remembered as the man who changed the system from totalitarianism to democracy; from a planned economy to letting the market decide; from social paternalism—with the favours handed to Party members—to individual responsibility.

He is proud of it all, he said. "We had to build our own state without parliamentary experience. We had no representative parliament here. We had no parties, except for the Communists, so we had to start political parties." He had joined the Slovak version of the Czechs' Civic Forum, Public Against Violence, he explained, because it was the only way out of the past. The Velvet Revolution provided an exit from tyranny for both Czechs and Slovaks, but Havel was not interested in an equal partnership. He had been indifferent to demands for fair Slovak representation. His attitude to Slovaks had been, at best, patronizing.

Havel did not bother to appear in Bratislava till after he became president of Czechoslovakia. His first presidential visit, in January 1990, was to German chancellor Kohl. Only four Slovaks were included in his two-hundred-person entourage for a Washington visit in February 1990. Havel paid no heed to the calls for establishing a true federation, for the country to be named Czech-Slovakia. Yet he seemed genuinely surprised when he was booed, shoved, jeered and spat on in Bratislava in March 1991. It was a great opportunity for the international media (with a nod at my scribbling hand) to show primitive Slovaks assailing a beloved symbol of democracy in Central Europe.

The Public Against Violence group—Gal, Simecka, Bútora, Jan Langos and others—were for making a deal, keeping the partnership together, but Mečiar didn't believe it could last. Slovaks needed a voice—their own voice—in government. When it was not offered, the only option was independence. Mečiar spoke of his battle with VPN leader Fedor Gál over the "Velvet Divorce": "Gál talked of democracy, but he assumed he could control the outcome. When he didn't like what freedom of choice brought, he left. So Gál ended up in Prague and got rich."

"In the beginning, Gál supported me, then, he changed his mind. He and Havel tried to get rid of me. And look..." He spread his broad palms to show he is still here.

"In 1992," Mečiar said, "we had a 20 per cent decline in our economy. The big industries, the backbone of this country, were lost. It was worse for us here than for the Czechs because we had the heavy industries. The Communists had us build factories here, far from the West's prying eyes," and, perhaps, in hopes of buying Slovak loyalty. Havel's famous ethical decision to end all armaments manufacture in Czechoslovakia meant irreplaceable job losses for Slovaks. No Slovak politician was consulted.

Strangely, for a man of such broad vision, Havel seemed unaware of the smouldering resentments, unaware of the Slovaks' bug-eyed irritation with what they saw as Czech snobbery.

If Czechs and Slovaks were not going to be equal in Czecho-slovakia, then there would be no Czechoslovakia. That staple of Czech literature, the backward, simple-minded Slovak, was about to sever Masaryk's Czech-Slovak partnership.

The Public Against Violence group split apart, some say over Mečiar's hunger for power; others talk of the inevitable demise of an idealistic, charismatic group that was unprepared for leading a country once the battles for democracy had been won.

Mečiar was elected HZDS chairman in June 1991. Backed by his new political party, he successfully blocked the re-election of Havel as president of Czechoslovakia.

A formidable speaker, Mečiar revived nationalist neurosis, pre-senting a picture of a beleaguered small country with enemies both inside and outside its borders. He once claimed that he had thwarted a planned Czech invasion in 1992. He opposed the Czechs' fast eco-nomic transformation program. He insisted that Slovaks would have to be masters in their own house and dictate their own terms for their own reforms. Václav Klaus was happy to oblige.

Today, Mečiar is proud of the peaceful, negotiated end of that artificial country and the realization of its two successor states. "Once we had our own country, what I saw as my main task," he said, "was to wrestle hyperinflation to the ground and build a new state. The challenge was to stop inflation, to avoid a meltdown. We had to evaluate our currency. We had no national bank..."

But his own rule was marred by corruption and crony capital-ism. Foreign investors fled. His isolationist speeches fuelled Slovaks' resentment of the EU. He fed their fear that their country would vanish into the EU's vast population, that they would once more be obeying someone else's rules.

There were also the scandals that showed that Mečiar had made peace with the bully boys of the old regime. The August 1995 abduc-tion of President Michal Kováč's son was rumoured to have been ordered by Mečiar and executed by Slovak members of the old StB. The reason for the botched kidnapping: to embarrass Mečiar's chief political rival, the young man's father. Kováč Jr. was dragged from his Mercedes-Benz, forced to drink a bottle of whisky, dumped into the trunk of another car and driven across the Austrian border. The young man was located in the abandoned car by the Austrian police. Their investigation concluded that the set-up was the work of the Slovaks, likely following orders from their government. A key witness who was willing to testify was murdered.

In the end, Kováč was able to oust Mečiar, but it was a pyrrhic victory. When Kováč's term was up, Mečiar assumed the role of president and all charges against those accused of perpetrating the kidnapping of Kováč's son were dropped.

The man who almost succeeded in keeping Slovakia out of NATO and the EU told me he believes in Europe: "Look, this country became the darling of the European Union. We were ahead of everyone else in this region in terms of our economic achievements."

He failed to mention that it was not until he was ousted by the voters that Mikuláš Dzurinda, allied with the Party of the Hungarian Coalition after 1998, was able to bring Slovakia into NATO and in line for the EU fold.[13] Dzurinda, who was greatly admired in the West, reduced foreign debt, renewed privatizations and built some sorely needed investor confidence. Following the 2002 parliamentary election in Slovakia, the Party of the Hungarian Coalition joined the Slovak government for the second time. Mečiar had been quick to accuse Dzurinda's government of enriching themselves at the expense of the people.

"Now, with this financial crisis, everything must be re-evaluated. "Perhaps we have become too open to foreign influences. Perhaps it is time to revisit our relationships with the rest of the world," Mečiar said to me, rising from his chair. "We have adopted too many of the West's false values, the stupid values of the capitalist system. Western civilization relies on an insatiable consumer market. That, in my opinion, is a deformation of life. The stomach is not the only organ of the human body."

"You know," he said, shaking my hand, "the world will be a better place after this," referring to the international financial crisis, and I had a sense of how he had won all those elections. He has a sunny self-confidence that invites agreement, and it is easy these days to be critical of a mindless consumer economy. But would the world be a better place after the U.S. subprime disaster that spread a financial crisis throughout the world? I doubted whether the rural poor in eastern Slovakia would imagine their lives had been improved by the hard lessons learned. But, upon reflection, there was a germ of truth in his parting remark. In the future there will be some barriers to the use of empty financial instruments, and those with the means to do so will be more careful with where they invest.

THE UNLIKELY REVOLUTIONARY

Miklós Duray was immaculately courteous with his political adversary. He did not interrupt or argue while Mečiar was there, though they have been on opposite sides of most issues. Duray had been a federalist and outspoken Havel supporter, one of the few in Slovakia who had signed Charter 77 and a member of the Czechoslovak parliament from 1990 till the end of Czechoslovakia. His party supported Dzurinda's coalition that defeated Mečiar in 1998.

Duray stood politely when Mečiar left his office. Then he spoke of the recent presidential elections of 2009, of how Ivan Gašparovič's campaign had been redolent with nationalism, seeking popular support by naming an enemy. What simpler way is there to unite a people while distracting attention from the corruption, the decline of the economy, the lack of job opportunities? These elections speak clearly about the kind of society "some politicians" wish to build. Still, he added, democracy was working fine in 2004 when Mečiar failed in his bid to become president.

Miklós Duray is a most unlikely revolutionary. When I met him, he was carefully dressed in a dark grey suit, soft-spoken, with a nearly unlined, tanned face (it was the beginning of a long summer in Slovakia), sprightly blue eyes behind wide-framed glasses, and carefully groomed white hair. He walks with that straight backed, arms at his sides, stiff-shouldered European male stride, so different from the American shoulder-swinging walk. He seemed young for his sixty-five years.

We drank coffee in the restaurant down a few steps from the entrance of the parliament building. He kept glancing at the Danube, too blue and swollen from the spring thaw, then up at the sharp angles of the parliament building's windows.

Duray was born into a well-to-do Hungarian family in the southern part of Slovakia, where almost everybody used to be Hungarian.
After World War I, when Hungary lost half its population and two-
thirds of its territory, about a million Hungarians were left in what
used to be Upper Lands and now belonged to Czechoslovakia, soon
to be divided by Hitler into the Moravian and Silesian lands and the
Reich protectorate (*Schutzfreundschaft* on German documents) of
Slovakia. The Hungarian army invaded Slovakia in 1938 and 1941 to
successfully regain parts of its lost lands.[14]

The peace treaties that ended the Second World War confirmed
the Versailles borders to create Czechoslovakia and a small Hungary.
The 1945 Beneš decrees imposed collective guilt on the Hungarian
and German populations of Czechoslovakia, stripping them of their
citizenship, rights and property. (According to Gustáv Husák, former
Communist president of Czechoslovakia, Josef Stalin gloried in the
Red Army's destruction of Budapest and commented that this was
the best way to deal with Hungarians.)

The Duray family was one of thousands marked for deportation
from their home. They had already packed their belongings and
awaited their turn when the extraditions ended. His parents lost
their jobs because they were both bourgeois and Hungarian. His
father, a lawyer, and his mother, a schoolteacher, were able to find
some menial work to keep the family alive. Young Miklós worked in
a warehouse before he was able, finally, to go to university.

In a slim volume about his life, *Összefonódó Ujjak* ("Interlocked
Fingers" is the literal translation, but I doubt that is what he meant),
he talks of the painful loss his family and the other Hungarian families feel when they think about the Beneš decrees: "They took our
lives, our destinies, our family savings, our homes, our land, our
past, our heritage, our cemeteries, our future..." All that because
they had been born Hungarian in what was then Hungary.

There has not been a suggestion of restitution or compensation for
what happened. Nor, he says, is there likely to be. The fact that the
Hungarian minority was federalist and supported Havel's dream of a
united Czechoslovakia has added ammunition for the haters.

The battle for minority rights, schools, newspapers, books and
street signs has been ongoing for most of this century. Wanting to

keep their language, to be able to go to school with Hungarian texts, had not seemed such a huge request. Yet Duray was jailed in 1982 for organizing to keep Hungarian language rights—demanding autonomy in culture, the use of Hungarian in schools where Hungarians are a majority. In his book *Kutyaszorító*, he writes about the indignities of house searches, the beatings, the terrible boredom of 407 days' jail. He credits his daily yoga exercises—joined by some of the other inmates—with saving his sanity.

He was not surprised by today's vote. His minority party was unlikely to convince Fico's majority of any significant amendments to the proposed new language laws.

Now that he can't be imprisoned for advocating rights for his minority of some 500,000 people, he is certainly not going to give up the fight. It is a significant base for a party in a nation with only 5.5 million people. He was elected to the Slovak parliament in 1994 and has been here ever since. His Party of the Hungarian Coalition has put several proposals before the government. One of those proposals was that the area near the Hungarian border, where most of the country's Hungarian-speakers live, be united with Hungary.

In recent years, Duray has moved closer to the Hungarian FIDESZ party leader Viktor Orbán, a brilliant speaker who talks of the common interests of all Hungarians in the Carpathian Basin, as if the Trianon borders had become meaningless.

"If I take it personally, I have nothing against political autonomy for the Hungarian minority in Slovakia," journalist and political commentator Martin Simecka says. When Duray was jailed by the Communist government, Simecka was one of his most vocal supporters. "But in reality, it can lead to a serious nationalistic tension between Slovakia and Hungary," he adds. In this context, Miklós Duray has become a dangerous man.

ANTI-SEMITISM WITHOUT JEWS

Terezín is thirty-five kilometres northwest of Prague. It was built in 1780s as a fortress town to defend Prague from invasions and named Theresienstadt, in German, after the Habsburg emperor Joseph II's beloved mother, Maria Theresa. After the invasion of Czechoslovakia, the ss converted Terezín into a Jewish ghetto.

A film was made of Terezín to show the world that this camp was an ideal location for Jews from all over Europe. The prisoners were dressed in good clothes for the occasion; empty shop windows were filled; an orchestra played; children were made to skip around looking happy. The same masquerade was repeated for the June 1944 visit of the Red Cross, whose representatives did not look behind the facades or ask questions. The truth was that almost 200,000 men, women and children passed through Terezín's gates on their way to their deaths.

The vast majority of Czech and Slovak Jews taken to Terezín never returned home; some died of starvation, some of disease, others by execution, but most were transported to Auschwitz once the capacious gas chambers had been built to accommodate the large crowds to be murdered by the newly perfected scientific method of Zyklon B.

The site's official website claims that 97,297 human beings died in Terezín, among them 15,000 children. Only 132 of those children were known to have survived. Fedor Gál was one of the lucky ones.

Gál's mother was on the last transport of Jews to Terezín from Bratislava, during the winter of 1944. She sat on the boxcar's wooden floor, surrounded by dead bodies, cradling her four-year-old son, Fedor's older brother. She was pregnant with Fedor.

When the camp was liberated in May 1945, he was three months old.

Gál never knew his father. When he was a child he used to dream that he was the son of a partisan who died in a gun battle with the Nazis. It would be many years before he discovered the truth.

WE MET for the first time in a Cuban café in Prague, with large, gaily painted windows that half blocked out the sun, dark brown walls with pink and white handwriting, a tiled floor, a chocolate brown bar and high stools and tables with vintage Camel ashtrays. The place was full of young people smoking powerful-scented cigarettes, shouting at each other or into their cellphones. It was hard to be heard over the voices, the sound of the drums and the cheery Spanish music. Though he was almost seventy years old, Fedor Gál seemed perfectly at home here. He wore a loose black and white hand-knitted sweater that flowed around him, the sleeves too long, the neck too slack. His hair and beard were bushy and almost white. He drank tequila with gusto.

After he graduated from the Slovak Academy of Science, he worked in various chemical factories, the usual reward for being a dissident during the last two decades of the Communist regime. He was one of the leaders of Public Against Violence, the Slovak sister organization of Civic Forum, both founded in 1989. His twenty-video series about 1989 in Slovakia was to be released as an eighty-two-minute full-scale movie. "It will be accessible online and will be shown on television," he said. "We have not paid attention to the usual broadcast rule of faked objectivity. The film is made by three frankly opinionated people. Our heroes are not the usual celebrities, the well-known political faces, but the ordinary man." He wanted to record the emotions of people struggling with their acceptance of change, the mass protests, the irrepressible hopefulness of the crowds that occupied Hviezdoslavovo Námestie, the cutting down of the border's metal fences. "The Iron Curtain was a tangible symbol of our powerlessness," he told me. So much had changed in just a few days that the border guards brought their own wire cutters to help remove that symbol.

I asked him about Vladimir Mečiar, the man who had become his sworn enemy when Gál opposed his dictatorial style.

"After 1989—and you have to understand that we did not expect the government to give up so quickly—we had to fill thousands of positions vacated by the Party faithful. That is when we found Mečiar. I was fascinated by him. He had the ultimate work ethic. Twenty hours a day did not seem too long for him. He has extraordinary recall. He is fast. Unemotional. Unsentimental. One day he came to me and said one of the army officers in the department had shot himself." Gál composed his face into a mask. "All Mečiar could utter by way of pity was 'You should have seen the mess...'" By contrast, Gál's every movement as he spoke to me was emotional. Ferocious, then sad, then indignant, suddenly cheerful. It must have been a pairing made in hell. And yet Gál supported Mečiar as minister of the interior, at least at the beginning. In fact, as Miklós Duray remembers, "Fedor Gál, personally, presented Mečiar as the most qualified of us all. Three and a half months later, he changed his mind. The next February, they got rid of Mečiar for turning against the very views that made him seem qualified for the job." Duray was there the day Mečiar was chosen, and he was there when Gál turned against him.

While Mečiar campaigned for an independent Slovakia, Gál opposed the breakup of the country. He thought of the 1991 demonstrations as a throwback to the war years of extreme nationalism, of pointless, nasty rhetoric. It was the same symbols, the same enraged faces, the same songs, the same signs, like watching an old black and white movie come to life. In answer to my question of why he didn't oppose Meciar publicly and run for the leadership, he said, "How could I, a Jew, run for parliamentary office? How could I have won? Mečiar offered them the right words, not I."

This was the rift that split Public Against Violence. When it was all over, Gál said, "I could not get used to the hate mail, the death threats, the obscene graffiti outside my apartment."

Martin Simecka said he, too, had been frightened of the outpouring of wild-eyed nationalism. "It's a stupid, dangerous ideology. It has killed people. Suddenly, Fedor Gál and I became enemies of the nation. We were judged to be anti-Slovak."

"Mečiar was elected twice, democratically," Gál told me, "and I became the most hated man in Slovakia. He had the answers they wanted to hear. And he talked about the economy. What could I, an intellectual and a Jew, offer?"

"I had the charisma," he added, with no hint of irony, "Mečiar had the talent for the technology of power. He was tenacious. In the end, I was not." Vladimir Mečiar became prime minister of the Slovak Republic in 1992. Fedor Gál, who had been one of the best-known faces on Slovak television screens during the 1989–90 rapid change to democracy, felt unwanted in his country. He left Slovakia and took up residence in Prague. There he made his fortune in a television privatization deal, and now he finds himself an uncomfortable celebrity.

The last time I see him, in late 2009, he has just returned from Bratislava where he was given the Jan Langos Award, for having

"endeavored for human dignity and freedom," at the National Theatre. Gál had been a friend of Langos, a fellow dissident and former
Interior minister in the Czechoslovak government who established
the Slovak Institute of National Memory. "Jan Langos encountered
strong opposition. The way in which he went public with StB documents on the Internet caused a wave of aversion, not to mention
numerous court cases. As a result, Jan Langos had many enemies. I
think that in essence he was a lonely person. His public work was
risky," Gál said, as if he were talking of himself. Langos was killed in
a car accident in 2006.

The fact that the Dalai Lama also received the award makes the
connection even clearer. Gál, like the Dalai Lama, had rarely considered his personal safety a major issue when taking a public stance.

All five hundred seats in the theatre were filled and at least
another five hundred people were standing. "So many of them were
surprised that I am still alive," he says, grinning. "I am just a symbol
for events in their past. But," and he lifts his hands in a display of
stage astonishment, "for history, symbols are very important, that
they are unconnected to reality is unimportant." He laughs.

WHEN GÁL found out how his father died, he went on a pilgrimage
that connected him with that unclaimed part of his history. His father
was taken by boxcar to the Sachsenhausen concentration camp and
died on one of the many death marches near the end of the Second
World War. There is a mass grave with a modest memorial at around
the two-hundred-kilometre mark on the road from Sachsenhausen to Schwerin. This is where Fedor Gál thinks his father is buried.

He and his philosopher brother walked the distance about five
years ago, filming what would have been their father's last views of
the world. Fedor placed a couple of pebbles from his garden on the
memorial. He told his father about his first granddaughter, Sofinka.[15]

In 2010, there are still Slovaks who passionately defend the
nationalist state under Father Tiso, whose government encouraged
the deportation of Jews and gypsies. If you need to find reasons, the
most commonly believed excuse here is that after the First World
War, Jews were associated with Hungarians and Hungarians were

determined to regain their lost territories. If you seek another reason: Jews lived in cities and small towns; they were not part of the
rural poor.

The Slovaks did not resist Nazi ideology; they were quick to issue
their own anti-Jewish decrees. The government limited the role of
Jews in the professions and passed a new law making it impossible
for Jews to own land. Then it began to expropriate Jewish property.
In 1942, the government paid the Germans 500 Reichsmarks a head
to have the first 57,628 Slovak Jews deported to Poland.

Tiso said he stopped the deportations when he learned the truth
about Auschwitz. Some Slovak histories claim that he, personally,
saved thousands of Jewish lives with the use of "presidential excep-
tions." But the fact remains that about 90,000 Slovak Jews were
killed in German extermination camps.

In 1947, Father Tiso faced charges that ranged from splitting the
Czechoslovak state to betraying the 1944 Slovak National Uprising
against the Germans, an operation that involved the mobilization of
about 80,000 fighters of all Slovak political factions. It is interesting
to note that, even then, "crimes against humanity," or assisting the
Germans with the "Final Solution," was not at the top of the list.

The trial, a veritable quagmire of Communist manoeuvrings, neither proved not disproved Tiso's guilt on all counts, but it did succeed in driving another wedge between the then Soviet-friendly,
Protestant Czechs and the conservative, Catholic Slovaks. Tiso had
been a persistent and vocal anti-Bolshevik. As a Catholic, he consistently voiced his unequivocal opposition to Communism.

In his defence at the trial, he declared that he had accepted the
lesser evil—the deportation of Jews and gypsies—to evade the greater
evil of the total devastation of his country by the Germans. In that
event, he claimed, *all* Jews and gypsies would have been murdered.
He protested that treatment of Jews was "never brutal, inhumane,
or done out of racial hatred." He had merely wanted to give Slovaks
the positions of power long occupied by Jews. If the Slovak Uprising
hadn't happened, he might have been successful.

Father Josef Tiso was executed on the morning of April 18, 1947.
His legacy included more mutual distrust between Czechs and

Slovaks and the Communist Party's crushing attack on the Slovak Catholic Church. Priests and even bishops were tried and convicted on numerous trumped up charges; Church property was confiscated; Church publications were censored; monasteries and convents were dissolved. Driven into defying the law, many Catholics joined the "secret Church," a resilient resistance movement undeterred by the Party's assault.[16]

In February 2000, the Žilina town council decided to place a Tiso memorial plaque on the wall of Catholic House, home of the Sisters of St. Francis. Žilina, a stronghold of Slovak nationalism, had elected the fulminating populist Ján Slota mayor. Slota, later to become leader of the Slovak National Party, had already achieved considerable renown for his openly anti-Semitic and anti-Hungarian statements. The council backed down only after a storm of international protest, and in deference to the country's impending membership in the European Union. The Slovak prime minister Mikuláš Dzurinda announced that "the Slovak government considers glorification of Tiso incompatible with the values Slovakia adheres to."

It is a sentiment many of his countrymen would argue is anti-Slovak. In 1991, ten thousand people showed up to lay wreaths on Tiso's grave. Whatever his faults, Tiso did deliver them a country with its own territory and its own flag. He was a follower of Slovak patriots Štúr and Hlinka. For some Slovaks, including Slota, Father Tiso remains a martyr.

Prime Minister Robert Fico has increased fourfold the funding for the nationalist organization Matica Slovenská, which vociferously condemns Father Tiso's critics and bemoans his execution.[17]

ONE OF the problems with democracy, Fedor Gál told me, is that anti-Semites and gypsy-haters are free to voice their opinions in public and there is nothing you can do. There is a pig farm at the site of the largest Roma concentration camp in the Czech Republic, Lety, next to the memorial to the Roma dead.[18]

There are about 400,000 gypsies in Slovakia.[19] Most of them are unemployed. In one of the poorest regions—Sabinov, Michalovce—residents have erected concrete walls between the Roma and the non-Roma. They claim that the walls are there to protect their own possessions, that no chicken or egg was safe from thieves until the wall went up. On the Roma side, the misery, the hunger, the dirt are unimaginable.

The Roma have been treated as inferior beings for centuries. Their suffering under the Nazis' extermination program has never been recognized.

Prime Minister Fico, when pondering the Romas' problem in March 2010, said that the best solution would be to take away all their children and put them into boarding schools.[20]

THE DISSIDENT INTELLECTUAL

Martin Simecka, former editor of the Czech weekly newsmagazine *Respekt* and of the popular Slovak-language daily SME, says he used Slovak for his banned writing during the Communist era because it's a language purged of "clichés and ideological connotations." It is, he says, "soft and good natured," ideally suited for simply expressing one's views about the world as it is. As he did not expect his writing to be read by anyone other than friends, he did not need to reach for literary artifice. Czech, on the other hand, creates reality by its elegant expressions. Czechs, like Slovaks, are obsessed with their language, but for the Czechs, language is intended for enjoyment.[21]

We met at Simecka's home, only a fifteen-minute drive from the centre of Bratislava, but the area feels like the country—small houses with large gardens, imposing trees, dogs running behind picket fences. The Simeckas live in one of the small houses at the end of a long, narrow garden. It is warm and cozy inside, with bulging bookcases and the study piled high with papers. Marta Simeckova was cooking garlic-basted chicken pieces on an old-fashioned woodburning outdoor fireplace in the front yard, where we settled. She is an editor at *Salon*, an independent online magazine that features news, politics and culture. The Simeckas' yard is overshadowed by a giant chestnut tree, and food and wine are served on a long wooden table that feels like something out of a Chekhov play. Former dissidents and Czech and Slovak intellectuals still meet here and talk about the post-Communist world of the late twentieth and twenty-first centuries. Václav Havel and Adam Michnik have argued and drunk under this tree, as have László Szigeti and Béla Bugár, the leader of Most-Híd, the new breakaway faction of the Party of the Hungarian Coalition. They have debated the role of the past in defining the future, the function—if any—of the former dissidents in determining how history is to be viewed in Central and Eastern Europe, and the expectations of a moral vision that the new additions to the EU were expected to bring from their experience of suffering under dictatorships. More recently, they were trying to make sense of the ferocious nationalisms of the early twenty-first century, the rapacious selfishness of capitalism and the raging corruption here and in the Czech Republic.

Martin talked with me about the Slovaks' need for recognition as a people, for belonging to their own country and enduring their fear of being parcelled out, once more, among other countries. Slovaks need their own national security. The constitution starts with "We the Slovak nation," unlike the Czechs' "We the citizens of the Czech Republic." It is not that the Czechs are less nationalistic—it's that they are less afraid.

The Simeckas' son, who studies at Oxford University, came by to hear his father's stories, occasionally dropping in a correction or a better English phrase. He listened as if he was hearing ancient history. He is the same age as or younger than Martin was in some of these stories, but their realities at the same age have been dramatically different.

Martin, a dissident's son, could not have gone to university and he could not have travelled. His father, Milan, a famous philosopher, would not sign the Czechoslovak government's condemnation of Prague Spring and would not denounce Charter 77. For his stubborn resistance, he lost his job at the university and all his writings were banned. "I think he felt guilty about me," Martin said. "Guilty enough that he arranged for his friends who had all been professors and teachers before 1968 to give me a fine education at home." They must have done an amazing job because Martin was described to me as "an icon of Slovak journalism," one of the dissident intellectuals who have thought and written extensively about both the experience of totalitarianism and the meaning of the fundamental changes that have occurred since 1989.

While studying at home, Martin worked as a stoker. For our meeting, he was comfortably attired in dark blue overalls and a grey T-shirt, the kind of clothes he would have worn for his old job. "Not a terribly demanding occupation," he said, with an easy smile, "and somewhat idle in the summers." He had time for meetings with other dissidents, the disillusioned, the post-1968 "normalization resisters." They did not dare to hope for an end to authoritarian repression until the Czech students began their open resistance in 1989. "There was no dissident movement in Slovakia," he said, "only meetings of like-minded people who dared to dream."

The realization of that dream was 1989 and the changes that would occur with democracy. It was perhaps inevitable that the decision makers in Central Europe would rush headlong into the market economy. "Our aim was to adapt as fast as possible," Simecka recalled. The Copenhagen criteria (rules that define whether a country is ready for inclusion in the European Union) and the Washington Consensus (economic policy prescriptions that could lead to acceptance by the International Monetary Fund) were read and evaluated by every politician and economist in the region—all without questioning how these rules would affect society, whether Central Europe was ready for such drastic change. "That is why we put up with daylight robbery that passed for privatization, believing it to be an integral part of western capitalism," Simecka wrote in *Eurozine*. He is still a favoured speaker at international conferences such as the Economic Forum in Poland, where various European leaders debate the efficacy of the astonishing changes their world has enjoyed or endured.

The rush toward EU acceptance meant that most people gladly left their past behind so that they could focus on the future. The half-hearted efforts at "lustration" were intended merely to lend legitimacy to the transformations, to prevent former agents from gaining legitimacy in the new, post-Communist world. Once Slovakia separated from the Czechs, they stopped most efforts to deal with the former Communist apparatchiks. What Simecka himself thinks is that it is difficult to deal with the future without acknowledging the past—no matter the moral dilemmas of this process.

He was the editor of *Respekt* when the magazine revealed the story of Milan Kundera's disastrous act as a secret police informer. It became one of the most explosive stories of that year and even now will move some Czechs and Slovaks to rage against the ease with which the old regime manipulated, intimidated and somehow induced people to become informers, or the ease with which some people accepted the role, or the futility of rehashing these old sins when so many were sinners, so few refused the temptations of an easier life. The motives of the young historian who dug up the story in the StB archives has remained somewhat suspect, but Kundera's brief romance with Communism and his guilt are certain.

No one had prepared for the day when the Communist government gave up control. Simecka remembers how the members of VPN discussed who could be chosen as leader in Slovakia. "Gál was a Jew. My father was Czech. Jan Budaj, an early favourite, had been disqualified when it was revealed that he, too, had signed something agreeing to report for the StB. All I wanted was to be able to travel at last. Mečiar really wanted the job. And he was one of us. No one had any notion of what he would later become."

Martin Simecka talks of the Western assumption that Communism would, somehow, have made Easterners "better human beings, more inquisitive, sensitive and intellectual. Today, that hope looks pathetic." But during the 1990s, post-Communist societies were too busy becoming what they thought the West wished them to be: market economies and, as a reward for good behaviour, candidates for membership in the European Union. Their hopes for quick changes produced corrupt privatizations and new kleptocracies. Their wish for swift adaptation landed them with a seemingly endless stream of Western consultants who siphoned EU cash for advice that rarely produced anything but sheaves of incomprehensible paper. Now, as the world economy has stumbled, perhaps there will be time again to reflect on the past and allow it to inform the future.

THE MIGHT OF WORDS

Robert Fico's left-leaning SMER, or Social Democrats, won the most seats in the 2006 elections on promises to reverse some of the economic reforms initiated by Mikuláš Dzurinda's right-leaning government. SMER announced an odd mixture of leftist financial measures and nationalist paranoid xenophobia. Fortunately for the country, most of the economic measures were not implemented, but unfortunately for the Hungarian minority, the xenophobia has found a welcoming echo within the unhappy grumbling classes that have not had their expected rewards from the capitalist transformation and membership in the EU.

A former Communist, Fico has pointed out that the old system was kinder than its successors. He realized that the tough side of capitalism caught Slovaks unprepared; the deregulation of commodities meant price increases, and reforms to social assistance meant there would be less for those who have the least. He has referred to the Velvet Revolution as "an ordinary coup." He appears to be indifferent to the Communists' human rights violations, and rather nostalgic for their control of the press. Oddly enough, from 1994 till 2000, Fico represented Slovakia at the European Court of Human Rights, a fact that says as much about that judicial body as it does about the task of monitoring human rights offences by member states.

Once in power, Fico made almost no changes, except to expand the coalition government with Slota's extremists. So long as Slota was a fringe party, his behaviour was merely embarrassing, but once his party became part of the ruling coalition, the country began to take him seriously. When he accused the Americans of running a "world dictatorship, liquidating entire nations and bombing whomever they wish," the press had to report his ramblings. On September 20, 2007, the Slovak Parliament adopted one of Slota's resolutions confirming the Beneš decrees.

His followers seem to overlook Slota's penchant for driving an expensive Mercedes that he could not have afforded on his salary,[22] his summer place on the Croatian coast; they may forgive his drunken speeches, his absences from Parliament; and they may even accept his lies about history. The prime minister, however, has tried to distance himself from some of Slota's people by eliminating them from government positions.

Robert Fico proved to be no better disposed toward freedom of the press than his predecessor, Vladimír Mečiar, had been. He proudly pronounced Gašparovič's 2009 presidential victory a defeat for the critical press. He is in the habit of referring to journalists as hyenas and whores. He has done his best to tame the newspapers by encouraging libel suits.

Protesting the muzzling of the press, newspapers appeared with blank front pages—a form of public dissent they had previously tried during Mečiar's rule. A new law makes it mandatory for all media to publish contrary views, at equal length, by people who have been criticized, or the paper, television or radio station that refuses will be banned. In fairness to Prime Minister Fico, I should mention that he is not the only prime minister of an EU country who is determined to muzzle the press. In 2009 Italy's Silvio Berlusconi instituted legal proceedings against *La Repubblica* for asking ten embarrassing questions of the prime minister, including one about his proclivity for very young women. But in Rome, vociferous mass protests greeted Berlusconi's libel suit, while Slovaks have remained relatively quiet about Fico's tactics.

Perhaps it is no accident that the only post–Second World War pogrom in Slovakia, on September 24, 1945, was perpetrated in Topol'čany, Fico's hometown. It is easier to accuse shadowy figures— the mythical Jewish conspiracy, international finance, the West— than to face up to the country's real financial problems, including the ubiquitous corruption that plagues most transactions, no matter how small. No political party has remained untainted.

"They can blame the dark forces for the country's problems," Frantisek Sebej told me. Sebej is a former member of the Czecho-slovak parliament, a psychologist, a karate instructor, a columnist at the popular weekly *Týždeň*, a another Slovak intellectual with a yearning for the democracy they had all envisioned in the heady days of late 1989. In an interview he said, "We are becoming an authoritarian country run by people with no ideology, just an insatiable hunger for power. The word fascism doesn't fit, but this is becoming an intolerant, highly centralized nationalist state."[23]

Perhaps because of the bright sunshine that day, he chose a dark bar for our meeting. It seemed to be a student hangout—some young people working on their computers, others discussing books and papers in ever louder tones as the afternoon wore on. Sebej squeezed his tall, broad-shouldered frame onto one of the narrow benches and announced that he hoped I would like Slovak beer.

He had not anticipated the return of the decrepit, discredited ghosts of Hlinka and Tiso, nor the resurgence of their Old World anti-Semitism. "Our prime minister seems permanently angry," he said. "His voice, his vocabulary resonate with hatred of "the other"— the bad Slovaks like me, the Hungarians, the EU, who have not given us enough. Some of us think he has forgotten how to smile."

When leading Slovak intellectuals Martin Bútora, Grigorij Mesežnikov and Miroslav Kusý warned of the racist rhetoric in politics in an open letter, Fico rebuked them for being anti-Slovak.

On a more hopeful note, Sebej thinks Slovakia will pass through the eye of the financial needle. Its banks are not toxic, its institutions are solid, its larger companies are healthy. Corruption here is no worse than elsewhere in Central Europe and maybe less than in some southern European countries where people have become used to their system of bribes. That some judges have become unseemly rich while wealthy criminals walk free is a little unusual, but no more so than the gargantuan payments top executives have enjoyed in the United States.

As Beata Balogová has written in the *Slovak Spectator*, Slovak politics has a strong digestive system: "It can tolerate quite a lot without suffering fatal effects. But people like Slota are a dangerous infection whose behaviour can cause serious deformation of the system."[24] This is an interesting twist on Slota's assertion that "Hungarians are the cancer of the Slovak nation, without delay we need to remove them from the body of the nation."

THE CRAZINESS OF LANGUAGE LAWS

On August 25, 2006, an ethnic Hungarian student named Hedvig Malina was severely beaten and robbed in the city of Nitra, Slovakia, after she spoke Hungarian on her cellphone. "Hungarians are parasites" was written on her clothes when she first reported her injuries to the police. A two-week-long police investigation concluded that Hedvig had made up the whole incident. The minister of the interior, accompanied by Premier Fico, stepped in front of TV cameras to announce that her claims were baseless. In November 2006, the police charged her with perjury. Amid cries of outrage and charges of political interference, Hedvig appealed her case at the Constitutional Court. In August 2007, a former high-ranking police officer accused the government of meddling. In 2008, Hedvig took her case to the European Court of Human Rights.

On September 1, 2009, the government's new language law came into force. It imposes hefty fines—as high as $8,000—on those who use their own minority language in public. Even a Hungarian doctor treating a Hungarian patient in a hospital must speak Slovak. All dealings with public officials must be in Slovak, irrespective of the fact that in towns along the country's southern border most people speak Hungarian. All signs and monuments, including tombstones, must show Slovak first and at least as large as any other language. Street signs are to be changed. Radio programs must be translated and broadcast at the same time as the original. There are odd exceptions for places where 80 per cent of the population is Hungarian, but I have no idea how you calculate the percentage or the exceptions under the complicated rules or how often the government runs counts to determine whether a place has passed its 20 per cent marginal Slovak quotient or not. Mordecai Richler should be alive and well and commenting on these language laws!

In September 2009, I visited Dunajská Streda, one of the Hungarian towns near the southern border. There is nothing remarkable about the place, except perhaps the fourteenth-century Catholic church and the fact that everybody—in the park, the schoolyard, the shops, the cafés, the library—speaks Hungarian. Dunajská Streda, formerly Dunaszerdahely, was Hungarian for some nine hundred years, then was transferred to Czechoslovakia at the Versailles Palace (Trianon) Peace Treaties of 1919-20, returned to Hungary in 1938 courtesy of a pact with Hitler's Germany and given back to Czechoslovakia after the Second World War; now it belongs to Slovakia. It was in the Dunajská Streda arena that the notorious 2008 soccer match between Dunajská Streda and Slovan Bratislava was interrupted by riot police, who managed to injure more than sixty people, all of them Hungarians. Péter Pázmány, a former mayor, had been there with his son. The police, he told me, were not locals. They had been brought in to create an incident. Little kids cradled their heads in their arms to ward off the truncheon blows.

A government-sponsored public inquiry into police brutality was unable to show sufficient provocation, unless the waving of the ancient Hungarian flag of King Árpád, the conqueror, so inflamed the police that they simply couldn't help themselves.

When Pázmány's friend's daughter fell off a horse, the paramedics argued about whether to send her to Hungary, ignoring the fact that she is a local kid who speaks Slovak as well as they do. "My family has lived here for six hundred years, and no matter what happens we are not leaving," Pázmány told me. They were among those to be deported after the last war, but his mother bribed the soldiers. His father lost his lands and worked as a bricklayer, but he would not give up and would not leave. "We have a strong attachment to this land," Pázmány says with a wide, sunny smile. "Our ancestors' graves are here. This is where we belong."

On August 21, 2009, Hungarian president László Sólyom was to speak at the unveiling of a statue of St. Stephen in Komárno, the Slovak part of the Hungarian town of Komárom, an hour's drive from Dunajská Streda. A crowd of a few hundred people waited on the square around the statue—"an atmosphere of celebration for both Hungarians and Slovaks," Tünde Lelkes, a young lawyer from Komárno, told me. "St. Stephen had, after all, been honoured by both Slovaks and Hungarians as a just king"—when a busload of rowdy hooligans descended and started heckling, waving placards and shouting insults. Meanwhile, the police stopped Sólyom's car at the border and told him he would not be allowed to enter Slovakia, despite the EU's core principle of freedom of movement and a previously approved official invitation.

Prime Minister Fico was characteristically unrepentant. He said the day chosen for the unveiling was also the day when Warsaw Pact forces (including Hungarians) invaded Czechoslovakia to end Dubček's "Prague Spring." The prime minister, as is well known, was a supporter of the invasion and, unlike hundreds of others, kept his Communist Party membership afterwards.

By strange coincidence, Sólyom had been a dissident under his country's Communist rule, yet he had assumed the role of penitent when he apologized for the invasion he had opposed.

The three high school students I met in Bratislava said that they are now scared to speak Hungarian on buses when they travel to school, that they are wary of giving their Hungarian-sounding names, that even when they are alone they do not make cellphone calls home in Hungarian and that they are worried when they see Slovak-flag-waving young men. But not one of them has given a thought to moving to another country.

Leading Slovak intellectuals have warned in an open letter published in liberal daily SME that the racist, xenophobic rhetoric used by Slovak politicians is sinking the country to "a dangerous level." According to Martin Simecka, the new laws are intended to show Hungarians that they are second-rate citizens. Hungarians are meant to feel afraid—and they do.

Yet even Miklós Duray is reasonably convinced that Slovaks have no natural antipathy toward Hungarians, that recent incidents are use only as political ploys. During his 407 days in a Communist jail, he did not experience hatred, only a lack of knowledge and understanding by his Slovak fellow prisoners.

On September 12, 2006, ignoring the laws about presumptions of innocence, Slovak prime minister Robert Fico accused Hedvig Malina of inflicting her own injuries in order to create an anti-Slovak atmosphere in the country and internationally.

Hedvig Malina, in the meantime, completed her degree, married her ethnic Slovak boyfriend and gave birth to their healthy Slovak-Hungarian baby.

LÁSZLÓ SZIGETI defines himself as Hungarian, though he was born after the Second World War in Czechoslovakia. His family is from Dunajská Streda. Szigeti runs his Bratislava publishing company from walk-up offices in a narrow, elderly building not far from historic Michael's Gate—the only remaining medieval entrance to the Old Town. He publishes books in both Slovak and Hungarian. Despite all he has seen, he is optimistic about the future of Slovakia, Hungary and Central Europe. He does not think that the "Velvet Divorce" was a great loss. The conjoined country was Tomáš Masaryk's pre–World War I invention. "Everyone who has ever bothered to look closely at this part of the world knows it has always been two nations," Szigeti says.

The anti-Hungarian card is just a way for Slovaks to define themselves, he tells me, a political ploy that will have lost its value once this part of the world realizes that it needs to belong to itself—not to the West, nor to the East, but content to be in the middle of Europe. "Our civility, our civic values are vital. This is why there will never be a civil war here. Nor real violence against the minorities. Unlike their predecessors—the Nazis and the Soviets—our governments have recognized individual human rights." That these rights do not extend to collective or community rights, as Szigeti had once wished, is not vital to life here. He is disappointed with the Fico government's ongoing vilification of the Hungarian minority, with the difficult-to-understand language laws, with the harassment, the mindless incitement of Slovaks against Hungarians. Yet he is determined to continue with "patience, empathy and a sea of tiny acts" that can bridge the divide between the two peoples. "It is vital to understand that the roots of these politics extend to the nineteenth-century soil of Hungarian assimilation promoters," he says. They were as zealous about their endeavours to eliminate Slovak as the Mečiar and Fico governments have been to eliminate Hungarian. "The basis of Hungary's own national politics remains [almost a hundred years after Trianon] the retrieval of lost territories."

"My life's purpose, if I may say so without becoming pompous," he tells me as he leans back against the wide bookcase displaying both Slovak and Hungarian titles, "is to hold a mirror to each, so they can see how they seem to the other."

In a recent article celebrating his sixtieth birthday, Szigeti is compared to Sisyphus, condemned by the gods to push a massive stone up a mountain only to see it topple down again before it reaches the top. Undaunted, Sisyphus starts again the next day, and the next. Oddly enough, in the myth, Sisyphus is punished for his hubris in deeming himself to be smarter than the gods.

THE ECONOMIC MIRACLE

In 2005, Slovakia was the poster child of Western economic transformations. It had wrestled with the ghosts of central planning, welcomed sufficient privatizations to convince the European Union that
it would meet the conditions for entry into the eurozone —it entered
on January 1, 2009—and its prime minister, the likeable Mikuláš
Dzurinda, a lithe marathon runner, had proven to be an excellent
speaker on the international circuit. Where Fico seems to have been
right is that Dzurinda's government also handed out favours and
enjoyed its own brand of corruption.

Four years later, the Slovak government is awash in scandals;
corruption is now viewed as endemic to a system that can neither curb nor legislate against it. You can buy a driving licence for
about five hundred euros and a secondary-school graduation cer-
tificate for a thousand. It's almost impossible to get any government
contract—even at the city level—without a 20 per cent cut for the
man who chooses you. Martin Simecka says it is a "new mutation of
an ancient disease... It has mutated into a separate system which is
invisible but all-pervasive." Under the Communist system, societies
became used to proclaiming that lies were the truth and vice versa.
"This is another system based on lies," he says. Simecka relates that
the Slovak taxpayer has been cheated out of millions of euros but
seems to ignore the reports of the obvious cases. He is as outraged as
Jan Urban at the public indifference to the enormity of abuse. "I can
only hope that a younger generation will lose patience," he wrote in
a recent newspaper article that engendered little reaction from its
numbed readers.

Prime Minister Robert Fico's cabinet managed to combine Slota's
and Mečiar's xenophobic nationalists with his own left-wing populists in a dull brew of tired rhetoric and mutual suspicion. Yet Fico
was able to force a couple of his more obviously corrupt ministers to
resign, and he has never granted either Mečiar or Slota the kind of
power they asked for. According to surveys by the Institute of Public Affairs, he continues to garner popular support from all walks
of life. People like his direct ways, his dictatorial tendencies, his
attacks on the press, and his disregard for human rights seem not to
have affected his popularity. "Unpredictability remains his defining

characteristic," according to Martin Simecka in *Salon*. "His lack of a clear ideological background or political goals has so far been something of a pleasant surprise."

Populism is a sign of frustration with local conditions. Here, as throughout Central Europe, it appeals to those who have lost out in the fast transition to capitalism: the elderly, workers in dismantled industrial complexes, the rural poor. Many of them yearn for the security of their former lives—what Simecka and Michnik refer to as the "prisoner complex." You never have to worry about your next meal while you are in jail. Out in the world, trying to make a living, it is easy to become nostalgic for the comfort of having no worries: the state will take care of you.

Grigorij Mesežnikov, who works for the Institute of Public Affairs, talks of the nostalgia for the Communist regime when there was guaranteed work for most people and social assistance for those in need: "There is a lost generation who do not feel they need what the future offers. They need neither NATO nor the European Union. They are disappointed with the trade-offs of democracy." But it is an old generation. The young did not experience Communism and do not long to be ruled by dictators. For them a nation is a political framework, not a homogenous block of people who all believe in the same gods, the same cultural legacies. It is, eventually, the young who will write the history of Communism; perhaps it no longer belongs to those who lived it.

Mesežnikov remains hopeful. He is the father of seven children, all enjoying opportunities that would not have been there before. "We have never before been masters of our own country, defining our own destiny, our position secured by NATO," he says, "living in a democracy where you can change those in power for a new bunch you prefer." As for Fedor Gál's fears, Mesežnikov thinks the "Jew stuff" was thrown at him only because people were opposed to his politics. He believes the racist card will fail to attract Slovaks. In the long run, this country will succeed in carving out a comfortable, perhaps even ordinary, place for itself.

In an effort to see themselves as meaningful contributors to history rather than its victims, Mesežnikov says, Slovaks cling to nineteenth-century romantic notions of exclusive nationhood. They are easy targets for politicians who can produce resounding poetry and ancient symbols.

The average Slovak's salary is still lower than what a labourer can earn in France, and the cost of everyday things is as high as in the rest of Europe. And yet George Soros, who had given millions of dollars' worth of scholarships and medical equipment to Slovakia, is not wanted here. Press criticism of the government is greeted with rage, and the new rules to curb freedom of expression are ludicrous.

Mid-afternoon in the late fall of 2009, all the outdoor restaurants along Hviezdoslavovo Námestie are full; tour buses disgorge their cheerful passengers in front of the creamy-white portals of the Radisson Blu Carlton Hotel; the baroque National Theatre (next door to a better-than-standard McDonald's) features Dvořák's *Rusalka* and Eugen Suchoň's *Svätopluk*, and all the best seats are sold. In the main square, dominated by the red-and-green-roofed Old Town Hall, crowds of tourists have their photographs taken with one of Bratislava's ubiquitous statue people, this one attired as Napoleon and leaning over a bench. In the centre there is a fountain where students who can't afford the café prices talk and hang out. The sidewalk cafés are packed, many of the old palaces are enduring facelifts and there are lineups in front of the exchange stores. Away from the pedestrian areas, a range of expensive European cars denotes that the economy is not yet in the kind of trouble that everyone predicted. Looking around Bratislava, and driving east along a well-maintained highway, stopping in tidy villages and towns, it seems to me that Slovaks have never had it so good.

Mark Landler of *The New York Times* referred to Slovakia as "still in its gawky adolescence as an independent state," still trying to find its way through the thicket of rules for grown-up states to the west, and wishing to assert its independence of the past—the old Habsburg Empire and the Hungarian Kingdom that had once been its masters. So, perhaps, we should overlook its missteps and assume a brighter future.

In the *Frankfurter Allgemeine Zeitung*, Michal Hvorecký writes of the end of the economic miracle in Eastern Europe: "The central European tiger is tired. And the [Slovakian] government is proving itself incompetent, ill-prepared and corrupt in these difficult times. The great rhetoricist Fico is silent while his government wallows in scandals." Well, perhaps, but on a sunny day in the capital, the city seems hopeful.

On November 18, 2009, when Václav Havel came to Bratislava to commemorate the old partnership of Czechs and Slovaks opposed to state violence in a country some of his young audience had never known, he talked of "love and truth" as the true ideals of his life and of any life of lasting value. During the years of his incarceration, he had begun to write of the importance of "living in truth." Now, he explained, he had added love to counteract consumerism. In Hviezdoslavovo Námestie, across from the National Opera building, Bratislava had erected a monument to the Velvet Revolution and its Slovak version, Public Against Violence. It was a giant heart on a pedestal. (The giant heart stayed there only for couple of weeks.) Havel was greeted with a standing ovation.

Perhaps in the midst of economic turmoil, corruption scandals, daily reports of cronyism, judiciary influence peddling and rising unemployment it has been, temporarily, useful to seek a common enemy, but there are signs that the Slovak public may, indeed, tire of the game and demand a change.

The splitting of the Party of the Hungarian Coalition into two parties has signalled that not all Hungarians in Slovakia are a threat to the national aspirations of Slovaks. Béla Bugár's Most-Híd party is even attracting some Slovaks who are fed up with the corruption and xenophobia of the leading parties. The greatest challenge is for the soul of the nation: will the people see that they are being manipulated, just as they were in 1939? Will the extremists be voted out of Parliament? Will the efforts of people like Frantisek Sebej, László Szigeti and Martin Simecka bring together charismatic intellectuals like the ones who once united to end the Communist dictatorship? And will the people listen?

One of the advantages of democracy, as Grigorij Mesežnikov said, is that every few years there is another chance to vote for change. Fortunately for Slovaks, the June 2010 elections opened the windows of their parliament to let in fresh air. Robert Fico lost his position as

prime minister, Vladimir Mečiar's party failed to hold on to its voters and Ján Slota's excitable nationalists were reduced to a minority.
The country will welcome a new face to the prime minister's office:
blond, statuesque sociologist Iveta Radickova, nicknamed the "Tatra
Tigress," is offering a fiscally conservative, ethically transparent,
peaceable government that seeks common ground with the Hungarian minority. Béla Búgar's Most-Híd (bridge in Slovak and Hungarian) party has gained 8 per cent of the popular vote, proving that the
civic values so treasured by many of those I met can hold out against
populist agitation.

FOUR

HUNGARY

BURYING THE DEAD

*I share the helplessness that constitutes Europe
today. This empty head, this shoulder shrugging,
this shy gaze towards the ground—this is Europe.
Therefore, my answer can only be a practical one,
and rather suspicious too. I prefer to cite my friend
who says, he would like to live in a country like Tos-
cana inhabited by Englishmen speaking Hungarian.*

PÉTER ESTERHÁZY in an interview from 1992

THE PLACE is called *parcella* 301. It is the 301st plot in the far-
thest corner of the Rákoskeresztúr cemetery, about a half-hour's
drive from downtown Budapest. The drive took us out of recognizable cityscapes into rough, muddy country with a smattering
of low-slung concrete storage buildings and scrapyards, past fallow
fields and the high walls of the old prison block. *Parcella* 301 is up
against the far walls, next to the zoo and circus animals' plot.[1]

This is the burial grounds of people executed by the state after the
1956 Hungarian revolution. Given the secretive nature of the regime,
few knew of the cemetery's existence until the 1980s. Visits were

strictly forbidden. For several years, when families came to mourn, they were beaten back by truncheon-wielding policemen or arrested for unlawful mourning.

In one corner, there is now a squat, white stone monument. It's close to the unmarked pit where the body of Imre Nagy was dumped, wrapped in a shroud, face down, hands and feet tied with barbed wire. Nagy had emerged as one of the reluctant heroes of the revolution when he assumed, again, the role of prime minister by popular demand. The post had been hastily abandoned by Moscow hard-liner Mátyás Rákosi when he and his greatly loathed sidekick, Ernő Gerő—two leftover Stalinists—fled to Moscow.

Imre Nagy, another Old World Communist, had joined the Party and volunteered for the Red Army while in a Soviet prison camp after the First World War. He returned to Hungary in 1921 to work with the illegal Hungarian Communist Party, moved to Vienna in 1927, then back to Moscow as a Party delegate in 1930. During the 1930s Stalinist purges, he was expelled then reaccepted by the Party. Some books and articles have suggested that he cooperated with the secret services to gain his freedom, denouncing several fellow Communists as counter-revolutionaries or "reactionaries." More recent research shows that these accusations first appeared in Soviet ambassador Yuri Andropov's hastily prepared dossier given to Nagy's former cabinet colleague János Kádár in case he needed some pretext to quash Nagy's popularity in 1957.[2]

In 1944, Nagy returned to Hungary with the Soviet army as it advanced across the country. He was minister of agriculture in the postwar provisional government, in charge of distributing large estates to the peasantry, and was prime minister between 1953 and 1955. He had seemed to be a gentler, kinder Communist leader than Rákosi, perhaps in Czechoslovakia's Alexander Dubček's mould, with notions of reform Communism.

It is difficult to imagine all the thoughts and doubts that must have crossed his mind before that fateful day of October 23, 1956, when Nagy gave in to the crowds that shouted for him to become their parliamentary leader again.

Nagy stepped out onto the balcony of the parliament buildings and spoke to the thousands gathered in Kossuth Square. The now famous speech began with "Comrades," but that quickly changed to "My dear young friends" once the crowd shouted that they no longer wished to be comrades. I was there. I remember being puzzled by hearing that form of address. In Hungary, in the '50s, it was always "Comrades."

On October 31, Nagy announced that the Soviet troops were leaving.

On November 4, when the Soviet army reasserted control over the breakaway satellite, Pál Maléter—the commander of an army brigade that refused to follow orders to shoot at demonstrators—was arrested by the Soviets and handed over to Hungarian military police. Nagy and a few of his associates, along with his wife and daughter, took refuge in the Yugoslav embassy. He was kidnapped while attempting to negotiate terms of surrender with the Soviet commanders and hustled out of the country to Romania's Lake Snagov.[3]

Kádár, who became Hungary's longest-serving prime minister and general secretary of the Communist Party, assumed power at the point of Soviet armour. His own ambitions fulfilled, it was Kádár who proposed, in April 1957, that Nagy be brought back, interrogated, tried before a secret court, pronounced guilty, sentenced to death. The Soviets opposed it—not because they had a lingering affection for Nagy, but because they thought the execution would make a martyr of him. Imre Nagy was hanged on June 16, 1958. Maléter was also tried and disposed of in the same way.

Nagy's and Maléter's bodies were buried in the courtyard of the prison. Three years after the Hungarian revolution had come and gone and most of the world had forgotten about it, they were exhumed and reburied in the unmarked graves of plot 301 alongside the other victims of the post-'56 purge.

In 1988, Gyula Horn, the last minister of foreign affairs of the Communist government of Hungary, allowed the families to claim and rebury the remains. Paul Maléter's legs had been broken to force his six-foot-four frame into a standard-size wooden box. Rumour has it, though this particular rumour was sternly quashed by others, that some of the bones were mixed with the bones of a giraffe.

Kádár was himself ousted in 1988. During the thirty-three years of his reign, he never mentioned Imre Nagy by name. He kept the records of Nagy's trial in a locked box in his bedroom. In 1988, when one of his last interviewers asked whether Nagy could now be rehabilitated, he said no. Even at the end of his own life, he would refer to Nagy only as "the dead man."

BY JUNE 16, 1989, the slow disintegration of Communism in Hungary had reached the point when Nagy could be granted a hero's ceremonial farewell by the government. The solemn occasion took place in Budapest's gigantic Heroes' Square, under the balustrade of the Palace of Art, near the grand national Millennial Monument commemorating the Magyars' settlement in the Carpathian Basin. This is the same square where Kádár held his first mass demonstration on May 1, 1957, celebrating the triumph of Communism over the "counter-revolution."

On that warm summer day, six coffins were on the podium, for the five martyrs of the 1956 revolution: Nagy, Maléter, Miklós Gimes, József Szilágyi and Géza Losonczy, who died under interrogation some days before the hangings. The sixth, empty coffin was added for the rest of the victims dumped into plot 301 and for all the young people whose lives had been stolen by the dictatorship. The young leader of FIDESZ (the new political party that called itself Young Democrats), Viktor Orbán, spoke on behalf of those young people and demanded that Soviet troops leave. Then the names of 277 identified victims[4] were read aloud while a crowd of thousands stood in silence.

Kádár survived his most famous victim's ceremonial reburial by a mere three weeks. He died during the same hour when Nagy was formally rehabilitated by the Supreme Court,[5] and was buried in the old Kerepesi Cemetery among the Communist great.

Someone dug up Kádár's grave in May 2007 and stole his skull, several bones and his wife's urn. This message was left in place of the bones: "murderers and traitors may not rest in holy ground 1956–2006." The grave robbers have never been discovered. Oddly, Mátyás Rákosi's ashes have also vanished from the vault where they lay.[6] Given the number of both men's enemies, it is impossible to point a finger, but there is a rumour that the family of one of their early victims, executed during the Stalinist purges and reburied in October 1956, wreaked macabre revenge on their remains.

When Minister of State Imre Pozsgay announced on a radio program in early 1989 that the 1956 revolution had been a "popular uprising" and not a "counter-revolution," I wonder if he realized that the Communist era was over.[7]

THE REVOLUTION I remember began as a noisy demonstration of placard-waving, flag-carrying people yelling that they wanted a change of government, democratic elections and freedom of speech. They shouted to protest the dictatorship, the lack of food and clothes in the shops, the forced idolatry of Marx, Lenin and Stalin, of Comrade Rákosi, whose huge photographs decorated factories, schools, stores and bridges (there was one—pasty-faced, piggy-eyed, bald, unsmiling—in our school gym). They wanted the Soviets to go home and their puppet dictatorship dismantled. Within a few hours, demonstrators from the downtown universities and offices were joined by auto workers from Csepel, factory workers from the rest of the country and, once the schools let out, a whole lot of young kids. There was an air of celebration at first, as Hungarian flags were gutted of their Communist emblems and Soviet flags and massive hammer-and-sickle symbols were dislodged and tossed off buildings.

Several units of the army, reluctant to obey orders to fire on fellow Hungarians, joined the revolution. I still remember that jubilation, people rushing down the street shouting, "Máleter is with us!"

There was a battle for the radio building. The news became the real news rather than the censored pap the dictatorship allowed people to hear. Stalin's gigantic bronze statue was toppled onto Dózsa György Road. I was there a short time after the thunderous fall of the Georgian monster, and I pocketed a small piece of him for my grandfather Vili, who had been jailed for eighteen months during one of the government's attacks on the intelligentsia.

State police, the much-feared AVO, fought back. They were aided by hastily assembled militia, recognizable by their puffy black jackets, armbands and heavy machine guns. There were street battles, some fought house to house; there were kids with Molotov cocktails attempting to stop tanks and armoured vehicles. There were some deaths, but the sense of jubilation persisted, as did the unaccustomed joy of freedom.

On October 31, Nagy declared Hungary's withdrawal from the Warsaw Pact and requested the United Nations' help to ensure the country's neutrality. At first the Soviet Union seemed unwilling to interfere, but that lasted only a few cheerful days. Soviet archives of the time reveal some hesitation and Khrushchev's anger at Rákosi and Gerő for allowing the situation to become uncontrollable.

On November 4, the Soviet army invaded in overwhelming numbers. I remember the rumbling of their monstrous turret-swivelling armoured tanks, the deafening boom of their shells and the rat-tat-tat of their machine-gun fire. Molotov cocktails, while enormously satisfying to toss, were no match for tanks.

Most of the deaths occurred in the last few days. It was difficult to estimate the exact number of dead, but it's now reported as 19,226. More than 100,000 were arrested, a few hundred deported to the Ukraine.[8]

Of the 35,000 people tried, 26,000 were sentenced.[9] Almost three hundred were executed.[10]

In 2008, fifty years after the Revolution, I visited Corvin Köz, a gathering place for very young self-declared revolutionaries. It faced the long yellow army barracks, whose soldiers would join us. In front of Corvin Köz, there is now a bronze statue of a kid with cap and grin who looks about fifteen years old. He wears running shoes and carries a gun. I had seen a lot of those kids on the streets of Budapest during the first few days of November 1956. One of them is in plot 301 of the Rákoskeresztúr cemetery. His name was Péter Mansfeld. He was fifteen when he was tried and sentenced to death. The government, not wishing to appear brutal, in case the rest of the world was watching (it wasn't), waited till Mansfield turned eighteen before they carried out the sentence.

My aunt Édi was one of the lucky ones. She was convicted of spying for helping the British embassy staff leave the beleaguered city and for taking part in the storming of the radio building. She, too, was condemned to death. Her two young children were placed in state orphanages. But her sentence was commuted to life and she was able to reclaim her two unforgiving boys in 1967. By then, her hair had turned white and her hands curved inward.

My mother and I left Hungary in late November 1956, our departure hastened by a well-aimed Soviet shell that transformed our one-room apartment into a large open-air hole. By 1956, courtesy of a Communist regime, we had progressed from house to apartment to single room and three of our family members had served jail time. My mother, who had been jailed earlier for trying to leave the country, was keen to avoid another stint in prison.

The government had a few of its own 1956 martyrs, most of them defenders of the Communist Party headquarters on Republic Square, near the Kerepesi Cemetery. The Party faithful surrendered after a long firefight with the revolutionaries. They were killed with their hands up. It was a moment frozen in time by the camera of a *Life* magazine photographer.[11] The pictures were featured in a special edition of *Life*, and the news about the killings reverberated around the world.

The Kádár government erected a gargantuan monument to the victims of what they termed the "counter-revolution" in the middle of Republic Square, where it remained until its move to the bizarre Sculpture Park, also known as the Sculpture Cemetery, outside the city limits, joining other ideological memorials of fifty years of Communism.

The 1963 general amnesty tried to end the matter of '56. Life under the Kádár regime had become a great deal more comfortable than life before the revolution and less restrained than in the other satellites. Kádár, unlike his predecessors, was ready to give the people a little more than they expected. Some land became available for private use; there were opportunities for advancement in government organizations and a chance to start shops and small businesses. Kádár's cheerful saying that "those not against us are with us" became a mantra of those who wished to get along. As one writer put it, the Hungarians "were the happiest barracks in the camp." It was as if a whole society had decided to bury its ideals and make an accommodation with the regime that imprisoned it.

That the revolution was not forgotten, nor its aims left behind, was clear only to those who chose to resist the enticements of the regime. George Konrád, a leading Hungarian intellectual and author, wrote about the aftermath of the revolution: "Leaving the Pipacs Bar one morning in early summer I have a few words for the Petőfi statue: 'Europe is quiet, Mr Petőfi, quiet again. We're keeping our mouths shut as we did in 1848, after your revolution and at least no one is getting shot into the Danube. But as you know, Mr Petőfi, they hanged our prime minister, Imre Nagy, two years back. We were terribly broken up when the news was announced and could think of nothing to say.'"[12] Sándor Petőfi, the lyric poet, had been the hero of another uprising, against another power in 1848. He too had been killed by Russians invited to help the Habsburgs put down a nationalist army. That too was followed by a period of peaceful coexistence, the Compromise of 1867, when the Habsburgs agreed to a new name for a joint country—Austria-Hungary—and granted the rebellious Hungarians rights they had failed to be awarded in battle.

Each year, over 200,000 refugees and their families around the world commemorated 1956, but it was not until the '80s that Hungarians could talk about it at home. In 1990, I was there when a small group of Canadians who used to be Hungarians unveiled a statue of Imre Nagy across from the Gothic towers of the parliament building. Nagy is round-shouldered, bespectacled; his hat and coat seem a bit shabby in the sunshine—such an unlikely man for a hero.

When the speeches were over, the orchestra struck up the tune from the slaves' chorus of Verdi's *Nabucco*. The crowd sang and cried. I wondered at the time why this particular music would make all these people weep. Was it the lonely bronze figure on the small bridge, looking out at the city? Was it the '56 resolve that no people should be enslaved by another? Hungarians have thought of themselves as victims for so many decades—denied their rights, excluded from decisions that determined their fate, surrounded by unfriendly Slavs and Germans, betrayed by allies and the Allies. The words of the national anthem bemoan that they have suffered enough to pay for whatever their past and future sins may be. People wept while singing those words during Sunday-morning church services. My whole family, not great churchgoers, would reach for their handkerchiefs and bow their heads in shared understanding of the tragedy of Hungarian life.

OCTOBER 2006 was the fiftieth anniversary of the revolution. It provided a grand public stage for battles between various political interests, all of whom claimed the revolution as their own. The far right portrayed it as a continuation of a pre–World War II line from the arch-conservatives of Admiral Miklós Horthy. The post-Communists claimed Nagy as one of their own. In this narrative, Nagy remained an idealistic Communist to the end of his life, wishing, like Dubček, to fulfill his country's destiny under the protection of the Soviet Union but on more lenient terms than those accepted by Kádár. In the right-wing narrative, on the contrary, he saw the truth and, finally, opposed Communism.

Prime Minister Gyurcsány (prime minister from 2004 till 2009), leader of the MSzP, the Hungarian Socialist Party, invited dignitaries from various countries to celebrate inside the parliament building. There would be speeches, films, a light-and-sound display. But protesters occupied the square in front of the building. Opposition leader Viktor Orbán, leader of FIDESZ, planned his own commemoration a few blocks away and took the opportunity to demand the government's resignation on "moral grounds."

Less than a month before, a speech Gyurcsány had made in a closed meeting of his recently re-elected colleagues had been leaked to the media. The public could hear Gyurcsány admitting that, like all politicians, "we were lying day and night" during the campaign and in their years in power. The leaked speech led to stunned fury, aggressive protests and Orbán's insistence that Gyurcsány resign. Although the prime minister fought back, explaining that the speech was not meant to be taken literally, he had clearly failed to impress those gathered in the square on that October day.

The crowds included supporters of the extreme right, some violent skinheads, furious old-timers whose lives had not been improved by democracy and offended '56ers who had been excluded from formal events.

The demonstrators commandeered an old 1956 tank on Deák Square. On Szabadsag Tér (Freedom Square), they invaded and thrashed the former stock exchange palace, now occupied by Hungarian Television, all in full view of police, spectators and foreign television crews. They set fire to files, dragged computers into the street, burned cars and vandalized stores. Still, the police stood around as if awaiting orders. Demonstrators moved from the parliament building toward the Hotel Astoria, where Viktor Orbán was holding his own open-air rally. At around the time that the two crowds began to mix, the police responded with tear gas and truncheons, beating some of the demonstrators and a few elderly Orbán supporters. Anyone wanting to know how Hungary was dealing with protesters needed only to switch on the news.

The government's efforts to claim a piece of 1956 for itself failed, not only in front of the parliament buildings, but also on Dózsa György Road, where Stalin's massive bronze statue had once ruled. A brand-new monument to the events of 1956 was commissioned to occupy the same general area near the stone lineup of Hungary's historical greats on Heroes' Square. But from the moment of its unveiling, the monument was derided as an insult to the dead. Its massive steel columns, meant to symbolize the street fighters who faced the might of Soviet tanks, are just an assembly of rusting pillars; it has no sense of heroism, no feeling that this signifies a momentous event in Hungary's history. What the country's aging '56ers had hoped for was a heroic, figurative sculpture, one that Rome's Bernini might have created had he been alive for the commission.

To some, the closely packed, tall, standing steel pillars look remarkably like gallows, just another way for Gyurcsány to dishonour the memory of those the old regime billed as counter-revolutionaries, disturbers of the peace. I thought the memorial was stark, grim, unforgiving, its lack of emotion less reminiscent of October 1956 than of its grey, relentless aftermath—as the words on the massive plaque say, "the repression of subsequent decades." No quarter here for the compromises of goulash Communism.

The 1956 Institute, the office that claims to represent the freedom fighters, stayed out of the fray.[13] It had its own problems with the raging debates about who played the major roles in the revolution: the students, the Petőfi Circle intellectuals, the workers, the "street."

George Konrád, who was arrested after '56, does not "feel close to people who dine out on the revolution ... Time has blown our frail stories out of proportion."[14]

THE SOVIETS' HUNGARY

My father came back to life in 1949, from a Soviet mining camp where he had been imprisoned since the summer of 1945. In 1945, he had been a healthy man of thirty-eight, a little thin as food had been scarce during the siege of Budapest. My family had been hiding in a basement bunker during the shelling that destroyed most of the city. He had climbed out in search of bread. For several months no one knew what had happened to him, though my mother suspected, rightly, that he had been picked up by a group of Soviet soldiers charged with finding "volunteers" for a little work—*malenki robot*, as they called it.

It is only during the past 20 years that historians have begun to delve into the stories of the around 600,000 Hungarians[15] who were pushed into boxcars and trundled off to the Soviet Union's slave labour camps. It was a world of fear, deprivation and debasement, of sadistic guards, intense cold and 20-hour workdays, a world that remained relatively unknown until Alexander Solzhenitsyn's *Gulag Archipelago*.

Some of those taken were disarmed soldiers, a few were Nazi-supporters, some were victims of local Communists who wished to acquire their properties, but many of them were picked up at random for work detail. For example, in the villages and towns of Transcarpathia, males between the ages of 18 and 50—approximately 45,000 men and boys—were deported.[16] In Transylvania, most men between the ages of 18 and 50 were deported. Stalin had ordered a "collective punishment" of the Hungarian people; the army was following orders. Soviet foreign minister Vyacheslav Molotov, one of the signatories of the 1939 Nazi-Soviet Non-Aggression Pact—another bit of Soviet history never mentioned in the former satellites—said openly that the guilt for collaboration with the Germans was to be borne by the "Hungarian people."[17]

When my father returned, he was a skeletal creature seeking a place to hide. He was one of the lucky ones. Many died of starvation or froze to death—about half of those taken never returned. Their families have not been able to trace where they were buried, if they were buried. Those who were allowed to go home were afraid to talk of their fate, nor would there be any acknowledgment of their suffering by the Soviets or their own government. To this day, I do not know where my father had been during those missing years of his life, or how he endured. When I asked him, shortly before he died, he merely shook his head to indicate that the subject was closed.

Memories of the Red Army occupation and its galling description as "liberation" added to Hungarians' hatred of Soviet rule. The deportations were not mentioned in any histories, and personal memoirs were suppressed. The public, if it was interested in the matter, was assured that all those who returned had served time as war criminals. It is only since the demise of Communism that there has been open discussion of victims of Soviet policies. A few recent memoirs attest to the terrible brutalities visited on the survivors. A few books talk of the mass rapes of the deported women and girls, some as young as ten, some in their seventies. Rape was one of the Red Army's favourite pastimes in the "liberated" countries. Soldiers raped thousands of women of all ages. Some even raped Jewish concentration-camp survivors they encountered along the roads home. In one account, a mother and daughter on their way home from Ravensbrück were raped ten times before reaching Budapest.

A school friend of my mother's, Mariette Gerlóczy, spent five years in a slave labour camp in Romania. Her father, a former aide to Regent Horthy, was executed. Her husband died of typhoid. Her two young children died in the camp of starvation and disease. Their tiny bodies were buried in cardboard boxes, in shallow graves dug by their mother's bare hands.

The Soviet enthusiasm for collecting Hungarians extended to all former Hungarian territories, now ruled by Romania, Ukraine, Czechoslovakia and Yugoslavia (Transylvania, Transcarpathian Rus', Upper Hungary and Lower Hungary). Precise numbers are difficult to arrive at because so many died on the way to the camps. During longer journeys to Siberia, many prisoners froze to death. As they were picked up from towns and villages at random, they had not come prepared for the extreme cold, had no clothes or food or water, and had not been able to tell anyone that they had been captured. In Kolyma and Vorkuta, temperatures were often −60 degrees centigrade. There was no medication for the sick and escape was impossible.

It is little wonder that Hungarians were eager to consign Soviet memorials to the strange Sculpture Cemetery—the "Totalitarian Monuments Theme Park," according to my recently aquired guidebook. There they are, the massive sculptures that had once confronted people at street corners, Marxes and Engelses and thick-thighed men and women with high cheekbones and threatening frowns, and a few monuments of Red Army soldiers dedicated by the grateful people of Hungary. As for seeing the Soviets as "liberators," few Hungarians were willing to keep even the military memorials erected in their honour. While *Liberty*, a fourteen-metre-tall statue of a woman holding a palm leaf aloft, is still there at the top of Gel-lért Hill, the bronze Red Army soldier that used to guard her base has been dismissed from his post.

THE HOUSE OF TERROR

You can discover a great deal about the Hungarian state police—the dreaded AVO (State Protection Agency), as it was known to post-war Hungarians—in the House of Terror at 66 Andrássy Boulevard. The boulevard is one of Europe's most beautiful streets, lined with trees and the porticoed, pillared mansions of the pre-war wealthy; it's now a UNESCO World Heritage Site. Number 66 itself was once a fine example of neoclassical architecture. Now its facade is painted grey and its roof is framed in gleaming black with the word "Terror" cut out of the background. Ironically, the building served as a club-house, then as headquarters, for the Arrow Cross, Hungary's home-grown Fascists, who ruled in late 1944 and early 1945, as well as for the state police after the war. It saw the interrogation, torture and murder of hundreds, perhaps thousands, of people until it was shut down at the end of the '50s. Its basement drains were often clogged with blood, and prisoners stood knee-deep in gore, waiting their own turn with the interrogators.

Near the entrance, in the high-ceilinged central hall, a Russian tank greets visitors. The surrounding semi-circular wall, three storeys high, displays photographs of the state's victims—not all of them, as the walls could not accommodate the thousands who passed through this building and other buildings like this on their way to death.

Throughout the building are stark reminders of the deeds of the former occupants and the suffering of their victims.

One side of a large, divided room displays video and photographs of the Fascist years, deftly connecting the country's turn toward racism and its drift into Hitler's net to the injustices of Trianon—a sideshow to the Versailles Peace Treaties that ended the First World War.

As the war ended, Hungary elected a Communist government of vitriolic reformers who hanged and shot opponents. Miklós Horthy, an admiral in the defeated Austro-Hungarian navy, organized a conservative counter-revolution and became self-styled regent after the Communists were ousted by the Romanian army in 1919, thus establishing a monarchy without a monarch and an admiralty without a sea. He loved to parade wearing his admiral's uniform, riding a white horse and being saluted by incongruously overdressed armed guards.

The texts introducing visitors to Hungary's wartime past pay scant attention to accuracy with respect to Hungary's active role supporting Hitler's war in order to regain territories lost at Trianon, where the fate of Hungary was decided in 1920—the piecing off of the country and three million of its inhabitants to neighbouring countries.

There is no mention here that the Hungarian parliament introduced its own anti-Jewish law, the Numerus Clausus Act, as early as 1920. It was the first anti-Semitic legislation in twentieth-century Europe. The Act, which was mostly ignored, limited the number of Jews who would be admitted to universities to 6 per cent, their proportion of the total population. In May 1938, 1939 and 1941, in addition to reintroducing the 1920 law, parliament went on to define Jews as a race rather than as followers of a religion and added an array of other laws to circumscribe what Jews could and could not do. The new laws prohibited Jews from holding government and judiciary positions. They also established the notorious labour service system that would eventually force Jewish men into military service on the side of the Germans, only without guns or rights.

In the summer of 1941, Reichsführer Himmler, who was answerable directly to the Führer, called for the "Final Solution to the

Jewish question": the annihilation of all the Jews of Europe and, after the war was won, all the Jews in the world.

Hungary's 1941 entry into World War II was pinned on the Soviet bombardment of the town of Kassa (today's Košice, Slovakia). This attack, historians have revealed, was most likely ordered by German military, their way of making sure the Hungarian army joined them on the killing fields of the Don River valley, where the Second Hungarian Army was wiped out—40,000 dead, 35,000 wounded, 60,000 taken prisoner.

Here in the House of Terror, Admiral Horthy's post–World War I regime is credited with keeping the Germans out until March 19, 1944.

Adolf Eichmann's Sondereinsatzkommando arrived in Budapest on March 19, 1944, with the army of occupation. Over the next few weeks, they obtained the assistance of two senior men in the Ministry of the Interior and the chief of the gendarmerie to divide the country into deportation zones. Deportations began at the end of April.

There is no mention here of the role the gendarmes played in assembling Jews into ghettos, beating them to extract confessions of where their valuables had been hidden, in the terrible screams of the tortured that rent the nights around the ghettos, the suicides, how children were beaten in front of their parents; nor is there any notion here of guilt—only a confirmation of the view that Hungarians were, throughout the war and its aftermath, the victims.

You would not learn in the House of Terror that Jews were isolated, ordered to wear yellow stars and forced into ghettos, that all their property was confiscated, that close to half a million Jews were packed into boxcars holding eighty to one hundred human beings each and that they were transported, mostly standing, and without water or food, for five to six days from Hungary to Auschwitz-Birkenau. The journey claimed the lives of many children, the elderly, the sick and hospital patients who had been thrown into the carriages. The trains arrived day and night, disgorging their dazed passengers onto a wide platform guarded by dogs and ss men, lit by powerful strobe lights, in case someone still found the energy to try to escape. At the end of that ramp there was a selection, separating those who would be killed immediately from those destined to die more slowly through overwork and lack of food. Women with children had no chance of survival.

By July 7, 1944, when Admiral Horthy ordered the transports stopped, most of the deported were dead.

I have visited Auschwitz II-Birkenau, the extermination camp where Hungary's Jews were murdered. When you stand on that Birkenau ramp today, you face the two ruined crematoria where the bodies were burned. To the right are the remnants of the showers where new arrivals were gassed with Zyklon B, one of the local inventions that replace the messy business of shooting, clubbing and carbon-monoxide poisoning.

According to German records, the combined daily capacity of the furnaces was 4,416 bodies. The ashes were used as fertilizer. The hair was used for lining coats, though about 7,000 kilograms—7 tonnes—were found packed into bags when the camp was liberated. Gold fillings from teeth were removed and melted into ingots. There is an exhibition of hair, another of children's shoes; a mountain of small suitcases; and a few personal effects in one of the exhibition rooms of Auschwitz I, the original camp. The ruins of two crematoria were still standing in Auschwitz II-Birkenau when I was there. They had been hurriedly blown up in 1945, when the Red Army approached from the east, but the guards still took time to order a forced march of prisoners to other camps inside the Reich. Most of the prisoners did not make it.

On October 14, 1944, Admiral Horthy made his speech attempting to extract his beleaguered country from Germany's war. His admission that day, that "today, it is obvious to any sober-minded person that the German Reich has lost the war," was indeed obvious to all but the madmen hiding in the Reich cellars under Berlin. Horthy's announcement was realistic, rather than heroic. He was forced to resign his leadership of the country, and his family were kidnapped by the ss and hastily shipped off to Germany, where he survived the war.

In the Hall of the Arrow Cross, the ghostly figure of Ferenc Szálasi hovers at the head of a table set for dinner. Under the self-styled "national leader" installed by the Germans to replace Horthy, the last remaining Jews of the capital (except for those in hiding) were locked into a ghetto. Szálasi's Arrow Cross thugs forced their way into buildings protected by foreign embassies and marched the Jewish inhabitants to the banks of the Danube, where they were shot and dumped in among the drifting ice. It's where my friend György Vámos almost died, except for the capricious change of heart of an Arrow Cross man who responded to the question of a six-year old boy: "Mr. Arrow Cross, how long do we have to stand here?"[18]

A strange memorial has been erected on the Pest side of the Danube to commemorate those who were not so lucky: a bunch of bronze shoes where those about to die were told to take their shoes off.

This is a part of Hungarian history that people here still find difficult to confront. Of the twenty rooms in the House of Terror, only two and a half tell stories of Hungarian Fascist times.

But then, Jews seem not to be a big part of this house's narrative.

Historian Maria Ormos told me that the chief problem with recognizing the Jewish trauma is the population's own sense of the catastrophe that was 1944–1945: the year of the Arrow Cross and the horrific siege of Budapest. The siege lasted from Christmas 1944, when the first Red Army soldiers were spotted in Buda, till February 13, 1945. The bombings, the destruction, the starvation, the deportations for forced labour to the Soviet Union, the mass rape of women all contributed to the feeling that "we have all suffered"—equally.

Unlike the Poles, the Germans and the French, Hungarians have not yet argued about, confronted, let alone admitted their own part in the Holocaust. These words by Attila József, a well-loved Hungarian poet, grace the first page of the House of Terror book: "The past must be acknowledged..." The end of that sentence could be that, unacknowledged, the past festers in the mind.

Despite numerous academic studies, the public has remained strangely disengaged from the truth. Unlike Poland, this country was ruled by men who—however reluctantly—cooperated with the Nazi plans for Europe. There was no underground army, no resistance, little organized opposition. Miklós Horthy's autobiography takes great pains to explain that he had no choice, that he did what he could, that his attempts to make peace with the Allies were honest and honourable, as they no doubt were; but he did not tell the whole truth, or confront his government's role in the deportation of its Jewish citizens. However, his October announcement did provide him with the opportunity to claim credit, along with a whole lot of other people who wished to be remembered, for saving about 100,000 people still alive in the Budapest ghetto.

In 1993, Horthy's ashes were returned to his hometown of Kenderes and reburied in his family crypt during a tearful ceremony that attracted many government leaders, including then–prime minister (from May 1990 until his death in December 1993) József Antall. Since 1993, there has been a veritable orgy of Horthy celebrations, including his adoption by the Hungarian Guard, a brand-new Fascist group of mostly young men in black uniforms and boots and spouting racist slogans, whose presence terrifies those with unhappy memories of Hungary under the Arrow Cross. In 2009, the Guard rented a feisty white horse for a special commemoration in front of the old Hotel Gellért, which had been the favourite haunt of ss officers during the Horthy era.

The other side of the House of Terror's double-occupancy room displays videos and photographs of the Communist regime's instruments of rule. After the war, 60 Andrassy Boulevard's victims became more varied. There were political opponents of the Stalinist system, leading Communists who needed to be prepared for the show trials that characterized the late 1940s and early 1950s, people caught in the elaborate networks of informers, members of the intelligentsia who had not agreed to support the regime's rules of what could and could not be said/written/painted. Oddly enough, this was the building where János Kádár himself was interrogated and tortured over several gruelling days and nights in 1951, during one of Stalin's maniacal purges of his own followers. He was released in 1954 after Stalin's death.

It is in this building's basement cellars, reeking of fear, "sweat, blood, and human excrement," where George Faludy,[19] the poet, memoirist and social commentator, began his own endurance test of beatings, torture and humiliation, a journey that led in 1949 to the country's most feared prison camp at Recsk.

The underground cells today are recreations of the originals; the instruments of torture, the crude gallows are gifts from other institutions. Yet none of this takes away from the sheer sense of horror that visitors feel when they descend into the dark bowels of the building. My grandfather was interrogated here and sent to work in the stone quarries. He had no poems to escape to, so he became convinced that there was no escape from the system other than death or exile. Given the opportunity, he chose the latter.

In the dark Hall of Tears, tourists are invited to remember those who were executed. On the way out, I watched a short video excerpt from Imre Nagy's interrogation at the phony trial that he would have known would end in his execution. He seems astonishingly peaceful, seriously arguing his case in front of judges he knew were not going to listen to him. It seemed to me that he spoke knowing the time would come when this speech would be heard by the people. The fifty-two hours of tapes were played fifty years after the week-long trial during the exact time of the original trial.

The film of the Soviet forces leaving Hungary in 1991 is one of the last moments of the exhibition. Then, a reminder that all is still not well with the world: films of demolished Hungarian villages in Romania.

Near the exit is a display of mugshots identifying some of the Communist Party's chief victimizers. One of the photographs features Antal Apró, a hated member of the post-1956 Politburo, an outspoken opponent of reforms, a man whose voice urged death sentences for leaders of the revolution. Posthumously, he also became future prime minister Ferenc Gyurcsány's grandfather-in-law. Apró's daughter, Piroska—Gyurcsány's mother-in-law—lives on the top floor of Gyurcsány's home in the Buda Hills. The lovely house was Apró's state-provided home when he served the Kádár regime.[20] A nearby neighbour, slightly uphill, was Kádár himself.

Opening this museum in 2002 to the public was one of Viktor Orbán's proudest moments. The young prime minister (July 1988 to May 2002, and again beginning in April 2010) had personally guaranteed the government funds necessary for its completion. In his opening speech, heard by most of the country on radio and television, he declared that the House of Terror "slammed the door on the sick twentieth century."

His words were not prophetic.

DEALING WITH THE COMMUNISTS

It is ironic that in 1994, only five years after the 1989 transformation, the Hungarian Socialist Party (Magyar Szocialista Párt), a renamed successor of the Communist Hungarian Socialist Workers' Party, won more than 50 per cent of the seats in Parliament and formed a coalition with the Liberals to govern. Gyula Horn became prime minister. That was the same Gyula Horn who had served as a volunteer militiaman helping the state police during the 1956 revolution. Horn, like Kádár, had consistently characterized 1956 as a "counter-revolution" and its leaders as lawbreakers. (All schoolchildren learned to refer to 1956 as a counter-revolution, and citizens were told to be grateful to the Soviet forces for saving them from themselves.)

The pattern continued after a FIDESZ interregnum, when the Socialists returned with a majority and formed the government with the Alliance of Free Democrats. Péter Medgyessy, the new prime minister, had been an intelligence officer during the Kádár era. It is even more ironic that his popularity soared after the revelations about his past.

In Hungary, the former *nomenklatura* could and did retain their positions of power. Unlike in other former satellites, there were no formal processes to punish those who had interrogated, condemned, sentenced political enemies who, in Polish Solidarity's Father Zięba's words, refused to "live in a lie."

The disposal of the vast array of state police documents has remained a touchy subject for most politicians. In a system that worked because so many spied on their friends and neighbours, the question of what access should be granted to the archives and to whom is still, twenty years after the Communist government gave way, a conundrum. Some seven hundred researchers and hundreds of individuals looking for their own files were admitted to the Historical Archives of the Hungarian State Security; others have not been. Even those who have seen files complain that many are empty, that the documents are missing. Some files that were copied for other security agencies, such as the East Germans', have since been recovered in the Stasi files, but thousands have not.

I VISITED Péter Boross—head of State Security under Prime Minister József Antall, a former leader of the Hungarian Democratic Forum and the second prime minister of a democratic Hungary. Boross was the first non-Communist official to have been given the keys to the state police's secrets.

It was a long late-summer afternoon on Lake Balaton; his garden was overgrown with blue grass flowers and lazy shadflies too tired to move out of our way; the neighbour was grilling something intensely spicy on his barbeque. Despite the heat, it was surprisingly cool in the low-ceilinged living room of Boross's hundred-year-old farmhouse. The thick fieldstones walls, he explained, keep the place bearable even in midsummer. We sat on low sofas, looking out over the gardens and enjoying the breeze. My companion, a former bureaucrat in the Antall government, addressed him as "Mr. Prime Minister" and made a small bow when they shook hands.

Péter Boross is in his eighties, a broad-shouldered man with short-cropped hair and a painfully strong grip. Slow-moving but with a commanding voice, he announced right at the beginning that he was, himself, a victim of Communist jails. A member of the '56 revolutionary committee, he was sent to an internment camp in eastern Hungary. After his release he spent three years under strict police supervision. Not allowed to continue with law school, he found a job in a pub. He worked his way up to assistant manager during the '70s and met József Antall for the first time in a pub at the zoo. Antall was to become the leader of the Democratic Forum, the party that cobbled together a government from disparate parties in 1990. The Democratic Forum was astonishingly effective in bringing together a coalition that could make the changes necessary to build a country founded on democratic principles.

Antall and Boross didn't exactly become friends—they had nothing in common—but there was mutual respect and Boross was not surprised to hear from Antall once he became prime minister. "He told me he had no idea what to do with the state police, the intelligence services," Boross said with a smile. "He said he needed me to help sort out the mess. I said yes but for only two years."

Obviously, Antall, who was bookish, a dreamer, a historian, needed a man with a practical mind. Perhaps the only reason Antall had agreed to be a politician was that he loved history. István Rév told me, "He thought he owed it to history to restore something lost during the previous forty-five years." Rév should know: himself a professor of history, he has been fascinated with all the players engaged with the changes.

When Boross was appointed minister of the interior, he had not the slightest notion of what the job entailed. He arrived for his first day at the ministry building full of terrified men who had by now realized that their lives would be utterly changed, their privileges would be cancelled, their standing in society reduced, they may even face some form of retribution for following the Party's orders. The fact that they had already burned at least 50,000 cartons of state secrets, informer records and spy reports testified to their panic.

In early 1990, there were still 28,000 large boxes and four to five thousand individual cartons reported in government documents and six thousand files containing information about people who had "engaged in incitement activities against the state."[21] That thousands of documents had been moved to other secret locations and thousands more transferred from "internal" to "external" security areas was obvious. Most of these files have since disappeared. When he looked into some of the labelled file folders, Boross discovered that they were empty.

But there were still thousands upon thousands of cartons with millions of secrets about people. Boross said he wanted to have them all safely stored so no one could use them unfairly. "I knew that so many people had been threatened into becoming informers. Women were forced to spy on their own families or they could lose their children. I read one of those files. It was heart-breaking. So many people reported about nothing, irrelevant bits of information about their friends, to keep themselves safe. They did no harm. What were we to do with all that?" There were a few cases of judges who had condemned people to death after '56, he told me, but those who were still alive "were such pathetic old men now, it would have been senseless to prosecute them now. Communism lasted too long for justice to follow."

According to István Rév, some of the men in that ministry had been instrumental in promoting the changes that ended Communist rule—that of the very Party that had guaranteed their comfortable existence. They had been in a unique position to recognize that the government could no longer govern, that the economy would collapse, that the Brezhnev doctrine of preventing all the satellites from trying to leave the Soviet system was dead, that Gorbachev's perestroika had changed everything. These people, unlike the rest of the population, were aware of the changes in Poland. They knew that there was no turning back.

In May 1989, Gyula Horn,[22] then the Workers' Party's foreign minister, ordered Hungary to raise its piece of the Iron Curtain to provide safe passage for the East Germans who had been waiting to cross the border to Austria.

That summer, the number of East Germans in temporary camps, private homes, Red Cross shelters and the West German embassy's garden in Hungary had grown to 45,000.[23] Horn's decision to open the border was in direct contravention of Hungary's treaty with East Germany that called for the return, by force if necessary, of East German citizens to their home country. Many historians view Horn's decision as the immediate cause of the dismantling of the Berlin Wall. German foreign minister Hans-Dietrich Genscher later awarded Horn the Stresemann Medal, remarking that "everything that followed was a consequence" of Horn's brave decision.[24]

"The Soviet advisers were still there in 1990. They knew everything that went on. Of course, I fired the people who had worked with them, but those direct lines to Moscow were still there," Boross said, "and all the senior officers."[25]

But the low-level operatives remained in place; they swore allegiance to the new "legal" regime that succeeded the former "illegal" one-party rule of the Communists, and carried on with their work. Boross had viewed them as practitioners of a craft, much like electricians or plumbers. He believed the government would be able to use them. Espionage was not a useless profession.

What happened to the top of the pyramid where the real power lay? Almost nothing. There was no commission of inquiry; no Institute of National Remembrance, as there was in Poland; no lustration, as there was in Czechoslovakia and the Czech Republic. Those whom the Kádár regime and its predecessors had rewarded with lucrative university posts or foreign travel or expense accounts, the Party faithful whose children could be educated in London or Paris, could keep their homes, though they lost their privileged lives. They were not threatened by the advent of democracy. In this new world, they could continue to reap the benefits of their advantages and education. It was easier for them to transform themselves to fit the specifications of the new system. They could be bankers, investment brokers, real estate entrepreneurs. They spoke the language of the newly arrived European Union and United States advisers. They knew the language of capitalism. Many chose to remain in government posts until early retirement on generous pensions. No law bars them from "public service." The officers of the former dreaded III/III section of the state police were "lustrated" after 1994—the only ones—but they could keep their new jobs if they admitted what they had done under the Communist regime.

The injustice suffered by those the regime judged, imprisoned, marginalized, continues. They were left without adequate support, their jobs and pensions evaporated while they were in jail, and many of them never recovered from the beatings and isolation cells. Ferenc Vida, the judge who condemned Imre Nagy to the gallows, died in November 1990 without being forced to answer pesky questions in a court of valid law. The other judges and government appointed lawyers enjoyed comfortable retirements.

In Hungary, General Jaruzelski would be allowed to fade into the soft twilight of his life.

Péter Boross walked with us through the garden. He smiled when he told me he is now head of the freedom fighters' association—"You know, those who were condemned to death but survived get double pensions. You can get by on that."

THERE HAS been no general public access to the archives since, though bits of information have found their way to the press. The leaks have proven useful against enemies, political opponents, TV personalities, journalists. It is difficult not to sense personal spite in these occasions, a desire to bring down someone disliked or just envied.

In 2007, the sorely beleaguered Gyurcsány government commissioned a report on the state police archives by a nine-man committee headed by János Kenedi. Kenedi is described by others as an emblematic figure of the resistance before 1989 and a questioning and questing critic of government actions ever since. He quit his job as a journalist in protest against Hungary's part in the 1968 invasion of Czechoslovakia. He is the author of numerous books and hundreds of articles about a broad range of subjects, but returning, time and again, to examining the shadows the past casts over his country's present. Kenedi is in his early sixties, with salt-and-pepper, curly hair, a suntanned face, grey eyes behind round granny glasses and a quiet, gentle voice that belies his fierce determination to get at the truth in the secret files of the former state. Since 1990, he has worked at the 1956 Institute.

He lives on the top floor of what had once been the family's mansion in a verdant part of Buda. The garden is rather shabby now, the fountain clogged with dead leaves, but you can still see that this would have been a stunning place sometime pre-war. His apartment is sunny, casual, lined with books in several languages. Some of them attest to his passion to "lustrate" the secret services of the Communist regime.

He talks of the EU's advice to the former Soviet satellites: to examine the sins committed by their totalitarian governments so that they can create some distance between themselves and the past. Knowing and understanding the past is an essential part of their future. But finding the truth is never easy, and the current disposition to make peace between different views of history by drawing a line down the middle is a form of lying to oneself. There are always knowable facts, and unless these are faced by society, the danger of slipping back into old habits will continue. Here, where there are no ingrained democratic and judiciary traditions, the risk of reverting to old nationalist, populist, racist, irredentist habits is even greater. Those impulses die hard, and with the advent of free expression, they can become more attractive. It is obvious, he explained, that four decades of Communism provided a thick covering for those impulses to find and blame "the other," unless the other happened to be a former capitalist. Now newspapers can openly publish Arrow Cross propaganda; they can point fingers at left-wing intellectuals, accusing them of being anti-nation. Now there can be open season on gypsies.

In October 2008, the Kenedi Report weighed in at 438 pages and could be read in its entirety on the prime minister's website. But the recommendation that the secrets of the files should finally be made public has yet to be implemented. The recommendations at the end of the report include a new legal framework, definitions and accessibility. Some of these recommendations were already in previous reports ignored by Péter Boross, both as minister of the interior and as prime minister after Antall's death in 1993.

Kenedi has made a number of public statements about his findings. Among them is the allegation that the files demonstrate how far the rot penetrated every layer of society and to what extent the people who were spreading the rot then are still active in various branches of government, in the Church and in business.

He was not surprised to discover that Hungary was used as a money-laundering centre by the Soviet Union. Hungarian agents managed to hide millions of cleansed money in foreign banks, a fact that supports the enduring suspicions of those who have been most vociferous in their accusations against the *nomenklatura*'s elites. Hungary was viewed by the West as the most democratic of the satellites, so it was given more leeway when negotiating with Western companies. All this information was passed on to the Soviets.

Each satellite's secret service had its own specialties. Hungary's was information and disinformation and the theft of Western technology, particularly pharmaceuticals.[26] The Czechs specialized in stealing military secrets, especially those related to manufacturing armaments. The Bulgarians had responsibility for murders—a few writers, some suspected spies, overly active dissidents. Failing to kill the pope was one of their missteps. The East Germans were to keep tabs on their fellow Germans. Their penetration of most government offices, the intelligence network and the media in West Germany was almost complete. The files attest to the fact that the Russians never trusted the Poles; their menial tasks were limited to watching their own emigrant nationals.

Documents, Kenedi told me, continued to disappear throughout the various changes in government. He is dismissive of the so-called January 1990 Dunagate scandal when a TV crew revealed film footage of the shredding of files. The reason he is dismissive: it was assumed that after the revelations, the destruction stopped. In fact, it continued till late 1994, perhaps longer. During a 2005 BBC interview, Kenedi said that hundreds of thousands of documents were taken by members of the secret services and stashed for possible later use. A senior state police operative testifies in the Kenedi Report that at the end of December 1989, between Christmas and New Year's, Ferenc Pallagi, who was standing in for the minister of the interior, ordered the destruction of all III/III (internal security) files, without exception. This had to include citizens' reports, notebooks, names of all operatives past and present, the master lists of documents and the orders for their destruction. His unit packed the papers into crates and transported them—five crates at a time—to a specific location where they were to be burned. Unfortunately, as the agent says, they found two senior officers at the site already busy incinerating their own loads of files. They were told to take their load of about forty to fifty kilos of papers elsewhere. Other officers estimate the amount taken for destruction during that time to four to five hundred kilos.

Nevertheless, tons of material remained—32,618 documents—for the Kenedi committee's study and conclusion that it must all be available for individuals to read, that no government should assume the right to protect citizens from themselves and that historians can, and should, be able to use this material for their study. If he had his way, the entire mess (except for highly personal information about people's health or sex lives) would be available online to anyone who chose to read it. He would also exclude reports that could expose foreign informers, such as those in the Middle East, to possible execution.

A dangerous aspect of the current secrecy is that some files—no one knows how many—could be used by the unscrupulous. From time to time a radio station or newspaper is offered information by unnamed sources in exchange for cash. One such case may be that of István Szabó, the celebrated, Oscar-winning director of such memorable films as *Mephisto, Colonel Redl* and *Sunshine*.

In September 2008, I dined with Szabó at the Rosenstein Restaurant, near Baross Square (named after Gábor Baross, who had helped manage a tense relationship with the Habsburg administration after the 1867 Compromise and reorganized Hungary's railway system). Szabó had promised me a sumptuous meal at his favourite eatery. Rosenstein is an overwhelmingly friendly, cheerfully decorated restaurant—white tablecloths, blue plush chairs, peach walls and a long, open bar—with a wide range of local dishes, many of which are featured in the restaurateur's own book of recipes.[27]

Still recovering from an illness, all Szabó could do was to recommend dishes and watch me eat. In his black T-shirt, black jeans and loose black jacket, he seemed much paler and thinner than the last time we had met.

Szabó had been accused of being an AVH (state police) informer. The allegation first appeared in 2006, in the Hungarian cultural weekly *Élet és Irodalom* ("Life and Literature"), under the title "The Identification of an Informer." The author, András Gervai, had been researching material about film history in the secret services archives when he came across a series of reports Szabó had written between 1957 and 1963. While Szabó's reports themselves are downright boring, the fact remains that Szabó had supplied information—however uninteresting—about seventy-two fellow students and professors at the film school. He now repeated to me what he had told interviewers earlier: it is true that he had been forced to inform on colleagues, but he turned the reporting sessions to the advantage of those he was supposed to hurt. His reports were all intentionally dull.

His ordeal began in February 1957. He was arrested, held in custody without charges, interrogated and, finally, told to sign an agreement to inform on his classmates. There was nothing in the agreement that would force him to report anything of the remotest interest to the secret police. No one suffered as a result of his debriefings. He believes he helped one man who was on the scene where the Party stalwarts were gunned down in October 1956. Whether this is true or not, is impossible to prove as not much has remained of Szabó's file and as revelations about the murky past of prominent figures such as Szabó have become mired in controversy.

He said that his feelings about what had happened to him are the theme of many of his award-winning films, which tackle the dark spaces of the soul, the tough personal decisions man must make in his life. During a *New York Times* interview after the 1982 opening of *Mephisto*, he talked about the theme of making hard moral choices in impossible times: "We are often unable to carry out the more difficult tasks set for us by history... The human tasks set by history in this century may be unique in their difficulty..." Anyone who had taken the trouble to carefully study his films would have seen the signs of a man troubled by decisions, the compromises he had to make.[28]

Now he told me that he was not particularly surprised by the revelations' surfacing, as and when they did. A successful man is often the target of envy and resentment. When that man is also willing to acknowledge his Jewishness, he can become the target for all those reignited hatreds that fuelled the murderous rage of uneducated rabble during the last months of the Holocaust. "My enemies," he told me, "have been searching for an opportunity to destroy me and they were provided with one on a platter."

But if the aim was to sever his relationships within the international film world, his alleged enemies have failed. If the aim was the deprive him of an enthusiastic audience at home, that too has been unsuccessful. I was struck by the response his presence elicited from people in the street and on the subway. He nodded and smiled at the shouted hellos, the wishes to have a fine day, the anxious enquiries about his health. A woman stopped him to say how great it was to see him out and about. A man confronted him near the restaurant. "God bless you, and keep you," he said with tears in his eyes, and touched István on the shoulder.

ON MAY 26, 2009, the case of *Kenedi v. Hungary* crawled to its laborious conclusion in the European Court of Human Rights.

"The applicant alleged that the Hungarian authorities' protracted reluctance to grant him unrestricted access to certain documents, authorized by a court order, had prevented him from terminating a professional undertaking, namely, to write an objective study on the functioning of the Hungarian State Security Service..."

The court determined in Kenedi's favour.

In June 2009, the 1956 Institute released the names of just 110 Communist spies and informers, together with their code names. Some of the names—journalists, politicians—are well known; others are ordinary citizens who have benefited from the twenty years of silence. Strangely, after some short mentions in the press, there have been few repercussions. One reason, according to Kenedi, is that those exposed tend to sue, and judges have tended to side with them at trials. With so much evidence destroyed, the arguments for reasonable doubt have won over the tangible documents. The judges, it seems, have decided to move on.

I MET István Rév for the first time in 2008. He is a small man with lively grey eyes, a mass of grey curly hair and a wide smile that lights up his otherwise overly serious face. It is as if his mouth was denying the professorial mien of the rest of his personality. We went to a small, noisy restaurant on the Pest side of the Danube, close to the elaborately restored Four Seasons Hotel Gresham Palace.

His father, a Communist since 1935, had spent six years in the Gulag. He was picked up by Soviet soldiers on a street in Budapest after the siege. Undeterred, he remained a Communist throughout his imprisonment. He steadfastly clung to his admiration of Stalin even after Khrushchev's Twentieth Communist Party Congress speech revealed the truth about Stalin's persecution of his former comrades, and remained a member of the Central Committee of the Hungarian Communist Party. In October 1956, he had been on his way to Republic Square, a gun in his pocket, ready to join the battle on the side of the state police against the revolutionaries. István remembers how his mother cried when Imre Nagy was executed, but his father's faith in the Party was not shaken till the 1968 Soviet invasion of Prague. "I was in London then," István tells me. His hands fly when he talks. "I suddenly found myself answerable for the destruction of Prague Spring, for the Soviet response to a different way of interpreting Communism." Apparently he had no explanation, which meant his own disillusion with the system that had provided for the family.

István grew up on Rose Hill among the children of the privileged, in the leafy, tree-lined part of Buda where the Party faithful had their spacious homes. It was in stark contrast to my own childhood on the Pest side, where children played in the concrete, rubble, noise and dust of Rákóczi Avenue, Dohány Street and bits of what used to be the ghetto. Unlike István, I would not have been admitted to a university, let alone allowed to travel to London. My formerly bourgeois family was denied the opportunity to learn languages, other than Russian, which was compulsory for schoolchildren.

The two of us, sitting in that small, noisy restaurant, represented the two sides of the same self-proclaimed egalitarian regime and the two sides of the present arguments about the role of the old *nomenklatura*. For me, at least, that evening also represented the future, when those fears and mutual resentments are no longer important and the children, while knowing the history of this country, do not inherit the recriminations.

THE POLITICS OF AGGRIEVED MEMORIES

Most countries and the minorities within those countries celebrate grand moments in their history, raise monuments to their national heroes and mourn profound tragedies that changed the courses of their lives. Given the kind of history Central Europeans have endured, their greatest moments tend to be defeats and losses.

The greatest Hungarian tragedy, most Hungarians will tell you, is the Treaty of Trianon. It is named for the smaller Trianon Palace (now a top-end hotel) next to the grand Château of Versailles where the post–World War I peace treaties were signed. Hungary was not only on the losing side, but it was also, briefly, governed by a Communist minority that made it a pariah among the conquering nations. The main treaties of Versailles had already been signed. Germany was "contained." Poland was restored. Czechoslovakia had been carved out of the thousand-year-old Hungarian kingdom. Romania received one of the most beloved parts of Hungary's history: Transylvania, stronghold of the Hunyadis, who had supplied the last great Magyar king—or so the story goes. The thousand-year-old names of Kolozs-vár and Nagyvárad were no longer; they were renamed Cluj and Oradea. Hungary had ruled Transylvania since the ninth century, and while there are now more Romanians in the area than Hungarians, Hungary still claims that this is part of its historical land.

Hungary's loss was, undoubtedly, the most painful of all the national losses. In addition to two-thirds of its territory and more than half its population, it lost a large part of its industry and it was also forced to pay war reparations. Hungary's main preoccupation between the wars was to regain what it had lost. Given that focus, the alliance with Germany was inevitable. Of course, when that was over, every piece of land was lost again. And more war reparations were due to the Soviets.

Even today, the word "Trianon" starts passionate arguments in most parts of Hungary and the adjacent lands where there is a significant Hungarian minority.

The Slovaks' and the Romanians' desire to rebalance the scales of power is rooted in their own years as minorities, when they were denied active political roles in these lands. Several local historians blame the Hungarian nobility for setting Slovaks and Romanians against Hungarians during preceding centuries when they had a chance to invite them to be equals.

Historian Maria Ormos says that the Hungarian elite's politics were tough while they ruled. After the Turks killed more than half of the population during the sixteenth and seventeenth centuries, Hungarians were afraid of becoming a minority in their own country. Hungarians' lands became a Turkish colony. Buda was a Turkish bastion. Transylvania was a nominally independent principality, paying tribute to the Turks. Pozsony became the administrative centre of what was left of Hungary, and remained that way until 1848. After the Turks, defeated at the "gates of Vienna," decamped, the Habsburgs were eager to repopulate the devastated land. They invited thousands of Serbs, Romanians and Croats, and Germans, of course. In contrast, the Hungarian elites' overriding concern was to keep their country predominantly Hungarian. This is why Maria Ormos sees the 150 years of Turkish rule in Hungary as the nation's greatest trauma. The Treaty of Trianon is just what naturally followed.

As a result of Trianon, about 700,000 Hungarians live in Slovakia. Most of them were born after Slovakia was no longer part of Hungary, yet they still profess that their mother tongue is Hungarian and their sympathies are with Budapest. They endured postwar deportations, a lack of job opportunities, little infrastructure in their towns and the open animosity of those in government. Since the Slovaks split from the Czechs in 1993 to form their own country, the rise of Slovak and Hungarian nationalism has ignited battles between the two aggrieved groups. Hungarian soccer fans have a habit of displaying old maps of the Hungarian Kingdom that include the territories of Serbia, Croatia, Romania and Slovakia when they follow their teams to those countries. In 2008, Hungarian soccer hooligans showered Romanians with broken glass and waved the pre-Trianon flag from the windows of their train to Bucharest. At an October 2008 soccer match in southern Slovakia, Hungarians waved banners with the picture of "Greater Hungary," the one that included Slovakia before the First World War. Slovak police beat up both the visitors and their local Slovak-Hungarian hosts. It is this kind of provocation that makes it difficult for ethnic Hungarians in Romania and Slovakia to declare their neutral stance.

Slovak newspapers trumpeted that Slovakia must defend itself against its neighbour's revisonist tendencies. Viktor Orbán made a number of emotional speeches directed at Hungarians' sense of having been wronged. He claimed to speak on behalf of 14 million people, all Hungarians in the Carpathian Basin—an open challenge to the bordering states that harbour about 5 million of those people.

In 2006, he proposed voting rights for Hungarians irrespective of where they lived—an interesting idea that was nixed by a referendum.[29] In May 2009, following another nationalist speech, he called for EU support for Hungarians living outside the borders. Meanwhile, he suggested territorial autonomy for Slovak Hungarians. Slovak prime minister Robert Fico rose in Bratislava's parliament to condemn Orbán's attempts to fire up "Slovaks of Hungarian origin."

The Hungarian daily *Magyar Nemzet* expressed its indignation at the new Slovak language laws by comparing them to Romanian laws of the 1980s, when Hungarian place names disappeared from the press, all maps and textbooks.

When I was in Cluj (Kolozsvár) in 1998, mayor Gheorghe Funar had ordered excavations under the bronze statue of Hungarian King Mátyás (Hunyadi) in the main square. He was hoping, it seems, that an old Romanian monument would be found underneath to validate his conviction that a Hungarian king's statue had no business to be here. He may also have hoped that St. Michael's, the Hungarian church next to King Mátyás's statue, would slide into the massive hole his machinery had created.

Under Romanian Communist dictator Nicolae Ceauşescu's rule, Hungarian villages close to the border were bulldozed and their populations moved to new locations, mostly to bleak prefab apartment blocks on the outskirts of cities. But there is one major difference. While Romania was a dreary dictatorship at the time, today's Slovakia is a democratic country and member of the European Union.[30] In the late 1980s, thousands of Romanian Hungarians fled across the border to the relatively prosperous Hungary. But there are still more than two million Hungarians in Romania, and most of them still cling to their language and traditions.

Given how Ceauşescu had dealt with them, it was not surprising that the end of his dictatorship began in Timişoara (Temesvár), Transylvania. In his fiery sermons, the Reformed Church's Reverend László Tőkés denounced the repression of Hungarians and the government's efforts to disperse them. Buckling to government pressure, religious authorities ordered his own relocation from Timişoara to an isolated parish. Tőkés refused to leave. On December 15, 1989, when the Securitate (Romanian state police) attempted to arrest the pastor, crowds of supporters, both Hungarians and Romanians, surrounded the church to protect him. The next day, the Securitate attacked, shooting hundreds of unarmed demonstrators. This is the day that sparked the revolution against the regime and its enforcers. The army joined the protesters; the Ceauşescus were arrested, given a short military trial and executed on Christmas Day 1989.

Unfortunately, not enough has changed in Romania since the defeat of the Ceauşescus. This is another country where the transition did not sweep the ex-Communists from power, where the Securitate's massive files have not been opened to the public, where corruption is rife and the old Securitate, though officially disbanded, is still feared. Its army of agents and informers has found top positions in business and government.

December 16, 2009, was the twentieth anniversary of the Timişoara rebellion against the Ceauşescu regime. "In the past two decades nothing fundamental has changed," wrote Vlad Stoicescu in *Evenimentul Zilei*, "although we should by now have banished the demons and communist reflexes. Society today is as forgetful as it has always been, we live in the same body politic eaten away by dictatorship, we suffer from the same terrible ignorance... [P]ain doesn't go away because of press freedom, or US comedy series, or even full supermarkets. What the eyewitnesses of 1989 need is the truth."

On a more postive note, Tőkés became one of Romania's Protestant bishops. He was elected to the European Parliament as an independent candidate in 2007, and cultural and territorial autonomy for Romanian Hungarians is still central to his political platform. In 2008, the Greater Romania Party, a persistent group of vocal Magyar-haters, lost all its seats in Parliament.

One of several matters on which Churchill, Roosevelt and Stalin could reach unanimous agreement was the expulsion of ethnic Germans from largely non-German countries. In a December 1944 speech to the British parliament, Churchill argued that "a clean sweep" would help ensure lasting peace. After the war, 200,000 ethnic Germans were expelled from Hungary. They left in carts and by trains, took only what they could carry and could never return to their homes. Andy Brandt, who became a Conservative politician in Canada, remembers the trek, and also recalls how his parents gave up all they possessed except for the impotent anger they carried with them to the new world. Novelist Herta Müller's family had been part of the German-speaking minority in Transylvania. Her seventeen-year-old mother was deported after the Red Army's arrival in her hometown in 1945. Like the Sudeten Germans of Czechoslovakia and the Germans expelled from Poland, the Hungarian Germans have never accepted their loss of homeland. It is this anger that continued to fuel conservative politics in West Germany and Austria after the war and that continues today in the form of arguments about compensation and reclaimed homes.

In Hungary, Slovakia, the Czech Republic and Romania, there are vast differences in what history is taught. Each country celebrates different versions of crucial events, and each mourns ancient hurts and wrongs that others had inflicted. Polish philosopher Leszek Kołakowski spoke of the dangers of modern historians' assumption that there are no facts, only interpretations. This belief abolished the idea of human responsibility for genuine standards of historical inquiry: "Historical knowledge is crucial to each of us... if we are to know our place in the universe, to know who we are and how we are to act."[31] He would have applauded the attempt by Slovak and Hungarian historians to write a new, joint history of their countries.

In what used to be southern Hungary, there has been news of Hungarian-baiting by Serbs, but the Serb parliament moved to calm relations between Serbia and Hungary by granting the country's approximately 300,000 ethnic Hungarians (and other minorities) almost full cultural autonomy.

Former prime minister Ferenc Gyurcsány tried to be philosophical about the aggrieved nationalities. If you can't remove your country from its borders, he said, it's advisable to live in peace with your neighbours. It's a thought that should work even when dealing with the Russians: "They do not respond well to hectoring. They are a proud people. It is understandable that most Russians feel distressed by their loss of international influence. Their grief is not all that different from how many Hungarians still feel about the loss of "Greater Hungary."

As George Soros said, nationalism is catching; "it flourishes in the absence of a universal idea, such as human rights or civilized conduct."[32] The problem is that while nationalism comes with ready-made symbols and slogans, with drums and uniforms, memories and poetry, it is difficult to dress civilized conduct in a flag and sell it with fervour from a podium. It is equally difficult to advocate Soros's or Karl Popper's ideas of an open society with the kind of passion they would need to counter the strident voices of ethnic nationalism.

VÁCLAV HAVEL thought of Poland, Czechoslovakia and Hungary as "a single unbroken region in Central Europe... historically and culturally very close to one another."[33] During his early years as president of Czechoslovakia and, later, the Czech Republic, he tried to unite them in the single powerful unit: the Visegrád Group.[34] But, despite these countries' common goal to transform themselves into democracies, Havel failed to convince them to apply together for memberships in the European Union. Each was determined to be seen as superior to the others in terms of qualifications for entry.

In late February 2010, defying grim predictions of the Group's demise, they met again in Budapest to discuss energy problems, the need to share infrastructure for the transport and storage of gas and crude oil, and the usefulness of solidarity in case of a crisis. They discussed common economic issues and the possibilities for greater influence in the European Union. In a hopeful sign for the future, there was no mention of Slovak-Hungarian troubles, Slovak prime minister Fico's language laws or Orbán's dreams of Greater Hungary.

In the March 24, 2010 issue of *Salon*, Adam Michnik wrote of the nationalism left behind by Eastern Europe's Communist regimes: "It lives on in the form of nostalgia, a phobia, an anti-democratic, anti-liberal, anti-European and anti-American ideology... Their common denominator is invariably a resentment of the liberal rule of law, of the philosophy of dialogue, of the spirit of tolerance."

THE TWO GLADIATORS

During the second decade of the post-Communist era, two charismatic, determined, politically astute young men have dominated Hungarian politics. Both were born into poverty. Both suffered at the hands of humiliating fathers. Both are physically strong, athletic, attractive, well spoken. Both have devoted followers, though—as is customary for political followers—such support has ebbed and flowed with their political fortunes.

Viktor Orbán, the fourth prime minister of the newly constituted Republic of Hungary, was only thirty-five years old when he first marched into the highest office in the largest Gothic parliament building in Europe (excluding Westminster). He is short, but walks with straight back and wide shoulders, a man of confidence. In 1998, he was the youngest prime minister the country had ever had. His dark, tousled hair, hesitant smile, his freshness, his passionate delivery and his devotion to soccer made him an instant hit with the media.

In 1989, when he first appeared on national television at Imre Nagy's reburial, his words shook the foundations of the old order: "We, the young, fail to understand how those who only a short while ago heaped scorn on the Revolution and its prime minister, claim to be the followers of his reform politics... how these same people, whose textbooks taught us lies about the Revolution, are now shoving one another aside to touch this casket." Orbán was only twenty-five years old. The fact that the older men honouring the dead included Imre Pozsgay and Péter Medgyessy made Orbán's speech more poignant. Pozsgay had been minister of education and responsible for the textbooks that named Nagy a traitor to his country; but he was also the man who, in 1989, announced that 1956 had not been a counter-revolution after all. Orbán and a few of his student friends were arrested for mourning Nagy and the 1956 loss of lives. It was as if the emotional young man had decided that he would not play the game by the rules set out by those who seemed ready to hand over power. And even then, he was noticed and admired by thousands for his frankness.

Viktor Orbán grew up in a village where there were no prospects for a career other than the chance to grab some sort of a technical diploma, as his parents had. His father beat him regularly till he was seventeen years old.

"He was obstinate as a child," his mother said, "and remained obstinate as an adult."[35] His family history, as he described it, had nothing to do with the old nobility or the historical intelligentsia.

What he accomplished, he did on his own. "There is still something in me," he said, "of that lower-class roughness." During his compulsory military service, he picked fights with his officers and would not brook what he thought was unfairness.

Playing soccer was one way to escape from his unpleasant home. He was a talented player—fast, calculating, determined. He loved the game, but winning was everything. He worked hard to attain a law degree and worked harder at Oxford after winning one of the Soros Foundation's scholarships. It is that obstinacy, that determination to succeed on his own terms, that carried him to victory in 1998 and to his 2002 defeat at the hands of the voters. He took advice only from a chosen few—people who surrounded him then, and still do. When I met him in Canada in October 1999 at the tony Toronto Club, he fitted comfortably into the upscale surroundings, spoke reasonably good English and mixed easily with the somewhat overdressed guests. He carried himself with utter confidence, but he wore shoes or boots with slightly elevated heels.

His years in the prime minister's office, according to a recent biography by József Debreczeni, were characterized by corruption, the transference of public funds to FIDESZ party stalwarts, privatizations favouring his friends and supporters, a naked show of entitlement. A whole list of companies sprang up with millions of support from public coffers, all sharing the same directors, presidents, even to the point of family connections, and all with close ties to Viktor Orbán. When FIDESZ needed or wanted financial contributions, they stood in line to oblige. To gain their desired slant in the news media, FIDESZ funded Hír TV (a new national television station) and a news magazine, and supported a daily newspaper, *Magyar Nemzet* ("Hungarian Nation"), that became the country's highest-rated right-wing daily.[36] The young man who had spoken of moral imperatives from the podium at Imre Nagy's funeral had learnt *realpolitik*.

WHEN I first met him in 2007, I found Ferenc Gyurcsány disarmingly open, engaging, energetic and approachable, in contrast to the staid formality of his spacious, wood-panelled parliamentary offices. The high, wide windows give onto the Danube and face the verdant

Buda Hills, favourite homes of aristocrats before the wars and stylish villas of the Communist era's red barons.

For someone who had been at the vortex of a political crisis since his "lying day and night" speech in 2006, he seemed remarkably relaxed. He strode into the room with the smile of a man who fully and rightfully inhabits this historic space and has no intention of leaving it despite the opposition parties' ceaseless clamouring for his head.

It was difficult to imagine from his easy demeanour, his modish clothes, his layered haircut, the long-cuffed white shirt, the confident smile, that he too had risen from poverty. He too was born in an unhappy home; his grandfather, one of the ubiquitous indigent gentry of small-town Hungary, had committed suicide over an unpaid card-game debt. His father had little education, trouble finding what he considered suitable employment and a low tolerance for hard liquor, which he drank in satisfying quantities to salve his sense of failure; he was jailed periodically for various minor offences.

His mother was a piece-worker in a factory. "We lived in one room," Gyurcsány told me. "At night my parents had the couch; I slept next to them." There was no indoor plumbing. No running water. Despite his growing feet, he wore the same shoes for two years—there was no money for new ones. Eager to escape his home, he studied hard, earned a scholarship and, given his poor working-class background, he had no trouble entering a university. "I was an aggressive, pushy, ambitious kid," he said, his broad smile indicating that he still is. "Argumentative, like my mother." She was determined that the young Ferenc would have the opportunities for a better life than the one she had. Initially, he joined the youth-wing of the Communist Party, but while studying economics, he founded his own party of socialist reformers. After 1989, he worked in international finance: for CREDITUM Financial Consultant Ltd. until 1992, as director of EUROCORP International Finance Inc., then as CEO of his own holding company, Altus Limited.

He became one of the wealthiest men in Hungary—a fact that helped send all his young relatives to private schools. But this quickly achieved wealth added to an atmosphere of mistrust around Gyurcsány over the next few years.

"My success in business has its own critics," he explained. "There were privatizations, and they ask whether I succeeded because of my Party connections." He makes no secret of the fact that he was once a leader in the youth wing of the Party. He has proven his talents for making money.

In late 2008, I met István Stumpf, lawyer, sociologist, former minister in the Orbán government, now president of the Századvég ("End of Century") Academy of Politics and Foundation. He has a PhD in political science, writes columns for one of the right-wing dailies and appears on television as a commentator on public affairs. He had been one of the most respected members of the old FIDESZ leadership. A large, blond, bearish, immaculately polite man of about fifty, he was quick to mention that Ferenc Gyurcsány got his start in business thanks to his mother-in-law's *nomenklatura* connections and borrowing ability.

Piroska Apró, a Communist of the old era, daughter of the man featured on the wall of shame in the House of Terror, was Gyula Horn's cabinet chief and, later, on the board of the Commercial Bank when it financed some of Gyurcsány's most successful privatization investments. It is barely surprising to find her name on the board of Gyurcsány's holding company.

Business began to bore him, Gyurcsány told me. He started to take a serious interest in politics, presented himself as a candidate for the Socialist Party under Medgyessi. And won. "Now I belong among the very few fortunate enough to be engaged by the work I love... We can decide what kind of country we want. I really believed that I could help make the country over, as I had made myself over. We, Hungarians, blame everybody else for our problems, our wars, our history, our geography. We must," he said, "take hold of our own fate."

His party won its first election in 2002, succeeding FIDESZ, whose leader, Viktor Orbán, had been prime minister for, in his own opinion, not long enough. He had not had a chance to implement the fundamental changes he thought were needed—perhaps right down to a change in the constitution. The notion of vacating the seat of government to a Communist successor party was unthinkable. For forty days after his defeat, Orbán was in seclusion, refusing food and, some say, even water.[37] For three years following FIDESZ's defeat at the polls, he did not attend a single parliamentary session. "Our nation," he announced mournfully, talking about his own recently defeated party, "cannot be in opposition."

Shortly after the 2002 elections, a newspaper story revealed that Socialist prime minister Péter Medgyessy had been on the payroll of the Ministry of the Interior. When Medgyessy explained that during the 1980s he had been protecting documents from the Soviets, no one believed him. He retaliated by leaking evidence that several members of the opposition parties were also on the ministry's payroll and that many others have found gainful employment with state-financed companies.

Ferenc Gyurcsány succeeded Medgyessy in the prime minister's office in 2004 and became president of the Socialist Party in 2005, before the 2006 elections. It was a move Orbán criticized as unconstitutional, but he was unable to prove the point. Gyurcsány inherited most of the whispers and innuendos that had swirled around his predecessor. Add to that the rumour that he forced his predecessor out of office and, possibly, poisoned him, and you have a potent mix of nasty gossip that could have driven Gyurcsány out of politics and back to counting his millions. Instead, the challenges only served to bolster his resolve to stay the course.

And as for the kind of government he wished for? The country he wanted, he told me, "straddles easily between the Russian East and the European West, between capitalism and fair democracy." His admiration for Britain's former prime minster Tony Blair is well known—and, according to the newspapers, mutual—because Blair had managed to convince the left that capitalist ideas are useful and that a market-driven economy is workable. The very mention of Blair's name makes Gyurcsány smile. But he would do business with whoever offered the best deals: "You don't have to love capitalism to benefit from it." He wanted to reform the health care system, close some of the half-empty hospitals, reform education, reduce pensions—the reforms he was convinced would prepare the country for the tough times to come.

Stumpf said, "Gyurcsány sees himself as a symbol of change." Yet his government was mired in a "public perception of corruption at the highest levels." Stumpf did not talk of the earlier public perception of Orbán's period of corruption, but I assume that, as one of those close to Orbán, he was aware of every move the insiders made. There was much nasty talk around his and his brother's business interests in the grape-growing, world-famous Tokaj wine area, and the talk has they not ceased during the years his party was out of office.

Gyurcsány was barely forty-five years old in April 2006, when, much to Orbán's dismay, his party won a second term. Shortly after the elections, he called a meeting of his MPs and informed them that the government's past record—including that of the government run by his predecessor, Viktor Orbán—was deplorable; that the economy was in shambles, spending was out of control; that major reforms were needed. He decorated his speech with a number of common swear words. This was the infamous "lying night and day" speech much derided by the media.

One example of "out-of-control spending" occurred during the election campaign, when Viktor Orbán promised a 70 per cent salary increase for all civil servants and a 400 per cent increase for doctors and, in the last days of his campaign, added another 5 per cent for pensioners. It was nuts, but it was equally crazy for Gyurcsány's own party to promise that they would match these offers. The country was in debt. They had to face the people and tell the truth. Party members, he hectored his newly re-elected colleagues, must stop playing politics and tell their befuddled countrymen the truth. What they had been doing throughout the past elections "day and night," he told them, was lying.

In answer to my question about the "lying day and night" speech, Gyurcsány explained that he had been attempting to light a fire under his colleagues' assembled asses with a barnburner of a speech, one that would wake them from their post-election self-satisfied euphoria and force them to face the difficult tasks ahead.

IN SEPTEMBER, a member of Gyurcsány's party helpfully leaked a recording of this speech to the country's main radio station. After a stunned public reaction, the opposition launched itself at the government, demanding the prime minister's immediate resignation and a new election.

The president announced that the country was in the throes of a moral crisis, and Viktor Orbán added that the government was illegitimate. He accused the Gyurcsány government of stealing the country from its people, of representing foreign powers, of protecting criminals rather than the innocent, of condemning the sick to die rather than give them deserved medical care—all this without proof and with all evidence to the contrary. When Gyurcsány didn't resign, Orbán promised and delivered public disruptions. He spoke in town halls, in churches and at open-air meetings where his adoring followers shouted approval at his every patriotic phrase. He took ownership of national symbols, such as the "Holy Crown" and the red-white-and-green emblems of the 1848 and 1956 national uprisings. Orbán, according to Stumpf, had found a way to "revitalize the damaged relationship between ordinary folks and politicians." He took his issues directly to the public.

Orbán had managed to persuade himself and his followers that he represented the "people" and the elected prime minister represented corruption. Using the general trademark of populism, he went on to argue that he was merely an instrument of the will of the people and that their desire for change could be achieved only through his own success against Gyurcsány. Orbán seemed unconcerned with the lack of any factual basis for his statements. His rhetoric overcame all sense of democratic fair play.

He refused to sit in Parliament when the prime minister spoke. The moment Gyurcsány rose, all but one of his party's members marched out of the council chamber in protest. The task of the single remaining party stalwart was to let the others know when Gyurcsány had stopped speaking and it was safe to return. His followers tended not to mention the prime minister by name, referring to him as "the evil one," "the traitor," "the criminal" or just "garbage."

The problem with parliamentary democracy, of course, is that it presupposes debate and discussion even when the ideas of the other are abhorrent to you. Democracy—a willingness to accept that one's own views may not be preferred by the electorate—is a difficult habit to get used to in countries where there is little or no democratic tradition. Hungary is one of those countries. Orbán's decision that the government was immoral and illegitimate, his conviction that therefore the country must be led by him, made it impossible for him to abide by the rules of a democratic system.

Orbán's indignation at the government was more than matched by the far-right Jobbik party's and the fury of the Magyar Gárda (Hungarian Guard), the Jobbik's military wing. The Guard's 2007 founding ceremony in front of the president's palace was attended by only three thousand people, but its influence grew over the next two years. In 2009, Jobbik got 15 per cent of the vote during the European Union elections, an interesting phenomenon when Guard leader Gábor Vona declared that they would force a change of government and "rescue" the country from pro-Europe Communists. In an attempt to unite the right, some FIDESZ parliamentarians attended Guard rallies and Orbán failed to criticize the Jobbik's anti-Semitic and anti-Roma stance.

Orbán focussed his ceaseless attacks on the government to ever-larger crowds of his admirers. Loud, impassioned, abrasive and utterly devoid of humour, he talked of the "nation's interests." His slogan "One camp, one flag" was plastered over billboards and in right-wing newspaper headlines.

Gyurcsány's promised reforms, starting with education and health—the two most costly and contentious issues facing most Western governments today—were derailed by a referendum. His 2009 budget barely survived parliamentary debates and non-confidence motions. It had become difficult to govern through a democratic process, he told me. The democratic consensus, whereby rival politicians acknowledge one another's legitimate rights to govern once elected, has been destroyed. In a life-and-death struggle, the opposition honoured no rules; there could be no civil discourse. When back in power, they promised retaliation and prison terms for members of the governing party. As political commentator Debreczeni remarked, "We live in a country where the right holds the left in such contempt that it does not recognize its right to citizenship."[38]

Throughout the year, the demonstrations continued, culminating in September 2006 when crowds occupying the grand square in front of Parliament and the burning of the old Stock Exchange building. The arrests that followed, the police inaction and, later, police brutality charges, the inquiry into police actions and government instructions to senior officers heightened tensions in the capital. FIDESZ began to win local and municipal positions both east and west. The government seemed paralyzed.

WHEN THE Russians invaded Georgia in 2008, Orbán compared the brave Georgians to the Hungarians of 1956. Gyurcsány was slow to condemn the Russians—he told me he could see the Russians' point of view. The South Ossetians, of whom no one had ever heard until Russia sprang to their defence, are no more Georgians than they are Russians. "As a distinct people," he told me, "they should decide for themselves where they wish to belong. Russia needs to find its own way," he added with a shrug, "without our lectures."

Like most of Europe, Hungary relies on Russian gas, and here it is *only* Russian gas, with no alternatives. "When I last sat with Putin, I said to him, I dislike buying energy from only one source," Gyurcsány said. "Putin agreed: 'In your place, I would feel the same way. But you seem to have no choice.' It's Russian gas or none." Dealing with Russians is, after all, inevitable. One may as well do it with good grace. "Tony Blair told me," Gyurcsány said with a smile, "the Americans consider this [the buying of gas] to be an important foreign policy issue; for you, it's just a heating issue.'"

Gyurcsány, it seems, had invited Putin to his home for a private dinner. Orbán, no matter how high the stakes, would never entertain such a friendly, personal gesture to a Russian, even if it was good for business or foreign policy. Unlike Poland's Radek Sikorski, Orbán is not pragmatic about Russia. In fact, he would have been pleased to position NATO missiles on Hungarian soil.

It is ironic that in the midst of the worldwide economic crisis, Gyurcsány, the socialist, was struggling to excuse the failures of capitalism to his countrymen and that it was Gurcsány who had to go to the EU, hat in hand, begging for additional money. The $25-billion

IMF and European Union loans merely staved off imminent bankruptcy. Gyurcsány signalled that he had no choice but to freeze social expenditures for at least five years. The massive domestic debt has made it impossible to borrow more until he succeeds with the various changes, such as reforming the health system, eliminating unequal benefits to civil servants, the thirteenth month's pay, one of the best deals for women with babies—reforms he had tried and failed to implement earlier. Public reaction was foreseeable. Striking security guards picketed the Budapest airport; a railway workers' strike disrupted train travel; the ranks of the unemployed swelled to 10 per cent—and that was just the beginning.

Meanwhile, Orbán refused to take part in discussions with the government to find consensus on financial issues. He failed to mention what his own solutions might be to the country's economic woes, other than these few gems: he concluded that capitalism was exhausted, that market economies are crumbling, that no plan could fix what had to be replaced. He promised to change the role of banks and bankers, to stop capitalists' easy access to people's pockets, to make new arrangements with multinational corporations. All he needed was to replace the "enemies of the people" with his own selections.

Gyurcsány told me he understood the frustration, his countrymen's sense of betrayal, of grief—a case of lost illusions. Hungarians had expected more of the new era. Membership in the EU has not guaranteed the nirvana they see across their western borders. In Austria, the cars are better and the air conditioning works. Taxes are lower. People seem to live better. Democracy has not provided enough benefits to Hungarians yet, Gyurcsány told me, and they are tired of waiting. They don't understand that twenty years is not long enough to reach what took Western Europeans seventy years to build. But unlike his opponents, he still believes in democracy. Unlike Viktor Orbán, who thinks he was chosen, Gyurcsány was willing to accept a time out of his leadership role. Perhaps it was good, now, to reflect on all that had gone wrong.

On March 15, 2009, the anniversary of the beginning of the 1848 Hungarian revolution against Habsburg rule, Viktor Orbán gave one of his grand emotional speeches to a crowd of resolute followers. He compared the feelings of despair facing the economic crisis of 2009 to the anger and frustration of 1848. He reminded people of the will to reclaim their country to what had inspired "our people" to rise against the mighty Habsburg Empire to the need to resist now those who would claim the country for themselves. He was surrounded by green, white and red flags and the emblems of the 1848 revolution. All the symbols were called upon to compare him, favourably, to one of the country's great heroes: Lajos Kossuth, the man who called the nation to arms on 1848.

On Saturday, March 22, Ferenc Gyurcsány announced his resignation from the position of prime minister. The prime minister's chair would be occupied, temporarily, by a businessman ready to make the tough decisions that could no longer be evaded. "I am told that I have become, personally, the greatest obstacle to the sober behaviour of the opposition and, therefore, the realization of the necessary changes in this country. I am ready to remove this obstacle," he said in his parting speech.

As he left that grand monument to Hungarian hubris, the neo-Gothic parliament building, someone in the huge shouting, deriding crowd spat on him. A far-right (Jobbik) spokesman who witnessed this humiliation pondered in print that it would have been far better had Gyurcsány been shot and killed rather than just spat upon.

Two days later, Gyurcsány resigned from the leadership of his party.

I saw him last in April of 2009 in the garden of his Buda house, next to a kindergarten, surrounded by trees, with one over-friendly dog lolling about the grass. He seemed sad but not yet regretful. He still thought he had done the best he could and he had not yet tired of politics. No, he was not upset by the personal attacks, he said; there would always be those who hate him.

He now sat at the back of his parliamentary faction, observing the others. He did not even mind this new vantage point. He could watch and listen. He expected to return to the post of prime minister once Viktor Orbán has been tested at the post.

I did us both the favour of not asking how he now felt about his "lying day and night" speech. Irrespective of other explanations, I was sure that it was the moment when his government had begun its descent to defeat.[39]

The Pew Global Attitudes Project's 2009 survey indicates that Hungarians' enthusiasm for democracy has declined to 56 per cent from the 74 per cent of 1991; 72 per cent of those surveyed thought that life now is worse than it was during the Kádár years, and more than 90 per cent thought the country had taken the "wrong track."

András Göllner, a one-time lecturer at a Canadian university, has been living in Hungary for the past few years. He says he used to have hopes for the country, but the past few years have dampened his enthusiasm. "As far as I'm concerned," he says, "the frenzied intolerance that is riding roughshod over everything that smacks of a genuine civic culture, that scorns the concept of discursive democracy, is the sole responsibility of a small gang of ex-university students, headed by Viktor Orbán, who never had a day job in their lives. They have tested the sweaty, tepid waters of political power, and have formed an incurable obsession about its supposedly healing qualities. In the process, they discovered the key to exploiting the political immaturity, the justified frustrations of their fellow countrymen. He knows that a substantial number of his fellow Hungarians are not obsessed by the niceties of democratic governance, and simply want a strong man to lead them towards greener pastures."

In September 2009, Viktor Orbán rewarded his party faithful with some serious talk about Hungary's future under his leadership.[40] He urged them to take over the country and make it their own. Those who oppose them were to be hounded and declared enemies of the people. He asserted the need to end "superfluous value discussions" between the rival forces of socialism and his own brand of conservatism. The opposition is to be eliminated. There is no need, in fact, for opposition parties in Parliament. He said that in the long term—he foretold fifteen to twenty years—the country would be better served by only one governing party: a single, constant, stable government.

I wondered what had happened to that young democrat who spoke at the Imre Nagy funeral, and when he began to sound like János Kádár, the leader of the former single party that ruled Hungary for some thirty-two years.

In April 2010, Viktor Orbán became the prime minister of Hungary with over 50 per cent of the votes, a strong mandate to govern. He has finally inherited the role he has coveted since 2002. But it comes with a heavy price tag: the million new jobs he pledged to deliver and the "defeat of hopelessness" he promised .

Ferenc Gyurcsány's Socialist Party won just short of 20 per cent, a resounding defeat that may change the face of Hungary over the next ten years. István Rév calls Gyurcsány a tragic hero, a man who fell victim to his own idealism. He thought he could affect change with the support of the people, but the people were reluctant to give up anything they already had: "The cynical old Kádár system conspired to sink him." It was a system of spending and promises to keep the public unaware and quiet. In the end, Ferenc Gyurcsány lacked the courage of his own convictions.

The happiest winner in these nasty elections was Jobbik, with almost 17 per cent of the vote and the certainty of gaining entry into the Hungarian parliament. This was the first time since World War II that a Fascist party was elected to a position of power in this country.

THE NEW FASCISM

As the recession deepened, the crowds became angrier and more vituperative. Some demonstrations turned into armed battles with the police. The mayor of Budapest was assaulted while speaking at a festival, and during a speech in early 2010, a mob shouted "Jewish pigs" as the mayor attempted to be heard; in 2009, actors were chased from the stage at a riverside poetry reading. The 2008 gay pride parade was attacked by screamers, stone-throwers and club-wielders who hit and abused the peaceful marchers, including József Orosz, one of the country's best-known TV and radio journalists. Orosz ended the day in hospital with multiple abrasions and a fracture.

Kati Lévai, one of Hungary's representatives to the European Parliament, took refuge in a police car. "It was terrifying," she said of the moment a paving stone smashed through the window, "but more than that, it was profoundly humiliating." We met late one evening in the Marriott Hotel's bar. She was dressed for a reception, in black with lacy trim and high-heeled pumps, her dark hair flipped back over her shoulder. With her understated jewellery, her soft flowery scent, she seemed more a European lady than a revolutionary force resisting street violence.

"The past has come back to haunt us," she says. "That ordinary, once common Fascism is striding down our streets, becoming louder and more self-assured in its vulgarity. When it becomes acceptable that a group of citizens can humiliate and debase another, simply because it is different, we must resist. These Fascist groups are not unique to Hungary, but elsewhere there are laws that deny them the right to speak of their obsessive hatreds. Here, we have taken the right to free speech too far."

"My conviction is that until this country is ready to fully admit its own history, until the majority is ready to deal with what happened here during the Holocaust, we are not going to learn," she tells me. "It is astonishing that after forty-four years of silence, they, and their children, could crawl out from under the rocks and start the hate speeches again."

The Jobbik leaders are Euroskeptic, anti-Semitic and anti-gypsy. Their paramilitary wing, the Gárda, parade around in black uniforms that are reminiscent of National Socialists of a bygone era. The FIDESZ-supported paper *Magyar Demokrata* billed Viktor Orbán's critics as "left-liberal Jews," talked of 9/11 as a CIA plot and called Nobel Prize winner Imre Kertész "a stinking piece of human excrement."

In the spring of 2009, just before the elections to the European Parliament, I attended a Jobbik rally in a small town close to Budapest. The hall was packed. The garden and entranceway supervised by uniformed Gárda. The mood was festive. The speaker tonight was rising political star Krisztina Morvai, a graduate in law from Budapest's renowned Eötvös Loránd University, she had gone on to study at King's College in London and been a Fulbright Scholar teaching at the University of Wisconsin–Madison before joining the European Commission of Human Rights in Strasbourg. Between 2003 and 2006, she was a member of the Women's Anti-Discrimination Committee of the United Nations.

In 2006, Hungary's Socialist government decided to replace its delegate to a United Nations committee. The newcomer was a Jew. The incumbent was Krisztina Morvai. Upon learning that, after four years, her time in New York was up, the human rights champion with a Jewish husband fired off a surprising letter in which she accused the government of trading her for a "Zionist" because she was pro-Palestinian. Referring to the Israel-Palestinian conflict in Gaza, she sent a letter to the Israeli ambassador to Hungary expressing her wish that "all of you lice-infested, dirty murderers will receive Hamas's kisses."[41]

In 2009, the youthful-looking blond with a soft voice, a gentle smile and an alluring manner had her sights on a bigger prize. The Socialists were on their way out of power, Orbán's centre-right was rising and all indications were that there would be easy pickings for the Jobbik in the next elections.

I wondered whether Orbán confidant István Stumpf would still describe the Jobbik as a "fractious, insignificant minority" now that they had risen to about 17 per cent in popularity surveys. One of the important political functions of the extreme right, here as elsewhere, is to enable to slightly more moderate party to appear mild and benevolent. Thus, FIDESZ has been inching to the middle of the spectrum, while the Socialists have dripped off the left edge.

Morvai made her way to the podium with the ease of a celebrity, greeted by the affections of the crowd. Many of her fans had already been handed flyers asking if they minded being "beggars" in their own country—Jobbik has struck a chord with its attacks on foreign companies that enjoy tax-exempt status in Hungary. On another theme, the flyer asks, "Will you stand by while the government throws more aid at gypsy criminals?"

Party vice-president Zoltán Balczó, in a rambling introduction, complained that Jews have "colonized" the country and drew a cheer by cracking a joke about gypsies.

Professor Morvai (she teaches law at her alma mater) opened by distinguishing between "our kind" and "their kind," making it very clear that, as well as liberals, socialists and people employed by big corporations, the latter includes Jews and Roma. She told the crowd that it's time for Hungarians to "take back" what is theirs. *Barikad,* a Jobbik magazine, showed a photograph of St. Gellért holding a menorah with the tagline asking if this is what Budapest wants.

The Gárda glared at anyone who stirred and removed a rambunctious fan from the front row.

Two weeks before her forty-sixth birthday on June 22, 2009, Krisztina Morvai and two other members of the Jobbik were elected to the EU's ruling body carrying the standard of a party so far to the right that critics call it "neo-Nazi."

The Gárda has grown in tandem with the rising violence against the Roma—seven fatalities in less than a year, Molotov cocktails tossed into homes, a two-year-old nearly burned to death, a five-year-old killed by a hail of bullets. The killers' usual modus operandi was to throw a flaming bottle of gasoline into a house on the outskirts of a village and then shoot the occupants as they fled. But Jeno Koka, a worker at a pharmaceutical factory northeast of Budapest, was gunned down as he left home for the night shift. A few days later, five Roma children waiting for a bus were beaten by masked men.

In a surprise move, the Hungarian government banned the Gárda on July 3, 2009. To show solidarity and express outrage at the government's ban, Krisztina Morvai showed up wearing a Hungarian military costume for her maiden speech at the European Parliament. Another newly elected Jobbik member was proudly attired in Gárda uniform.

The Gárda ignored the ban and were cheerfully assembling again a week after some initial arrests. Television viewers were entertained by polite policemen attempting to remove seated Gárda protesters. The debate continued among lawyers, journalists and judges about the rights of Fascists to assemble and voice their views openly versus the rights of the public not to feel threatened. Freedom of speech and freedom of assembly were two essential achievements of the country's democratic constitution—people used to be imprisoned here for uttering certain words. Freedom of speech is one of the most cherished tenets of liberty. But how should a citizen feel when he is walking by a group of uniformed men (it isn't the uniform, what these people stand for would be equally appalling if they were all dressed as clowns) shouting at him that "his turn" will come and that he should pack his suitcase and run toward Israel while he has a chance?

Gábor Vona declared his intention to wear the banned Gárda uniform on his first day in Parliament.

THE ROMA MURDERS

With its cream-coloured houses, red tile roofs, grass verge, early spring flowers and narrow white church, Tatárszentgyörgy, just fifty kilometres south of Budapest, has all the trappings of the ideal bucolic village. But at the far end of the cemetery, near the marker where the village ends, there is a recently dug grave, still thickly covered with plastic flowers—a few bunches of waning lilies, a handful of wilted bluets, a large wreath of white silk roses over the simple marker: Csorba Robert 1981–2009; Csorba Robert Jr. 2004–2009: Rest in Peace.

Father and son share a grave, as they shared a death by gunshot during the night of February 23, 2009.

Tatárszentgyörgy has become a symbol of racial hatred in cultured, peace-loving Europe, in a country that recently entered the European Union with vast optimism for a bright post-Communist future. It was neither the first nor the last attack against unarmed Roma, but it was the one that finally drew the world's attention to atrocities that had grown in number and violence as the economic crisis deepened and the dark forces of racial hatred found receptive minds among people eager to find someone to blame for their disappointments.

The Csorba home was the last house along a row of other Roma homes, at the end of an unpaved road that leads to a small forest and a few patches of cultivated land. It was painted bright marigold yellow. All that remained of the roof were a few charred timbers; the windows were gaping holes; inside were mounds of glass shards, blackened bits of furniture, torn blankets; in one corner, face down, a doll. Near where the door had been blown in by the gasoline explosions, I could still see the bullet holes through the brushstrokes in the yellow paint. The holes that are close to the ground must have been from the shots aimed at the five-year-old boy.

The men came shortly after midnight, according the Robert Csorba's father. His granddaughter, Bianka, remembers something flying through the window, shattering glass, flashes. Then there was so much smoke and fire that it was hard to see. Robert must have grabbed his little boy and run out the front door. They were both shot at close range. Six-year-old Bianka was lucky: she was shot in the arm, but she survived, as did her mother and the baby. "She is a strong little girl," her grandmother told me. The grandparents live a few metres from their son's burnt-out home.

The gunshots had woken them. When they ran outside, their son's house was burning; their daughter-in-law and the little girl were screaming. Robert's father led me to the place where his son and grandson had fallen, a few steps from the door. "He was still breathing when I found him. But he was terribly quiet," Csaba Csorba said. "I felt the bullet wounds with my fingers. He tried to speak but the bullets had pierced his lungs." The first police car arrived about half an hour later. "It stopped up the road, and the men came strolling down here, as if nothing much had happened." Csorba is a small man, he seems much older than his forty-five years. His face a warren of lines, intense black eyes, he kept looking at his tearful wife for confirmation.

"The ambulance came about half an hour after. I kept telling them to get my boy to the hospital fast. I was in the army. I know about lead pellets. My son could have survived, but none of them believed us." Csorba tried to clean the wounds himself. "I don't know much about medicine, but lead will kill you if it's not removed fast."

The police and the medic seemed determined that the fireplace must have exploded on its own. The medic barely glanced at his son. When they tried to revive the little boy, he was already dead.

The fire brigade still insisted it was an electrical fire. No one would look at the bullet holes or pay attention to Csorba's telling them he had heard gunfire. As they moved around in the house, one of them stepped on the remnants of a bottle that could have contained the gasoline.

The Csorbas are too young to be grandparents, but Roma have children young. "It's one of our problems," Aladár Horváth told me.

He is a leader of the Roma Civil Rights Foundation, and he was one of the first on the scene after the police left. "Too many children, too young, and almost impossible to find work. The rules don't work when it comes to gypsies. The job is already filled when you show up and they see you're one of us. And the house is no longer available. They don't want us as neighbours."As the recession deepened, thousands of Roma lost their jobs—mostly unskilled labour—and depend increasingly on welfare. There are whole villages where no one works.

But Horváth, a self-described "troublemaker," refuses to accept that Roma do not deserve a better life. He made sure that the Budapest crime investigation headquarters sent down a unit of its own to ask questions. By then, of course, the traces of heavy boots had been obliterated, and there was only little Bianka to say that there had been a big black car outside.

The country's national police chief, József Bencze, announced a $50,000 reward for information leading to arrests and asked the FBI to help with the investigation. At the end of August 2009, Hungarian police arrested four men implicated in the Roma murders. The police claimed they found evidence in the men's homes that would help convict them.

Hungarian president Sólyom opined that everyone can now breathe a great sigh of relief. Aladár Horváth is not so optimistic. "I used to believe in a political solution," he told me. "I no longer do. There are too many lies, too much play-acting, pretending that you care does not add up to caring. The system itself is compromised. Politicians don't like to risk unpopularity by helping the Roma."

Meanwhile, national newspapers and radio shows continue with verbal assaults on Roma, and "gypsycrime" is blamed for all petty crimes in the countryside.

The Roma's situation in Hungary is similar to their lot in the Czech Republic and Slovakia. The language of hatred and exclusion has been on the rise in Europe. Here, there are fewer barriers to expressing loathing for other human beings. The press is less vigilant and some journalists are active promoters and practitioners of hate. I fear that the desire for a completely free press has succeeded in nurturing an environment unencumbered by a sense of civility and, as history has proven, inciting hatred is a powerful tool if used cleverly with the witless.

THE QUINTESSENTIAL EUROPEAN INTELLECTUAL

György Konrád was born in a small town in eastern Hungary, son of a well-to-do hardware store owner, a gentle, learned family man who had the foresight to send his two children to Budapest days before the gendarmerie got its orders to round up all the Jews in the area, confiscate their belongings and cram the people into boxcars bound for the Auschwitz-Birkenau extermination camp. Most of Konrad's friends and family were dead by the time he returned to the town a year later.

Since the age of eleven, he has been an adult. Once you face the likelihood of your own death, he wrote later, you are no longer a child.[42] Being a Jewish child of eleven in Budapest during the Nazi era meant facing death every day and learning not to pay much attention to it. As he points out, had he stayed in the bucolic little town where he was born, he would have died in May, when the first trains from eastern Hungary arrived on the ramp at Birkenau and Dr. Mengele sent all the children—except those he intended to use for his experiments—to die. "Dr. Mengele sent all my classmates, every last one, to the gas chambers," Konrád says. In the months that followed, he got used to seeing people he knew disappear with armed bands of marauding Arrow Cross lads who found it considerably easier to shoot unarmed women, old men and little girls than to defend the city against the advancing Soviet army. In the forecourt of the ghetto hospital, where he visited his elegant aunt Zsofi's mother, the mountain of corpses reached the first floor. Zsofi's mother, like so many others, was shot through the head and joined the mountain of corpses.

György witnessed the senseless destruction wreaked by the German and Soviet occupations, the rapes and killings that seemed to continue relentlessly from one reign of terror into another. His father, when he returned to the empty, looted hardware store that had been the family's support over the previous decades, imagined he could start again, but owning stores was considered bourgeois and was forbidden after the Communist Party established itself in power.

György did not join the Communist Party. Instead, in 1956, he joined the revolution, because, as he told me, he suddenly found himself with a machine gun. There was only one moment when he might have shot someone, but he did not. Armed and arm-banded as a student national guard, he practically walked into another young man, equally armed, but for the opposing side. They looked at each other for a moment, then they walked away, without mutual acknowledgment.

After the revolution, he was condemned to fifteen years' imprisonment. In his book *A Cinkos,* he writes of witnessing a hanging in jail. The guards encouraged witnesses to instill shock and fear in the inmates: "It's strange that family men in ordinary jobs consider it in a day's work to murder other men, who have done them no harm." After his release during the general amnesty, a government lawyer mentioned that he regretted failing to send Konrád to the gallows.

During the years of "goulash Communism," Konrád's books were banned, his manuscripts were taken, his home was regularly searched. He grew accustomed to daily harassment. Like Havel, he became so familiar with the government's agents, he no longer saw them as individually threatening; it was the system that dispatched them whose workings he knew were evil.

We meet in the strangest of places: a sports centre for a famous Hungarian soccer team. It's a big yellow building in Pasarét, a wooded, old-fashioned part of Buda. Long rows of sports equipment line the glass-enclosed area near the restaurant where Konrád sits under a gigantic TV screen playing endless soccer in silence. He regards me from behind rimless glasses, squinting, his thick, grey eyebrows raised, a small, ironic smile—suspicious, wary. My every question makes him squint more; he does not want to talk about his decision to join a political party in 1990, right after the end of one-party rule, nor is he interested in revealing why he left politics. He leans back in his chair when I tell him about Prague today. Then he leans forward to mention how he and a bunch of other so-called intellectuals went to Prague Castle to see Havel during the winter of 1990: "I tried to talk him out of becoming president. He didn't suit the role of politician." Havel seemed uncomfortable in the Castle. He relaxed only after they went to a nearby pub. Even there Havel was surrounded by guards—"a cloud of gnats," Havel called them. They seemed to Havel much like the men who used to follow him in the old days, when he was a mere dissident.

Konrád is a quintessential European intellectual.[43] His role: to comfort the afflicted and afflict the comfortable. He reminds his fellow Hungarians of their servile past, a "satellite mentality so deeply ingrained in our history, our sayings, our self-justifications, our selves." It is this mentality, this sense of victimhood, that must be destroyed. He warns against the possibility of relying on another authoritarian type to lead the country out of the recession. "Communist kitsch has given way to Christian-nationalist kitsch abounding in references to ... Saint (King) Stephen, the 'Holy Crown'"[44] and a bewildering nastiness in public discourse. He warns against the radical right, the demagogues of ultranationalism who have found someone to blame for the country's problems: the Jews, the gypsies and the liberals.

In 2008, members of his stalwart liberal group, including then-prime minister Ferenc Gyurcsány, gathered in the ornate Palace of Arts to sign something they called the "Hungarian Democratic Charter"—a public expression of support for democracy and against the politics of hatred, a demonstration for civility in political life. It advocates the survival of humanity and citizenship for all, regardless of religion or colour. The ideas are not so radical when you hear them with American ears, but in Central Europe twenty years after the Iron Curtain rolled up, intolerance is on the rise again.

In recent months, Konrád has achieved that pinnacle of success for a critic of his times: an ultra-right-wing magazine has recommended that his books, along with those of fellow travellers Faludy, Esterházy and György Spiró, be yanked from shelves and relegated to garbage heaps.

SPEAKING THE UNSPEAKABLE

During the first few years of the twenty-first century, there was a vociferous debate in Hungary about a man who has been dead for more than seventy years. Count Pál Teleki was a wartime prime minister of the country—a devout Catholic, honourable by most accounts, a gentleman whose word was his bond. Hence, he committed suicide when, after he put his good name to a treaty guaranteeing peace and mutual assistance with Yugoslavia, Hungarian troops following German orders invaded Yugoslavia.[45] The only problem with Teleki is this: he was an anti-Semite. Under his stewardship, twenty-two anti-Jewish laws were passed by Parliament. A group of political right-wingers initiated the raising of a statue of the former prime minister in the Castle area of Buda, close to where he died. The idea was opposed by an equally vociferous group of historians who pointed out Teleki's enthusiasm for anti-Jewish laws. During the melee that followed, the mayor put plans for the statue on hold.

Hungarian-born author Imre Kertész noted that he saw no difference between Teleki's polite anti-Semitism and Arrow Cross leader Ferenc Szálasi's rabid version—both led to the same end point: Auschwitz. Kertész's book *Fateless* is about that end point. When Kertész became the first Hungarian writer to receive the Nobel Prize for Literature in 2002, some Hungarians, instead of celebrating, expressed annoyance that the prize should be given for such a "foreign work," though Kertész was born Hungarian and writes in Hungarian. His work is only "foreign," or, as one newspaper columnist said, "foreign-hearted," because he chooses to write about what he knows. In all his books, he speaks of the world as he sees it.

In 2009, he spoke of what he saw in Hungary, that the country is bent on spiritual and physical suicide. If a country cannot examine its past, its tragedies, its sins honestly, it is committing a sin against itself. It is not enough to say, this too happened—and most Hungarians are not Holocaust deniers; somehow the knowledge of what happened and how has to become part of this country's history. It hasn't. As witnessed in the House of Terror, the general tendency is to blame the Germans for all the expulsions and murder of the Hungarian Jews. During the Communist years, textbooks had placed the blame on West Germany, in order to uphold the myth that the war was about the Soviet Union's Red Army defeating Fascism.

The fact that several senior Communist Party members, including secret police chief Péter Gábor and Party boss Mátyás Rákosi, were

Jews raised a whole range of post-'89 blame-the-victim opportunities that infused openly anti-Semitic publications, just as it had done in Poland. Add to the convenient trend of forgetting what does not fit a theory: that Gábor and most of the Jews in power fell to Stalin's change of heart about Jews. In 1954, Péter Gábor was sentenced to life imprisonment on charges of betraying the trust of the people. [46]

In a 2009 interview in *Die Welt*, Kertész said that in Hungary today, extremists and anti-Semites rule. As for himself, he said he is a metropolitan man, someone who belongs to a tolerant world—Berlin, rather than Budapest, "the city is completely balkanized." Therefore, he did not wish to be stamped "Hungarian."

The Hungarian press responded with predictable outrage. How dare someone abuse "the people," attack the "nation"! Only a few publications, such as the literary *Élet és Irodalom*, recognized the obvious: the attacks on Kertész served only to prove his point.

In December 2009, Elie Wiesel, another Nobel Prize winner, told the Hungarian parliament that those who foment hatred and racism bring shame on all Hungarians. Perhaps he was thinking about the FIDESZ parliamentarian and small-town mayor who had recently accused "Jewish capital" of "devouring the entire world, especially Hungary." Wiesel called on all politicians to strike at racism in all its forms, to make Holocaust denial a punishable offence and promote mutual respect among people. He talked of the danger of accepting extremists into a party to gain votes. It is difficult not to imagine that Wiesel was addressing these words to Viktor Orbán.

Wiesel had not set foot in Hungary since 1944 when his family was sent to Auschwitz-Birkenau from Sighet (Máramarossziget), Transylvania. His book *Night* is one of the most devastating yet life-affirming statements about the end point of racism.

During my several stays in Hungary, I was astonished both by the culture of nervous silence about the Holocaust and by the openly anti-Jewish statements in some of the mainstream media. As my last book concerned the 1940s,[47] I interviewed several Holocaust survivors who assured me that that such things are not talked about in polite company and who suggested that it would be best if I chose another topic to research. As Kertész said, "the cartel of silence" rules and people are, once more, afraid.

Professor Pál Tamás disagrees. As the Director of the Institute of Sociology at the Hungarian Academy of Sciences, he has studied Hungarians' attitudes to most matters, both immediate and long-term. While it is, he says, socially acceptable to talk of Roma problems, it is not socially acceptable to make overtly anti-Semitic remarks. Furthermore, he has never been afraid in Budapest. He was at the Hotel Astoria when the demonstrators clashed with police in 2009 and, though he was recognized by several noisy protestors, none threatened him. His face is familiar from newspapers, magazines and from his frequent appearances on Duna TV, yet he has never encountered violence and does not expect to even when he is at Jobbik rallies. "And I am openly Jewish. There is a vibrant Jewish cultural scene in Hungary," he says. "There are restaurants, like the Spinoza, and favourite bars. You can take a Jewish tour, featuring the famous sites in the city. And a recent survey indicates that only about a third of the population is anti-Semitic." He is a big man with sloping shoulders that shake when he laughs, and that's what he does when he adds, "Almost the same percentage that claims to be anti-anti-Semitic."

His mother, who was in the Ravensbrück concentration camp during the war, does not view the Gárda with as much equanimity.

THE DECEMBER 2009 Hanukkah festival in Budapest's 7th District—it used to be the Jewish area—was a resounding success. It featured over a hundred events: jazz, hip hop, klezmer, art, theatre, lectures, juggling and tours of the older historic buildings. The thirty different venues included galleries, cafés, the Jewish Museum and three reconstructed synagogues. The magnificent twin-towered Great Synagogue, the largest and one of the oldest in Europe, celebrated its 150th year in 2009.

On the last day of its last session before the April 2010 elections, the Hungarian parliament passed a law banning Holocaust denial.

HINTS OF HOPE

By the 1980s, there was a burgeoning black market economy in Hungary, tolerated, probably encouraged, by the regime. The transition from a single party with many factions to a multi-party system was a great deal less chaotic and more natural than in other Central European countries. Hungary was the most prosperous of the satellite states. Its government's trade links to the West allowed it to borrow easily. Miklós Németh, Hungarian prime minister in 1989, and Gyula Horn, the hero of opening the Western borders, had flown to Bonn to ask the West German leaders for more credit. The DM 1-billion loan was not announced till the first of October to distance West German generosity from Hungary's generosity to the East Germans.[48] The country looked good to foreign investors: about $600 million worth in 1989 and another $800 million the following year. The new democracy hurried to pass legislation for privatization, banking, new financial institutions.

What Prime Minister Antall had not learned from his history books was how to deal with the weight of those $200-billion loans, a legacy the Communist governments had given no thought to repaying. The massive foreign debt was increased after 1989, with individuals eager to take on loans to buy into the new capitalist world. In a country where owning a home was beyond everyone's horizon, the notion of now being able to buy a place of one's own was too tempting and foreign banks were offering attractive rates. Through the '90s, the devalued forint helped push exports. In 2001–2006, the EU invested in highways and the government offered subsidies for mortgages, doubled the minimum wage and added an extra month to pensions[49] while the deficit grew and unemployment climbed.[50]

By 2008 the bloom was off the rose; car manufacturing had collapsed; debt levels soared; unemployment reached over 10 per cent. Those attractive interest rates were to be paid in euros and the Hungarian forint declined with the economy. When then prime minister Gyurcsány went to the EU and the IMF to beg for help, the country was in the middle of a financial crisis, as were most of the recent converts to democracy in Central Europe and the Baltic.

Most people were no longer hopeful. According to the European Commission's Eurobarometer Report, Hungary was the only former Communist country where more than 50 per cent of the people surveyed claimed to be worse off now than before 1989. Transparency International listed Hungary among the most corrupt countries in Europe, with corruption an almost public practice that made all contracts that required government approval 20 to 25 per cent more expensive than they would have been without the bribery commissions. Most of the under-the-table amounts went directly or indirectly into the pockets of politicians, though the massive bureaucracy had created small interfering barricades that could be mounted only if the responsible officials were also paid. The openly requested bribes were not so much for speeding the approval processes as for not slowing them down. As one Hungarian businessman told me, bribery had been part of the old Kádár system—everyone was so used to it, few people objected.

When I last met him in 2008, Hungary's wealthiest capitalist, Sándor Demján, was still betting that the East would recover quickly and return to the path it chose in 1989. There were great opportunities here for anyone willing to stay for the long term. Demján is founder and chief executive of TriGránit, a vast real estate development empire that stretches across most of the former Iron Curtain countries and beyond. He saw no threat from the West's economic problems, nor from Putin's Russia, despite Russia's recent spats with the Ukraine over pipelines and the price of gas. He talked about Putin's "enlightened absolutism." The Russians, he said, have never had it so good. Most of them love Putin. The last election, Demján says, was planned so as to avoid an overwhelming vote for Putin. He installed Medvedev to offer if not a different a attitude, at least a different voice. He wanted the semblance of democracy. "For the Americans, it has been difficult to resist preaching democracy at the Russians, but resist it they must, if only for the sake of peace," he told me. Demján would have been pleased with President Obama's conciliatory gestures and willingness to listen to Russia's concerns.

Demján's offices occupy a large white building adjacent to one of his successful shopping centres in Pest. He owns one or more executive jets, has a chauffeur-driven limousine, but still dresses and lives as he used to before the system changed to accommodate his financial ambitions.

"Ten years from now—mark my words—Russia will be the most democratic country in Europe," he told me. "In thirty years St. Petersburg will be the cultural capital of Europe. To have democracy, all you need is for more than half your population to earn a reasonable living."

He is not alone in making the connection between wealth and democracy. For many years, economists and political scientists have drawn a line between a country's per capita GDP and its democratic tendencies, or its reversion to totalitarianism in the absence of wealth.[51] Yet in most countries where democracy took root, market economics preceded it. China has proven again that there need be no vital connection between these two ideas. But that, according to Sándor Demján, could change. All you need for democracy to thrive, he said, is a satisfied middle class.

When you examine the survey results more closely, as Professor Tamás has, you note that individuals are much better off than they were twenty years ago; that they own more, work for more, travel more for leisure; and that, despite their conviction that country is worse off, when they are asked specific questions about their own lives, it is obvious that perception and reality have parted company.

Michael Tippin is also betting on the East. He has bought the grand old Exchange Palace in Budapest. In 1905, it was the second-largest building in a city that still had the trimmings of an empire and pride in its baroque, beaux-art edifices that proclaimed greatness and a venerable history. "Economic recessions come and go," he said at a press conference announcing his architectural plans for the building. "Economies always come back stronger." Besides, he told me, in tough times construction costs go down and, should he wish to borrow, borrowing is cheap. He says he has not been asked for bribes and he does not expect to pay them should he be asked. I did believe him about the past but, given how close he was to the realization of a dream, I certainly didn't believe him about the future.

Tippin arrived here in October 2004 after a call from a business associate who suggested that no matter what grand plans Tippin had realized in Canada and the United States, he would never again find an opportunity like this.

Though the Exchange Palace has survived two world wars and the destruction of Hungarian Television's floors during the 2006 demonstrations; its facade is still one of the wonders of the city. Its grand staircase, though grimy and shabby after years of neglect, retains its classic lines and the rotunda, with its fine wall niches and starburst glass skylight, has retained its graceful lines.

The Tippin Corporation's new business partners include several U.S. Ivy League investment funds. The architects he has chosen for the project reflect his supreme confidence in the eventual success of his venture: Beyer Blinder Belle of New York are the top specialists in restoration. Their projects include Grand Central Terminal, the Rockefeller Center, the Empire State Building, the Morgan Library and the United States Capitol in Washington.

"In ten years," said Tippin, gesturing across the Danube, "this will be the greatest tourist destination in Europe." We were sitting on the terrace of another city landmark, the Hotel Gellért.[52] Tippin, Canadian born and bred, was in love with the city. The way he gazed at the river, at the grand Elisabeth Bridge and up at the Gellért Hill, where tourists were climbing to reach the viewing platform, you would think he was born here and proud of it. But hedging his bets on Budapest, he is also rebuilding Berlin's Humboldt transformer station and he bought the airport lands in Tbilisi, Georgia. "The Russians," he tells me with a wave of his long-fingered hands, "love Georgia. These troubles will pass, as they did for Eastern Europe." The love, however, does not extend to Mikheil Saakashvili.

Thirty-five-year-old Dávid Tibor, the CEO of thriving multinational Masterplast, has no doubts about what the future holds: continuing growth and profits for his 100-million-euro company (its 2008 income was 113 million euros), a quick reversal of his enviable 4 per cent 2009 drop in profits and going public in three to four years. He operates branches in Slovakia, Romania and Serbia and has no concern for any animosities between the various ethnicities of his workforce. Still, his management teams are mostly Hungarians. "Slovak-Hungarians are proud to work for us," he tells me. "They love our success."

His memories of Communist times under Kádár are of a peaceful greyness, the sameness of everything, for everybody. No stirrings of ambition and no notions that the other guy's life was going to be better than yours. Now life is less peaceful but a whole lot more exciting. He is busy planning the future and is optimistic about the political atmosphere for business. "FIDESZ, no matter what they may have said during the elections, will want us to stay in the European Union," he tells me. As for Viktor Orbán, "he will become the statesman he started out to be when he was young, rather than the dictator everyone fears he has become."[53] As if to confirm Tibor's prediction, a few days after the elections, Orbán vowed to defend Hungary from the far right and announced that "democracy in this country is strong enough to defend itself."[54] Let us hope it is strong enough to hold out against the new prime minister's own, earlier stated objectives.

By early 2010, the "caretaker" government of Gordon Bajnai, appointed after Gyurcsány's resignation, has made some of the public-sector spending cuts that neither Gyurcsány nor Orbán had been able to impose. He has raised the retirement age and removed some of the compulsory benefits burdens that kept companies from hiring more workers. Bajnai was not interested in a political career; he did not need popularity. The former banker's task was simply to rescue the country from financial crisis and debt default. At this, he has succeeded.

SPRING ARRIVED early in 2010. The Budapest restaurants, the Danube Corso, the famous hot spring baths and the picturesque Castle District were full of tourists. The grand covered market was still serving the best sausages and red peppers in Europe. The shops along Váci Street were busy and overpriced. The chestnut trees along Andrássy Boulevard and the Danube were in full bloom. The tourboat operators were shouting their daily specials. Lake Balaton's hotels and guesthouses were open for the season, and the horse shows on the Plain were already advertising the mastery of Hungarian riders.

Among young people—noisy, inquisitive, in love with music, travel, movies and one another—there is a growing sense of optimism. Even the usually grim Pew report noted that more than half of those under the age of thirty were generally happy with their lives. My thirty-year-old cousin speaks four languages. He spent a year studying in Holland, works in a software business, drives a German car, goes gliding in the Alps and imagines he lives in a fine place: Budapest.

An earlier survey of eighteen- to twenty-year-olds displays their muddled thinking about the past and their not-so-radical desire for a "third way," or "Hungarian way," between capitalism and socialism. Most of them are not interested in listening to history lessons about old wars and the end of the Communist era. But they are sure that life was easier under János Kádár than it is now.

That, according to Ferenc Gyurcsány, is Viktor Orbán's greatest mistake. Since 2002, Orbán has been busily convincing people that the country is in a terrible state, that they must not trust the evidence of their own eyes, that their politicians have been thieves and their lives have been wrecked. For those who believed him, he offered a messianic future in a new dictatorship. The government, Gyurcsány told a crowd at the Inner City University in February 2010, is there to serve the people, not the other way around. People need to take responsibility for their own lives. That, even in difficult times, is the secret of democracy.

OUTCASTS,
ÉMIGRÉS AND
EXILES

IN ALL autocracies, writers who wish to continue writing have a unique problem. They have to decide whether to leave the country where their language lives or to stay and risk harassment, imprisonment or, worse, becoming part of the regime's inevitably compliant human landscape.

Writers and poets became easy victims of their Communist regimes' uniform way of thinking about the world. Some agreed to tow the regime's narrow artistic line of socialist realism in order to be published. Others were banned. Polish poet Zbigniew Herbert said that the regime bought itself legitimacy by buying certain intellectuals; he "did not want to be part of it." More writers, poets, painters practised their art in secret. Their words were published in underground magazines, by underground presses, in *samizdat*, hand-copied by the writers themselves or their fans. Banned playwrights wrote for underground theatres; the best journalists were available only in underground papers. Some, like Václav Havel, Adam Michnik, George Konrád, George Faludy and Bronisław Geremek, were imprisoned for continuing to write. They took their role very seriously. And it is interesting, in hindsight, to see how seriously the regime took them.

"None of this would have happened if a couple of writers had been shot in time," said Nikita Khrushchev about the 1956 Hungarian revolution.

CZESŁAW MIŁOSZ, the great Polish poet and novelist, broke with Poland because there were some things he "could not stomach." For him, the moment came at a reception where people in the highest circle of the Party drank and danced while army jeeps carried away prisoners to the East. But he was never to become an émigré. He remained an exile until the day he was, finally, able to return home. He never believed in the "possibility of communing outside a shared language, a shared history."[1] In his uncomfortable U.S. exile, he described himself as permanently ill at ease: "I do not emulate those émigrés who shed one skin and language for another... My Polish served my pride in erecting a protective barrier between myself and a civilization in the throes of puerility." That is how he saw his California surroundings—a society in which talent and innate aggression have all been channelled in only one direction: the struggle for money. It left him, the moralist, the individual with a soul in search of freedom, an outsider, always at odds with his environment. His books, many of which are gathered in Jiří Gruntorád's Library of Prohibited Books, could not be published in Poland until after 1989.

When Sándor Márai's brilliant book *Embers,* set during the decline of the old empire, became an international bestseller, he was no longer there to enjoy the success. He had killed himself in California in February 1989, just before the Communism he had fled declined into obscurity. He wrote thirty-two books in Hungarian but refused to have them published in Hungary while the regime he abhorred was still in power.

Milan Kundera has chosen to remain a French citizen, even after he could have returned home.

Arnost Lustig left Czechoslovakia in 1968 for Israel, then the United States. Though he was a visiting professor at the American University, all his fiction was written in Czech.

Josef Škvorecký escaped Czechoslovakia after the Soviet invasion but continued to write in Czech from his new home in Canada. Like Kundera, he chose to return home after 1989, but only for celebrations and publishing events. He said he had become accustomed to a quiet existence in Toronto. Czech democratic politics are a noisy and often nasty affair; in Canada politics tend to be more polite.

George Faludy first escaped from his homeland in 1938. He was a Jew, and it did not take a genius (though he was a genius) to see that a Jewish poet had no future in Hungary. He lived in Paris for a while, and then went to the United States. He served in the American forces during World War II and arrived back in Hungary in 1946. In 1949 he was accused of fictitious crimes against the state, and tortured at secret police headquarters on Andrássy Boulevard. Yet he was happy to be at last "where, in a communist state, I ought to be. No matter what injustice or stupidity my jailers committed, they had finally put me in a place worthy of me." Like other imprisoned writers, he was relieved that he no longer had "keep silent when I should have raised my voice, or to praise that which I loathed." He preferred the labour camp of Recsk to the pretences of the totalitarian world. In *My Happy Days in Hell,* he wrote of his three years of back-breaking work in the stone quarry, his nightly punishments, the terrible stupidity of his jailers, some of whom had been Arrow Cross members during the previous era, and the excruciating simple-mindedness of left-leaning Western journalists who denied the truth about what passed for justice in Central Europe. When he was refused pencil and paper, he composed his poems in his mind and recited them to himself. He cajoled his fellow inmates into memorizing them. He lectured other prisoners in literature, history and philosophy.

Only three of his original group of three hundred survived the Recsk labour camp.

Faludy had been out of prison for only a couple of years when the 1956 revolution opened borders, and he was unwilling to take a chance that Hungary would escape the Soviets, or, for that matter, its own sadists.

I first met Faludy in Toronto, in 1975. He had already travelled the world, and he seemed settled enough, though he missed being among Hungarians. He was, then, living with a beautiful young man called Eric, who clearly adored him and, like the rest of us, hung on his every word. I had grown up with Faludy's François Villon translations, more resonant and lyrical than the originals, and I had loved his autobiographical book, *My Happy Days in Hell.*

When he felt it was safe, he returned home.[2]

Czech playwright Václav Havel refused the proffered chance to leave for the United States and chose, instead, to remain in prison. While he worked in the laundry, wringing out "those thousands of sperm-stained sheets each day," several Western universities bestowed honorary degrees on him. The thought of leaving his language did not tempt him, nor was he terrified of the alternative.

Polish intellectual Adam Michnik also chose to stay, refusing every inducement the regime offered to make him emigrate. He said afterwards that he feared that "by saving my neck I may lose my honour." Like Havel, he spoke of honour and dignity as the role of the intellectual in opposition.

Imre Kertész returned to Hungary from the Buchenwald concentration camp in 1945. He worked, briefly, as a journalist until his dismissal for not following orthodox Communist rules. He spoke of the sense of utter isolation he felt as a writer in Hungary: "On a lovely Spring day in 1955, I suddenly came to the realization that there exists only one reality, and that is me, my own life, this fragile gift bestowed for an uncertain time, which had been seized, expropriated by alien forces, and circumscribed, marked up, branded..." In 1956 he escaped to the West.

György Konrád elected to stay. As he pointed out to his Party accusers, he was "a Hungarian writer." He could not take advantage of the Party's permission to leave the country. Leaving was never an option: "Communism and I grew old together. Decades passed in active, disciplined resignation... I spent the best years of my life in the shadow of its stupidity. Still, I never watched my country from afar. I groped my way around it."[3]

As he said in his aptly titled essay "More than Nothing," "The intelligentsia is the keeper of legitimacies; it provides grounds for morality."[4]

Vacláv Havel is now campaigning on behalf of Chinese literary scholar Liu Xiaobo, who was sentenced to eleven years in prison for "inciting subversion of state power" through his writings and his signature on Charter 08. Not unlike Charter 77, Charter 08 is a petition advocating human rights, free speech and an end to one-party rule. In January 2009, Havel delivered a letter to the closed doors of the Chinese embassy in Prague, demanding justice for Liu Xiaobo. The letter was signed by several former Charter 77 signatories.

Havel tried to convince the leaders of the People's Republic of China that writers should be allowed to write: "We strongly believe, and we dare to remind your government that there is nothing subversive to state security when intellectuals, artists, writers and academics exercise their core vocation: to think, re-think, ask questions, criticize, act creatively, and try to initiate open dialogue." As Havel knows from his own experience, a totalitarian state is allergic to open dialogue of any kind, but especially to discussion of human rights, freedom and democracy. China has shown no interest in Havel's letter. It continues to imprison writers. As does Cuba. And Burma (Myanmar), where, despite international protests, politician, intellectual, writer Aung San Suu Kyi has been under house arrest for fourteen years. And Iran and Syria. The list is discouragingly long. In Russia, open criticism of the government tends to lead not to prison but to death. Anna Politovskaya, who had written of Russian human rights abuses in Chechnya, was murdered. As was Anastasia Baburova, a twenty-five-year-old journalist gunned down in the street, one of four *Novaya Gazeta* journalists killed in five years. There have been no convictions.

Writers in countries where democracy is still unknown are willing risk their freedom and their lives to prove that human dignity should be a right, not a rare privilege, and that writers have a duty to perform in shining a light on the truth.

In early 2010, Václav Havel nominated Liu Xiaobo for the Nobel Peace Prize. The nomination was supported by Herta Müller, the Romanian-born Nobel Prize winner for Literature. Müller's novels are strongly influenced by the violence and terror of life under the Securitate. Herta Müller, like Václav Havel, understands a writer's dilemma in a totalitarian state.

AFTERWORD

*The world is a dangerous place, not because of those who
do evil, but because of those who look on and do nothing.*

ALBERT EINSTEIN

THE 2010 World Economic Forum drew to Davos, Switzerland, the usual crowd of high-powered executives, politicians, statesmen, publishers and economists. But this year there was a difference in the tenor of the speeches: the worldwide financial crisis had shaken the boundless confidence of highly paid chief executives in the invisible hand of the market to smooth out the rough ridges of the capitalist world. A favourite word at the Forum was "values," the admission that people need to share some common moral convictions. There was talk of ethics, of the "common good," of building a "better society." The theme of the conference was how to improve the state of the world.

These topics would not be new for George Soros, idolized hedge-fund manager, billionaire philanthropist and the man behind the Open Society Institute and Foundation and the Central European University. Soros was a generous promoter of anti-Communists in Central and Eastern Europe, all the way from Poland's Solidarity activists to Georgia's Rose Revolution. By the late 1990s, however, he had begun to criticize the "belief in the magic of the marketplace" and "the uninhibited pursuit of self-interest."[1] In his fall 2009 Open Society lecture series, he talked of the injustice of favouring the "haves over the have-nots." In his ideal "open society," where ideas are given free reign and opposition is encouraged, the enemy now turns out to be capitalism. All this from the man who advocated "shock therapy" economic reforms, the man who famously broke the Bank of England. Times have changed, and Soros, who made his fortune in the United States, no longer sees America as the world's unequalled power as this new century unfolds, nor does he see American ideas as dominant on the world stage. This could be exceptionally bad news for countries that have only recently joined the West and still hope to benefit from its capitalist systems.

I end this book in April 2010 looking back on the past twenty years in Central Europe with anxiety rather than the exuberant, optimistic hopes for the future with which I greeted the dismantling of the walls and barbed wire barriers that separated West from East. My travels across the borderlands of Central Europe found not only new "open societies" (to quote Soros) but also fear, disappointment, anger, insecurity and cloying nationalism—chords that echo the murky past of these regions, a past that included Fascism and the rise of the Nazi Party. It's all about insecurity, I was told by students in Warsaw and Prague—anxiety about the future. The old generation was used to a stultifying controlled society that provided a warm blanket of security and does not know how to adapt to its absence. But the members of these new Fascist groups tend to be younger. The Hungarian Guard's affection for nifty black uniforms can't be regarded as a mere fashion statement, and the painting of swastikas on synagogue walls is more than youthful protest. As Adam Michnik pointed out, we should remember that this is where the last two world wars began.

When meeting people in Warsaw, Budapest, Bratislava and Prague, it is hard to escape the conclusion that the West has failed those who have escaped the tyranny of Communism by lacking the courage of our democratic traditions, the conviction that what we offered was more than material benefits. It is as though we believed that it was not democracy, equality before the law, an independent, reliable judiciary, citizens' rights, a free press and other benefits we enjoy that drew these people to the West but the desire for better cars and more job opportunities. We have neglected to offer an alternative set of beliefs.

Democracy, as an ideology, is a tough sell. Our Western intellectual weaponry has relied too much on economic arguments, on promises of prosperity, of free enterprise, the common good: all very appealing but none of which bring forth the kind of ardour that the old, single-dimensional ideas of the twentieth century—Communism, Fascism, nationalism—inspired. It is time to reconsider why we espouse our ideals, to learn to enunciate clearly, and without the time-worn cynicism that has plagued Western intellectuals of the late twentieth and early twenty-first centuries, why we believe in them. Perhaps Vladimir Mečiar was right when he told me that the economic crisis was good for us. Perhaps we have learned something useful about the need to reassert our values and re-examine why we hold them dear.

Those of us who are fortunate to live in democracies need to remind ourselves that democracy is hard earned, that people in countries like China, Burma and Cuba, Iran and Russia are willing to die for the everyday realities we take for granted. We forget that simple fact at our peril.

Nineteen eight-nine was not only the end of Communist rule in Europe, it was also the year of the Tiananmen Square massacre. We still do not know how many protesters were killed by police, or how many were arrested and not heard from again. What we do know is that China has proven that capitalism can exist without individual freedom in a society ruled by an authoritarian state, and that Western governments and corporations, eager to gain entry into a new market for their products and a new partner for their financial ventures, are willing to overlook China's indifference to their values.

As I complete my journeys through Central Europe, I hope that a world too long occupied with greed will rediscover its sense of moral responsibility to society. And I find myself thinking more and more about the wisdom of the great Czech philosopher Jan Patočka:

No society... can function without a moral foundation, without conviction that has nothing to do with opportunism, circumstances and expected advantage. Man does not define morality according to the caprice of his needs, wishes, tendencies and cravings; it is morality that defines man.[2]

ACKNOWLEDGMENTS

THIS HAS BEEN a long and difficult journey, and I have many people to thank for helping me with the complicated subjects in this book.

I am grateful to Eva S. Balogh, whose blog *Hungarian Spectrum* is essential reading for someone interested in what goes in Hungary, and immensely grateful for her careful reading of and suggestions for the second draft of the Hungary chapters; to Magda Cabajewska, whose assistance in reaching Poles is unmatched, as is her willingness to help a writer on a mission to understand; to Oldřich Černý, director of Forum 2000, who volunteered to read and correct dates and enlighten me about great moments he witnessed in the Czech and Czechoslovak history; to LDIC's Michael Decter for checking my references to the economic and financial worlds; to Fedor Gál for his documentary about the events of 1989 in Slovakia and for his film about his father, one of the most moving tributes a son can offer; to Kostek Gebert for his perspective on being a Jew in Poland today; to János Kenedi of the 1956 Institute in Budapest, who gave me invaluable advice on the events and aftermath of the 1956 revolution, and the fate of the secret police files; to Jeffrey Kopstein, head of CERES, the Centre for European, Russian, and Eurasian Studies, at the University of Toronto, who provided me with an office and a smorgasbord of advice about sources to read and books that were not only essential but enjoyable; to Richard Krpac, Czech consul general to Toronto, who suggested people to meet in the Czech Republic and read the manuscript to offer last-minute advice; to Martin Simecka and Marta Simeckova for their warm, welcoming hospitality in their lovely Bratislava home, and to Martin, specially, for his reading of the first draft of *Ghosts;* to Zsolt Szekeres and József Orosz for helping me meet some extraordinary people in Hungary; to Piotr Wróbel, professor of history at the University of Toronto, without whose animated comments the Polish chapters would have lacked some vital pieces of information and historical perspective (I am particularly grateful for his patience with my attempts at Polish, and his forbearance with my efforts to spell Polish names); to Krystine Griffin for her love and understanding of Polish history; and to Judy Young, tireless provider of news from Hungary—I am particularly grateful for her reading the manuscript and her detailed comments.

I want to also thank several people closer to home: John Pearce, my enthusiastic agent and first editor, who did not discourage me from setting out on this journey, though he did point out that writing fiction is easier; Barbara Berson for her keen editorial eye and encouraging words when it became obvious that there are several volumes in this one book and that it could take the rest of my life to finish them; Stephanie Fysh for being the kind of copy editor every author deserves but very few are fortunate to get; and especially, Maria des Tombe, a.k.a. my mother, who has a keen eye for nonsense and spotted some embarrassing bits in the final draft and saved me from having to explain them later; and, of course, my brilliant publisher, Scott McIntyre, for being a brilliant publisher (there are so few left in the world).

NOTES

PREFACE

1 The "Iron Curtain" was first mentioned by Sir Winston Churchill in his now famous speech at Fulton, Missouri, in March 1946: "From Stettin in the Baltic to Trieste in the Adriatic, an iron curtain has descended across the Continent..."

2 Ralf Dahrendorf, *Reflections on the Revolution in Europe* (Transaction Publishers, 2004).

3 Interview with Katrina vanden Heuvel and Stephen Cohen, *The Nation*, November 16, 2009.

4 The phrase "open society" is particularly beloved by George Soros, billionaire philanthropist, who set up his first foundation in Budapest in 1984.

5 For details, I recommend Janine R. Wedel, *Collision and Collusion: The Strange Case of Western Aid to Eastern Europe, 1989–1998* (Palgrave Macmillan, 2000).

6 "No less than 31 million people were permanently or temporarily moved," Magocsi writes in "Eastern, East-Central, or Central Europe: Where Is It and What Is It?" in National Slovak Society of the United States, *Národný americko-slovenský kalendár,* vol. 113 (2005): 128–40.

7 László Karsai, "The People's Courts and Revolutionary Justice in Hungary, 1945–1946," in *The Politics of Retribution in Europe: World War II and Its Aftermath*, edited by István Deák, Jan T. Gross, and Tony Judt (Princeton University Press, 2000).

8 Ralf Dahrendorf, *After 1989: Morals, Revolution and Civil Society* (St. Martin's, 1997). Lord Dahrendorf, as he became in later life, was one of the great intellectuals of his generation. He had the unique distinction of becoming both a member of parliament in Germany and a member of the British House of Lords.

9 *Der Kurier/Eurotopics,* November 26, 2009. On two separate days in mid-December 2009, EU workers went on strike.

10 It is interesting to note that European Muslims celebrated terrorist acts, including the 2004 Madrid train bombing and the murder of Dutch filmmaker Theo van Gogh.

NOSTALGIA FOR THE HABSBURGS

1 Ödön von Horváth was the author of, among other plays and operas, *Tales from the Vienna Woods.*

2 According to Samuel Huntington, the old Central Europe maintained a dividing line between East (mostly Orthodox) and West (mostly Catholic) for five hundred years.

3 Michael Roskin, in *The Rebirth of East Europe*, 4th edition (Prentice Hall, 2001), is only one example of many.

4 Niall Ferguson makes this point well in his *The Pity of War: Explaining World War I* (Penguin, 1998).

CHAPTER 1

1 Jacques Rupnik, *The Other Europe: The Rise and Fall of Communism in East-Central Europe* (Schocken Books, 1990).

2 Leszek Kołakowski, *Main Currents of Marxism: Its Rise, Growth and Dissolution* (Norton, 1978).

3 It remained in force until June 22, 1941, when the German armies invaded the Soviet Union.

4 Gregory Slysz, "Crafting a Suitable Past," TOL: *Transitions Online*, March 25, 2009.

5 Norman Davies, *The Heart of Europe: The Past in Poland's Present* (Oxford University Press, 2001).

6 Norman Davies, *God's Playground: A History of Poland*, vol. 2 (Columbia University Press, 1982).

7 Davies, *God's Playground*, vol. 2.

8 *The New York Times*, July 31, 2004.

9 Lech Kaczyński, who had been loudly critical of Putin's Russia, was not invited to the earlier Russian-Polish ceremony. He was planning to attend a separate memorial organized by the Polish government.

10 Author of *The Power of Symbols against the Symbols of Power: The Rise of Solidarity and the Fall of State Socialism in Poland* (Penn State University Press, 1994).

11 Czesław Miłosz, *The Captive Mind*, translated by Jane Zielonko (Secker and Warburg, 1953).

12 Adam Czarnota, *The Politics of the Lustration Law in Poland, 1989–2006* (International Centre for Transnational Justice, 2007).

13 *Układ* refers to an arrangement, system or power; the word is often used in Poland to describe the Party's workers, the old bureaucracy.

14 Archie Brown, *The Rise and Fall of Communism* (Ecco, 2009).

15 Stalin's version of this, according to contemporary wit, was this: The future is certain; it is the past that is constantly changing.

16 Cyril Bouyeure, *L'Invention du politique: Une biographie d'Adam Michnik* (Éditions Noir sur Blanc, 2007).

17 Konstanty Gebert, *Living in the Land of Ashes* (Austeria, 2008).

18 Thomas Cushman and Adam Michnik, "Antitotalitarianism as a Vocation: An Interview with Adam Michnik," in *A Matter of Principle: Humanitarian Arguments for War in Iraq*, edited by Thomas Cushman (University of California Press, 2005).

19 Bouyeure, *L'Invention du politique.*

20 Adam Michnik, *Letters from Freedom: Post-Cold War Realities and Perspectives*, translated by Jane Cave (University of California Press, 1998).

21 Kukliński defected to the CIA in 1981, taking along a treasure trove of Soviet documents.

22 *Gdańsk 2000: Bound for the Future* (City of Gdańsk, n.d.).

23 The Lenin Shipyards strike was, itself, a culmination of a series of other strikes in mines and factories, all of them fuelled by lack of food, poor pay and appalling working conditions.

24 The idea for a round table was proposed by General Kiszczak, who would be one of Jaruzelski's co-accused in the criminal proceedings against Party leaders.

25 Thirty-five per cent of the seats in the Sejm and all the seats in the newly constituted Senate were open to free elections.

26 Dahrendorf, *After 1989.*

27 Lech Wałęsa, *The Struggle and the Triumph: An Autobiography* (Arcade Publishing, 1992).

28 Misha Glenny, *The Rebirth of History: Eastern Europe in the Age of Democracy*, 2nd edition (Penguin, 1993).

29 Jeffrey Sachs, interview, *Commanding Heights* (PBS, 2000).

30 The Black Madonna was crowned Queen of Poland by King Jan Kazimierz in the cathedral of Lwów on April 1, 1656. But there is a much longer story...

31 Wałęsa, *The Struggle and the Triumph.*

32 Antony Polonsky and Joanna B. Michlic, editors, *The Neighbours Respond: The Controversy over the Jedwabne Massacre in Poland* (Princeton University Press, 2003).

33 Chodakieweicz, interview, *Rzeczpospolita.*

34 Daniel Jonah Goldhagen, *A Moral Reckoning: The Role of the Catholic Church in the Holocaust and Its Unfulfilled Duty of Repair* (Knopf, 2002).

35 Goldhagen, *A Moral Reckoning.*

36 Predecessor of the Soviet KGB.

37 There is another, larger annual Jewish Culture Festival in Kraków, featuring groups of cantors, bands, dance, cooking demonstrations, lectures, theatre and more.

38 Stanisław Krajewski, *The Bond of Memory: Polish Christians in Dialogue with Jews and Judaism* (Laboratorium Wiezi, 2008).

39 In 2006, the government proposed restitution at the rate of 20 cents on the dollar, excluding property in Warsaw.

40 Approximately 4.5 million Poles settled in the former German territories after the war. This number included people fleeing the devastation of their homes in central Poland.

41 Author of *Gulag: A History* (Doubleday, 2003).

42 Robert Kagan, *The Return of History and the End of Dreams* (Knopf, 2008).

43 *Der Spiegel*, June 1, 2009.

44 BBC News, February 4, 2010.

45 *The Economist*, January 30, 2009.

THE LAST OF THE GREAT RESISTANCE INTELLIGENTSIA

1 *Die Zeit*, January 2007.

2 The director of the IPN died in the April 10 plane crash near Smolensk.

3 Adam Michnik at Geremek's funeral, quoted in *The New York Review of Books*, September 25, 2008.

4 Timothy Garton Ash, *The Uses of Adversity: Essays on the Fate of Central Europe* (Random House, 1989).

5 Timothy Garton Ash, *History of the Present: Essays, Sketches, and Dispatches from Europe in the 1990s* (Random House, 2001).

6 Miłosz, *The Captive Mind*.

7 Czesław Miłosz, *To Begin Where I Am: Selected Essays*, translated by Bogdana Carpenter and Madeline Levine (Farrar, Straus and Giroux, 2002).

CHAPTER 2

1 "The Power of the Powerless" was the title of a discussion paper written by Václav Havel in 1978 and first published in *samizdat* in 1979.

2 Margaret MacMillan, *Paris 1919: Six Months That Changed the World* (Random House, 2002).

3 Bernard Wheaton and Zdeněk Kavan, *The Velvet Revolution: Czechoslovakia, 1988–1991* (Westview Press, 1992).

4 John Keane, *Vaclav Havel: A Political Tragedy in Six Acts* (Perseus, 2001).

5 The Czechoslovaks had signed the International Covenant on Civil and Political Rights and the International Covenant on Economic, Social and Cultural Rights. Havel maintained in his writings that these were binding and that the government had not honoured its undertakings.

6 Wheaton and Kavan, *The Velvet Revolution*.

7 *Samizdat:* Individuals reproduced the work of forbidden authors and passed them from reader to reader. Patočka's translated works include "Wars of the Twentieth Century and the Twentieth Century as War," *Telos; Body, Community, Language, World; Heretical Essays in the Philosophy of History*; and *An Introduction to Husserl's Phenomenology*.

8 Havel's prison experience forms the major part of his *Letters to Olga*, published by 68 Publishers in Toronto in 1985.

9 Wheaton and Kavan, *The Velvet Revolution.*

10 Timothy Garton Ash's book *The Magic Lantern: The Revolution of '89 Witnessed in Warsaw, Budapest, Berlin, and Prague* was published by Random House in 1990.

11 Klaus's official website says, "He embarked on his political career in December 1989, when he became Federal Minister of Finance." Nowhere does it mention Václav Havel.

12 Václav Havel, *Disturbing the Peace,* translated by Paul Wilson (Vintage, 1991).

13 Josef Škvorecký, "Red Music," introduction to *The Bass Saxophone* (Anson-Cartwright, 1977).

14 Havel, *Disturbing the Peace.*

15 It is named after Jan Petr Straka, one of the emperor's privy counsellors, who intended it to serve as a hostel for sons of the poor but aristocratic Czechs.

16 The Czech consul to Canada picks *"Můj koníček"* ("My Hobbyhorse"), also known as *"Krysy"* ("The Rats"), as his favourite track from Pražský Výběr's clandestine tape (and later from the album)—"Cool, funky and minimalist, with [Michal] Pavlíček's sparse guitar effects illustrating an apparent nonsense story of a guy whose hobby is to watch mice and rats snooping around his basement. Every single sound has its place. A song near perfection."

17 Václav Klaus, according an article by Erik Tabery in *Respekt,* talked of the Roma having been imprisoned by the Nazis because "they didn't want to work" and questioned whether they would rank as victims of persecution, as those in the camp died "only of typhus."

18 Keane, *Vaclav Havel.*

19 Krzysztof Persak and Łukasz Kaminski, eds., *A Handbook of the Communist Security Apparatus in East Central Europe 1944–1989* (Institute of National Remembrance, 2005).

20 Franz Kafka (July 3, 1883–June 3, 1924) is one of the great Czech Jewish writers; his novels include the terrifying *The Trial* and the utterly incomprehensible *The Metamorphosis.*

21 Martin Myant, *The Rise and Fall of Czech Capitalism: Economic Development in the Czech Republic since 1989* (Edward Elgar, 2003).

22 Translation from Jacques Rupnik, *The Other Europe.*

23 October 29, 2009.

24 Urban's book *A Tunnel of Blood* seeks to expose the complicated byways of the Diag Human case. In the early 1990s, Diag Human, a formerly Czech company that transferred itself to Lichtenstein, was prevented from trading in blood plasma at Czech transfusion stations after an unfavourable comment on the firm by then health minister Martin Bojar. The company sued. The government paid 326.6 million crowns—about $17 million—for harming the company's good name. Diag Human is currently seeking more.

25 Kožen's Harvard Capital & Consulting siphoned money from several businesses to his private company in Cyprus, used his wealth to acquire Irish citizenship and lives, mostly, in the Bahamas. He was indicted in 2003 in New York State

for stealing $182 million from investors. He has been fighting extradition to the United States and the Czech Republic ever since.

26 For one telling of this story, see John Keane, "The Abdicator: On the Retirement of Václav Havel from Political Life," www.johnkeane.net/essays/essay_abdicator.htm, originally published in Czech in *Lidové noviny*, February 1, 2003.

27 Jordan's King Hussein awarded her one of his country's top medals for saving her husband's life.

28 United States president Barack Obama also evaded meeting the Dalai Lama in 2009, undoubtedly for the same reasons that the Czechs and Slovaks demurred. When he finally met with the Dalai Lama, on February 19, 2010, it was in a back room of the White House, a puzzling message to send to the Chinese government.

29 Public Opinion Research Centre of the Institute of Sociology of the Academy of Sciences of the Czech Republic (CVVM), December 30, 2009.

30 Václav Havel, "Václav vs. Václav," *New York Review of Books*, May 10, 2007.

CHAPTER 3

1 Bratislava was the capital of Hungary from 1536 to 1784, the coronation town from 1563 to 1830 and seat of the Diet, or parliament, of Hungary from 1536 to 1848.

2 Robert William Seton-Watson, *Racial Problems in Hungary* (Constable, 1908).

3 Rupnik, *The Other Europe*.

4 Stanislav Kirschbaum, *A History of Slovakia: The Struggle for Survival* (St. Martin's Press, 1995).

5 A local Hungarian poetry buff told me that Pavol Hviezdoslav's poetry was written in Hungarian until his tearful mother asked him to write in Slovak because she could not understand what he was reciting.

6 Lubomir Liptak, "Monuments of Political Changes and Political Changes of Monuments," in *Scepticism and Hope: Sixteen Contemporary Slovak Essays*, edited by Miro Kollar (Kalligram, 1999).

7 Even that was in some contention: according to a few Czech scholars, Slovak is a dialect of Czech, the word *Slovak* meaning "Slav."

8 Many historians define the regime as "clerical fascist," though the only "cleric" involved was the leader himself. I find the following article interesting: Yeshayahu Jelinek, "Slovakia's Internal Policy and the Third Reich August 1940–February 1941," *Central European History* 4, no. 3 (1971).

9 This is a very short take on a long and complicated story that has been told by historians with varying points of view. Where even the more generous accounts agree is that Slovakia collaborated in the deportation of its Jewish population.

10 Oldřich Černý told me that Havel fired Gašparovič in 1991. When Gašparovič demanded to know what he had done to deserve being fired, Havel said, "I don't want to fire you because you have done something. I want to fire you because

you have done nothing." In the end Havel asked Černý to accompany Gašparovič down the stairs because Gašparovič was crying like a small child and Havel worried that he might trip and hurt himself.

11 "Slovakia Slips Backward," *New York Times*, August 14, 1995.

12 A result of the Beneš decrees (officially called "Decrees of the President of the Republic"), named after Czechoslovak president Edvard Beneš, who successfully petitioned Stalin to allow his expropriation of ethnic Hungarian and German properties and paved the way for the eventual expulsion of the majority of Germans to West and East Germany and Hungarians to Hungary.

13 Slovakia was admitted to the European Union in 2004 and entered the eurozone in 2009.

14 The notorious Vienna Awards, signed by Nazi Germany's foreign minister Ribbentrop and Italy's Count Ciano on November 2, 1938, allowed Hungary to reclaim an area of 11,927 square kilometres and about a million Hungarian inhabitants.

15 Fedor Gál made a film about his journey in search of his father, *Krátká–Dkouhá– Cesta* ("Short Long Journey"); see www.kratkadlouhacesta.cz.

16 See David Doellinger, "Prayers, Pilgrimages and Petitions: The Secret Church and the Growth of Civil Society in Slovakia," *Nationalities Papers*, vol. 2, no. 30 (2002): 215–40.

17 *The Economist*, March 13, 2010.

18 See chapter 2, on the Czech Republic, for more on the camp at Lety.

19 Some sources say only 300,000, but an accurate census is difficult here, as in Hungary, because many Roma do not admit to being Roma.

20 Perhaps the Slovak prime minister should study the effects of the nineteenth and early twentieth centuries' residential schools in Canada.

21 For more on this subject, read Martin Simecka, "Story about Language," in *Scepticism and Hope*, edited by Miro Kollar.

22 A Mercedes SLR McLaren 722 Edition, a car which carries a €650,000 price tag.

23 Stephen Kinzer, "West Says Slovakia Falls Short of Democracy," *New York Times*, December 26, 1995.

24 May 18, 2009.

CHAPTER 4

1 János Kenedi told me this is a popular myth—the zoo is too far away.

2 In 1989 the KGB's Vladimir Kryuchkov offered the Hungarian Communist Party some documentary evidence attempting to prove that Nagy's revelations to the secret service had been responsible for the executions of fellow Communists, but the file turned out to contain nothing to suggest that Nagy had ever denounced a fellow Communist.

3 Thirty-two other people left the country with Nagy, including his wife and his daughter.

4 The victims were identified and named by János M. Rainer in 1984–85 and the list published in *samizdat* at considerable risk to Rainer.

5 István Rév, *Retroactive Justice: Prehistory of Post-Communism* (Stanford University Press, 2005).

6 Rév told me the stories of both the grave robbery and the disappearance of Rákosi's ashes.

7 The interviewer was József Orosz, the program *168 Óra,* and, in Orosz's view, Pozsgay was fully aware of the implications of this statement.

8 András B. Hegedűs, eds., *1956 Kézikönyve* [Handbook] (1956 Institute, 1996).

9 One of the "fortunate," István Bibó—lawyer, political philosopher, writer, scholar, minister of state in the short-lived 1956 Nagy government—was arrested in March 1957, tried and sentenced to life in prison. He was saved from execution by the intervention of India's prime minister Nehru. Bibó had handed his essay on Hungary, written at the end of the revolution, to the Indian ambassador. His co-accused at the trial was Árpád Göncz, who became the first president of the post-'89 Republic of Hungary.

10 In his 2009 book *Uncivil Society: 1989 and the Implosion of the Communist Establishment* (Modern Library), Stephen Kotkin uses these numbers. 100,000 were arrested between 1956 and 1961; 35,000 were tried, 26,000 sentenced.

11 I saw the bodies, suspended by their boots, their cut-open bowels exposed.

12 Konrád refers to the 1848 Hungarian revolution against Habsburg domination and to the way the Hungarian Nazis used to shoot Jews and dump their bodies into the Danube in late '44 and '45.

13 The Institute for the History of the 1956 Hungarian Revolution (www.rev.hu) was established in 1990 to provide historians with research facilities for the study of Hungarian history since 1944.

14 George Konrád, "Letter from Budapest," *The Melancholy of Rebirth: Essays from Post-Communist Central Europe, 1989-1994* (Mariner, 1995).

15 Steven Bela Vardy and Agnes Huszar Vardy, "Soviet Treatment of Magyars, 1945–56: Hungarian Slave Labourers in the Gulag," *Hungarian Studies Review,* vol. 34, nos. 1–2 (2008): 15–54.

16 Paul Robert Magocsi, "The Hungarians in Transcarpathia (Subcarpathian Rus')," *Nationalities Papers,* vol. 24, no. 3 (1996): 525–34.

17 Vardy et al., p. 13.

18 Today György Vámos is head of the Carl Lutz Foundation in Budapest. Lutz, like Raoul Wallenberg, put his own life at risk helping Jews with "safe passes," protected buildings and hastily reproduced foreign identity papers.

19 Faludy, who had lived in the United States and volunteered for the army, was accused of spying. When his interrogators pressed him to name his American co-conspirators, he confessed to two contacts: Walt Whitman and Captain Edgar A. Poe.

20 Antal Apró died in 1994. His daughter and granddaughter purchased the home from the government afterward.

21 László Varga, "A Vizsgálat Lezarul," *Élet és Irodalom*, October 2008.

22 Gyula Horn was the founder of the Communist Party's successor, the Hungarian Socialist Party, in 1989, and was prime minister from 1994 till 1998.

23 Constantine Pleshakov, *There Is No Freedom without Bread! 1989 and the Civil War That Brought Down Communism* (Farrar, Straus and Giroux, 2009).

24 Mary Elise Sarotte, *1989: The Struggle to Create Post-Cold War Europe* (Princeton University Press, 2009).

25 Others I interviewed were amazed that Boross thought there were still Soviet advisers in Hungary in 1990. The last one—KGB general Boris Shumilin—left, according to József Orosz, in the spring of 1989. Shumilin first arrived in Hungary, at Kádár's invitation, in 1957.

26 These included Maripen, Cocom, other antibiotics and penicillin.

27 Tibor Rosenstein and his sister were the only survivors of a large and equally friendly family murdered during the Holocaust.

28 István Rév, "The Man in the White Raincoat," in *Past for the Eyes: East European Representations of Communism in Cinema and Museums after 1989*, edited by Oksana Sarkisova and Péter Apor (Central European University Press, 2008).

29 Professor Pál Tamás, interview, March 2010.

30 *Magyar Nemzet*, July 6, 2009.

31 From Kołakowski's speech on accepting the John W. Kluge Prize in 2003.

32 George Soros, *Soros on Soros: Staying Ahead of the Curve* (Wiley, 1995).

33 Havel, *To the Castle and Back.*

34 Named after Hungary's Visegrád Castle, where the kings of these countries had met in friendship some hundreds of years ago.

35 József Debreczeni, *Arcmás* (Noran Libro Kiadó, 2009).

36 Jozsef Orósz in a speech in Montreal, May 2010.

37 József Debreczeni, interview with the author, September 2008.

38 Debreczeni, interview with the author, November 2008.

39 With apologies to those who think he lost the people when he lost his chance to make fundamental reforms in education, health, benefits, etc.

40 The occasion was the annual FIDESZ picnic at Kötcse, attended by about five hundred people.

41 *The New York Times*, April 12, 2010.

42 György Konrád, *Elutazás és Hazatérés* (Noran Könyvkiadó, 2001).

43 Most of his translated works list his first name as George, the anglicized version of György.

44 Konrád, *The Melancholy of Rebirth.*

45 To this day, there are some who believe that Teleki was murdered by the SS for refusing to bless the invasion after the fact.

46 He was released from prison in 1959 and died in 1993.

47 *Kasztner's Train: The True Story of Rezso Kasztner, Unknown Hero of the Holocaust.*

48 A great deal of the DM 1 billion went to interest payments and to purchase Western goods.

49 The infamous "thirteenth" month.

50 Professor György Csáki, lecture, Toronto, 2010.

51 Jeffrey Kopstein, "1989 as a Lens for Communist Past and Communist Future," *Contemporary European History*, vol. 18 (2009): 289–302.

52 Yes, it's the same hotel where Admiral Horthy had his first headquarters in 1919, the same place where the SS and other German officers used to hang out between 1941 and 1944. It has the most fabulous art deco architecture and the best pools in the city.

53 Interview with the author, April 2010.

54 *The New York Times*, April 12, 2010.

OUTCASTS, ÉMIGRÉS AND EXILES

1 Miłosz, *To Begin Where I Am.*

2 Faludy went back to Budapest in 1988. He was given a hero's welcome, showered with literary prizes, given an apartment to share with his lover (who was succeeded by a nubile young woman, some fifty years Faludy's junior), adored by a young generation of writers and rewarded with the publication of all his thirty-three previously banned volumes.

3 György Konrád, *A Guest in My Own Country: A Hungarian Life*, translated by Jim Tucker (Other Press, 2007).

4 Konrád, *A Guest in My Own Country.*

AFTERWORD

1 George Soros, "The Capitalist Threat," *Atlantic Monthly*, February 1997.

2 Translation from Rupnik, *The Other Europe.*

BIBLIOGRAPHY

BOOKS

Anderson, Richard. *Postcommunism and the Theory of Democracy*. Princeton University Press, 2001.

András, Kanyó. *Horthy és a Magyar Tragédia*. Népszabadság Könyvek, 2008.

Antohi, Sorin, and Vladimir Tismaneau, eds. *Between Past and Future: The Revolutions of 1989 and Their Aftermath*. Central European University Press, 2000.

Applebaum, Anne. *Between East and West: Across the Borderlands of Europe*. Pantheon, 1994.

——. *Gulag: A History*. Doubleday, 2003.

Ash, Timothy Garton. *The File: A Personal History*. Random House, 1997.

——. *History of the Present: Essays, Sketches, and Dispatches from Europe in the 1990s*. Random House, 2001.

——. *The Magic Lantern: The Revolution of '89 Witnessed in Warsaw, Budapest, Berlin and Prague*. Random House, 1990.

——. *The Polish Revolution: Solidarity, 1980–82*. J. Cape, 1983.

——. *The Uses of Adversity: Essays on the Fate of Central Europe*. Random House, 1989.

Bawer, Bruce. *While Europe Slept: How Radical Islam Is Destroying the West from Within*. Random House, 2006.

Bouyeure, Cyril. *L'Invention du politique: Une biographie d'Adam Michnik*. Éditions Noir sur Blanc, 2007.

Brown, Archie. *The Rise and Fall of Communism*. Ecco, 2009.

Chodakiewicz, Marek Jan. *After the Holocaust: Polish-Jewish Conflict in the Wake of World War II*. East European Monographs; Columbia University Press, 2003.

Czarnota, Adam. *The Politics of the Lustration Law in Poland, 1989–2006*. International Centre for Transnational Justice, 2007.

Dahrendorf, Ralf. *After 1989: Morals, Revolution and Civil Society*. St. Martin's, 1997.

——. *Reflections on the Revolution in Europe*. Transaction, 2004.

Davies, Norman. *God's Playground: A History of Poland*. 2 volumes. Columbia University Press, 1982.

——. *Heart of Europe: The Past in Poland's Present*. Oxford University Press, 2001.

Deak, Instvan, Jan T. Gross, and Tony Judt, eds. *The Politics of Retribution in Europe: World War II and Its Aftermath*. Princeton University Press, 2000.

Debreczeni, József. *Arcmás*. Noran Libro Kiadó, 2009.

——. *Az uj miniszterelnok*. Osiris, 2006.

——. *Hazardjatek*. Bibor Kiadó, 2007.

Domosławski, Artur. *Kapuściński Non-Fiction*. Świat Książki, 2010.

Dubček, Alexander. *Hope Dies Last: The Autobiography of Alexander Dubcek*. Translated by Jiri Hochman. Kodansha America, 1993.

Duray, Miklós. *Kutyaszoritó I* and *II*. Püski-Corvin, 1982, 1989.

——. *Összefonódó Ujjak*. Riport, 2006.

Faludy, George. *My Happy Days in Hell*. Translated by Kathleen Szasz. Morrow, 1963.

Ferguson, Niall *The Pity of War: Explaining World War I*. Penguin, 1998.

Fonseca, Isabel. *Bury Me Standing: The Gypsies and Their Journey*. Knopf, 1995.

Funder, Anna. *Stasiland*. Text Publishing, 2003.

Gebert, Konstanty. *Living in the Land of Ashes*. Austeria Publishing, 2008.

Glenny, Misha. *The Rebirth of History: Eastern Europe in the Age of Democracy*. 2nd edition. Penguin, 1993.

Goldhagen, Daniel Jonah. *A Moral Reckoning: The Role of the Catholic Church in the Holocaust and Its Unfulfilled Duty of Repair*. Knopf, 2002.

Gross, Jan T. *Fear: Anti-Semitism in Poland after Auschwitz: An Essay in Historical Interpretation*. Random House, 2006.

——. *Neighbors: The Destruction of the Jewish Community in Jedwabne, Poland*. Princeton University Press, 2001.

Halík, Tomáš. *Patience with God: The Story of Zacchaeus Continuing in Us*. Doubleday, 2009.

Havel, Václav. *Disturbing the Peace: A Conversation with Karel Hviľz_d_ala*. Translated by Paul Wilson. Vintage, 1991.

——. *Dopisy Olze* [*Letters to Olga*]. Sixty-Eight Publishers, 1985.

——. *The Garden Party*. Translated and adapted by Vera Blackwell. Cape, 1969.

——. *The Memorandum*. Translated by Vera Blackwell. Cape, 1967.

——. *Open Letters: Selected Writings, 1965-90*. Edited by Paul Wilson. Knopf, 1991.

——. *Summer Meditations*. Translated by Paul Wilson. Knopf, 1992.

——. *To the Castle and Back: Reflections on My Life as a Fairy-Tale Hero*. Translated by Paul Wilson. Knopf Canada, 2007.

Hegedűs, András B., ed., *1956 Kézikönyve* [Handbook]. 1956 Institute, 1996.

Hockenos, Paul. *Free to Hate: The Rise of the Right in Post-Communist Eastern Europe*. Routledge, 1993.

Hoffman, Eva. *Exit to History: A Journey through the New Eastern Europe.* Penguin, 1993.

Judt, Tony. *A Grand Illusion? An Essay on Europe.* Farrar, Strauss and Giroux, 1996.

——. *Postwar: A History of Europe since 1945.* Penguin, 2005.

——. *Reappraisals: Reflections on the Twentieth Century.* Penguin, 2008.

Kagan, Robert. *The Return of History and the End of Dreams.* Knopf, 2008.

Kapuściński, Ryszard. *The Soccer War.* Translated by William Brand. Granta; Penguin, 1990.

Keane, John. *Václav Havel: A Political Tragedy in Six Acts.* Perseus, 2001.

Kenney, Padraic, ed. *The Burdens of History: Eastern Europe since 1989.* Zed Books, 2006.

Kirschbaum, Stanislav. *A History of Slovakia: The Struggle for Survival.* St. Martin's Press, 1995.

Kirschbaum, Stanislav, and Anne Roman, eds. *Reflections on Slovak History.* Slovak World Congress (Toronto), 1987.

Klaus, Václav. *Blue Planet in Green Shackles: What Is Endangered: Climate or Freedom?* Competitive Enterprise Institute, 2008.

Klein, Naomi. *The Shock Doctrine: The Rise of Disaster Capitalism.* Knopf Canada, 2007.

Kołakowski, Leszek. *Main Currents of Marxism: Its Rise, Growth, and Dissolution.* Translated by P.S. Falla. Norton, 1978.

Kollar, Miro, ed. *Scepticism and Hope: Sixteen Contemporary Slovak Essays.* Kalligram, 1999.

Konrád, György. *A Guest in My Own Country: A Hungarian Life.* Translated by Jim Tucker. Other Press, 2007.

——. *The Melancholy of Rebirth: Essays from Post-Communist Central Europe, 1989-1994.* Translated by Michael Henry Heim. Harcourt Brace, 1995.

Konrád, György. *Elutazás és Hazatérés.* Noran Könyvkiadó, 2001.

Kontler, László. *A History of Hungary: Millennium in Central Europe.* Palgrave Macmillan, 2002.

Kotkin, Stephen. *Uncivil Society: 1989 and the Implosion of the Communist Establishment.* Modern Library, 2009.

Krajewski, Stanisław. *The Bond of Memory: Polish Christians in Dialogue with Jews and Judaism.* Laboratorium Wiezi, 2008.

Kubik, Jan. *The Power of Symbols against the Symbols of Power: The Rise of Solidarity and the Fall of State Socialism in Poland.* Penn State University Press, 1994.

Kundera, Milan. *The Joke.* Translated by Michael Henry Heim. Harper & Row, 1982.

Lendvai, Paul. *Anti-Semitism without Jews: Communist Eastern Europe.* Doubleday, 1971.

——. *The Hungarians: A Thousand Years of Victory in Defeat.* Princeton University Press, 2003.

Lucas, Edward. *The New Cold War: Putin's Russia and the Threat to the West.* Palgrave Macmillan, 2008.

MacMillan, Margaret. *Paris 1919: Six Months That Changed the World.* Random House, 2002.

Magocsi, Paul Robert. *Historical Atlas of Central Europe.* University of Toronto Press, 1993.

Michnik, Adam. *Letters from Freedom: Post–Cold War Realities and Perspectives.* Translated by Jane Cave. University of California Press, 1998.

Miłosz, Czesław. *The Captive Mind.* Translated by Jane Zielonko. Secker and Warburg, 1953.

——. *To Begin Where I Am: Selected Essays.* Translated by Bogdana Carpenter and Madeline Levine. Farrar, Straus and Giroux, 2002.

Myant, Martin *The Rise and Fall of Czech Capitalism: Economic Development in the Czech Republic since 1989.* Edward Elgar, 2003.

Patočka, Jan. *Body, Community, Language, World.* Translated by Erazim Kohaĭk. Open Court, 1998.

——. *Heretical Essays in the Philosophy of History.* Translated by Erazim Kohaĭk. Open Court, 1996.

——. *An Introduction to Husserl's Phenomenology.* Translated by Erazim Kohaĭk. Open Court, 1996.

Persak, Krzysztof, and Lukasz Kaminski, eds. *A Handbook of the Communist Security Apparatus in East Central Europe, 1944–1989.* Institute of National Remembrance (Warsaw), 2005.

Pleshakov, Constantine. *There Is No Freedom without Bread! 1989 and the Civil War That Brought Down the Berlin Wall.* Farrar, Straus and Giroux, 2009.

Polonsky, Antony, and Joanna B. Michlic, eds. *The Neighbors Respond: The Controversy over the Jedwabne Massacre in Poland.* Princeton University Press, 2003.

Reid, T.R. *The United States of Europe: The New Superpower and the End of American Supremacy.* Penguin, 2005.

Rév, István. *Retroactive Justice: Prehistory of Post-Communism.* Stanford University Press, 2005.

Rosenberg, Tina. *The Haunted Land: Facing Europe's Ghosts after Communism.* Vintage, 1996.

Roskin, Michael. *The Rebirth of East Europe.* 4th edition. Prentice Hall, 2001.

Rupnik, Jacques . *The Other Europe: The Rise and Fall of Communism in East-Central Europe.* Schocken, 1990.

Sarotte, Mary Elise. *1989: The Struggle to Create Post-Cold War Europe.* Princeton University Press, 2009.

Sebestyen, Victor. *Revolution 1989: The Fall of the Soviet Empire.* Weidenfeld & Nicolson, 2009.

Seton-Watson, Robert William. *Racial Problems in Hungary.* Constable, 1908.

Sikorski, Radosław. *Dust of the Saints: A Journey to Herat in Time of War.* Paragon House, 1990.

——. *The Polish House: An Intimate History of Poland*. Phoenix, 1998.

Škvorecký, Josef. *The Bass Saxophone*. Anson-Cartwright, 1977.

——. *The Miracle Game*. Lester & Orpen Dennys, 1972.

——. *Two Murders in My Double Life*. Key Porter, 1999.

Smith. Adam. *An Inquiry into the Nature and Causes of the Wealth of Nations*. Modern Library, 1994.

Soros, George. *Soros on Soros: Staying Ahead of the Curve*. Wiley, 1995.

Stoppard, Tom. *Rock 'n' Roll*. Faber and Faber, 2006.

Taras, Ray, ed. *Postcommunist Presidents*. Cambridge University Press, 1997.

Thorpe, Nick. *'89: The Unfinished Revolution: Power and Powerlessness in Eastern Europe*. Reportage Press, 2009.

Urban, Jan. *Tunel plný krve: Aneb kauza Kiag Human*. Gema Art, 2007.

Vardy, Steven Bela, and Agnes Huszar Vardy. *Stalin's Gulag: The Hungarian Experience*. Word Association, 2007.

Wałęsa, Lech. *The Struggle and the Triumph: An Autobiography*. Arcade, 1992.

Wedel, Janine R. *Collision and Collusion: The Strange Case of Western Aid in Eastern Europe, 1989-1998*. St. Martin's Press, 1998.

Wheaton, Bernard, and Zdeněk Kavan. *The Velvet Revolution: Czechoslovakia, 1988-1991*. Westview, 1992.

Wiesel, Elie. *The Time of the Uprooted: A Novel*. Translated by David Hapgood. Knopf, 2005.

Wolff, Larry. *Inventing Eastern Europe: The Map of Civilization on the Mind of the Enlightenment*. Standford University Press, 1994.

Zamoyski, Adam. *The Polish Way: A Thousand-Year History of the Poles and Their Culture*. John Murray, 1987.

ARTICLES

Cushman, Thomas, and Adam Michnik. "Antitotalitarianism as a Vocation: An Interview with Adam Michnik." In *A Matter of Principle: Humanitarian Arguments for War in Iraq*, edited by Thomas Cushman. University of California Press, 2005.

Doellinger, David. "Prayers, Pilgrimages and Petitions: The Secret Church and the Growth of Civil Society in Slovakia." *Nationalities Papers*, vol. 2, no. 30 (2002): 215-40.

Havel, Václav. "Václav vs. Václav." *New York Review of Books*, May 10, 2007.

Jelinek, Yeshayahu. "Slovakia's Internal Policy and the Third Reich, August 1940-February 1941." *Central European History*, vol. 4, no. 3 (1971): 242-70.

Judt, Tony. "The Past Is Another Country: Myth and Memory in Postwar Europe." *Daedalus*, vol. 121, no. 4 (1992): 83-118.

Keane, John. "The Abdicator: On the Retirement of Václav Havel from Political Life." www.johnkeane.net/essays/essay_abdicator.htm. Originally published in Czech in, *Lidové noviny*, February 1, 2003.

Kopstein, Jeffrey. "1989 as a Lens for Communist Past and Communist Future." *Contemporary European History*, vol. 18 (2009): 289-302.

Kopstein, Jeffrey, and Jason Wittenberg. "Does Familiarity Breed Contempt? Inter-Ethnic Contact and Support for Illiberal Parties." *Journal of Politics*, vol. 71, no. 2 (2009): 414–28.

Liptak, Lubomir. "Monuments of Political Changes and Political Changes of Monuments." In *Scepticism and Hope: Sixteen Contemporary Slovak Essays*, edited by Miro Kollar. Kalligram, 1999.

Magocsi, Paul Robert. "The Hungarians in Transcarpathia (Subcarpathian Rus')." *Nationalities Papers*, vol. 24, no. 3 (1996): 525–34.

——. "In Step or Out of Step with the Times? Central Europe's Diasporas and Their Homelands in 1918 and 1989." *Austrian History Yearbook*, vol. 36 (2005): 167–89.

Michnik, Adam. "Renouncing Humanity." *Salon*, March 24, 2010.

Muller, Jerzy Z. "Us and Them: The Enduring Power of Ethnic Nationalism." *Foreign Affairs*, March 1, 2008.

Patočka, Jan. "Wars of the Twentieth Century and the Twentieth Century as War." *Telos*, vol. 30 (1976–77): 116–26.

Rév, István. "The Man in the White Raincoat." In *Past for the Eyes: East European Representations of Communism in Cinema and Museums after 1989*, edited by Oksana Sarkisova and Péter Apor. Central European University Press, 2008.

Simecka, Martin. "Story about Language." In *Scepticism and Hope: Sixteen Contemporary Slovak Essays*, edited by Miro Kollar. Kalligram, 1999.

Slysz, Gregory. "Crafting a Suitable Past." TOL: *Transitions Online*, March 25, 2009.

Vardy, Steven Bela, and Agnes Huszar Vardy. "Soviet Treatment of Magyars, 1945–56: Hungarian Slave Labourers in the Gulag." *Hungarian Studies Review*, vol. 34, nos. 1–2 (2008): 15–54.

Varga, László. "A Vizsgálat Lezarul." *Élet és Irodalom*, October 2008.

INDEX